ABR-NAHRAIN
SUPPLEMENT SERIES

Volume 5

AN ANNUAL PUBLISHED BY THE
DEPARTMENT OF CLASSICS
AND ARCHAEOLOGY
UNIVERSITY OF MELBOURNE

CULTURAL INTERACTION IN THE ANCIENT NEAR EAST

Papers Read at a Symposium Held at the University of Melbourne,
Department of Classics and Archaeology
(29-30 September 1994)

EDITED BY

Guy BUNNENS

PEETERS PRESS
LOUVAIN
1996

ABR-NAHRAIN
SUPPLEMENT SERIES

Volume 5

AN ANNUAL PUBLISHED BY THE
DEPARTMENT OF CLASSICS
AND ARCHAEOLOGY
UNIVERSITY OF MELBOURNE

CULTURAL INTERACTION IN THE ANCIENT NEAR EAST

Papers Read at a Symposium Held at the University of Melbourne,
Department of Classics and Archaeology
(29-30 September 1994)

EDITED BY

Guy BUNNENS

PEETERS PRESS
LOUVAIN
1996

ISBN 90-6831-786-5
D. 1996/0602/12

Copyright by
The Department of Classics and Archaeology
University of Melbourne, Australia

All rights reserved. No part of this book may be reproduced or translated in any form, by print,
photoprint, microfilm, microfiche or any other means without written permission from the
publisher

PRINTED IN BELGIUM

Orientaliste, Klein Dalenstraat 42, B-3020 Herent

CONTENTS

Foreword
    Guy BUNNENS VI

List of contributors VII

"The Highland Sheep Are Sweeter..."
    Charles BURNEY 1

The Rise of Social Complexity in East Central Anatolia in the Early Bronze Age
    Liza HOPKINS 17

Obsidian in the Bayburt-Erzurum Area, Eastern Anatolia
    Peter V. BRENNAN 27

Anatolia and Cyprus in the Third Millennium B.C.E.: A Speculative Model of Interaction
    David FRANKEL, Jennifer M. WEBB & Christine ESLICK. 37

Egyptian Stone Vessels in Syro-Palestine During the Second Millennium B.C. and Their Impact on the Local Stone Vessel Industry
    Rachael SPARKS 51

The Egyptian and Mesopotamian Contributions to the Origins of the Alphabet
    Brian E. COLLESS 67

Emar: A Syrian City Between Anatolia, Assyria and Babylonia
    Jean-Claude MARGUERON 77

Ethnic Movements in the Thirteenth Century B.C. as Discernible from the Emar Texts
    Murray R. ADAMTHWAITE 91

Syro-Anatolian Influence on Neo-Assyrian Town Planning
    Guy BUNNENS 113

Cultural Interaction in North Syria in the Roman and Byzantine Periods: The Evidence of Personal Names
    Graeme W. CLARKE 129

Red to Blue: Colour Symbolism and Human Societies
    Claudia SAGONA 145

FOREWORD

A three-day conference on the ancient Near East was organized by the Department of Classics and Archaeology at the University of Melbourne on September 29 and 30 and October 1, 1994. The first two days were devoted to discussing topics related to the problem of cultural interaction in the ancient Near East. The papers published in this volume are the immediate outcome of these discussions. The third day was concerned with reports on Australian archaeological excavations in the Near East, which will be published elsewhere.

One of the goals of the meeting was to bring together scholars from Australia and New Zealand who specialize in the study of the ancient Near East. It was hoped that, by establishing closer contacts between them, a forum could be created for further meetings. It was also intended to be a testimony to the interest raised by such studies in the Australasian region. As Australia and New Zealand are far away from the main centres of Near Eastern studies in Europe and America, it was probably not futile to show that it was possible to gather some thirty scholars to discuss for three days before an audience of about seventy persons problems relating to cultures that flourished more than two thousand years ago.

The success of this first conference is illustrated not only by the number of its participants and by the importance of the audience, but also by the fact that scholars from overseas accepted the invitation to participate in our debates. I especially want to thank Professor Charles Burney, Professor Jean-Claude Margueron, Professor Ilknur Özgen and Dr Madeleine Trokay for undertaking the long journey to Melbourne to contribute to our discussions. (Unfortunately, Professor Ilknur Özgen and Dr Madeleine Trokay's papers did not arrive in time to be included in the present publication).

The conference would not have been possible without the assistance of various people whom it is my pleasure to thank here. First of all Professor Homer Le Grand, Dean of the Faculty of Arts, and Professor Frank Sear, the then Head of the Department of Classics and Archaeology. They both gave their full support to the project. Ms Michelle Glynn assisted with the revision of the English text of Prof. Margueron's paper. My wife, Arlette Roobaert, helped in the organization of the conference and, above all, in the preparation of the present publication. The technical assistance of Mrs Angela Khoury, Ms Michelle Langone and Ms Sarah Myers has also proved extremely effective. To them all I express my gratitude.

Guy Bunnens

LIST OF CONTRIBUTORS

Mr Murray Adamthwaite: 4 Simone Court, Hallam, Victoria 3803, AUSTRALIA

Dr Peter Brennan: Department of Geography, The University of Melbourne, Parkville, Victoria 3052, AUSTRALIA

Dr Guy Bunnens: Department of Classics and Archaeology, The University of Melbourne, Parkville, Victoria 3052, AUSTRALIA

Prof. Charles Burney: Dept of Archaeology, University of Manchester, Oxford Road, Manchester M13 9PL, ENGLAND

Prof. Graeme W. Clarke: Humanities Research Centre, The Australian National University, GPO Box 4, Canberra, ACT 2601, AUSTRALIA

Dr Brian E. Colless: Religious Studies, Massey University, Palmerston North, NEW ZEALAND

Dr David Frankel, Dr Jenny M. Webb, Dr Christine Eslick: Department of Archaeology, La Trobe University, Bundoora, Victoria 3083, AUSTRALIA

Ms Liza Hopkins: Department of Classics and Archaeology, The University of Melbourne, Parkville, Victoria 3052, AUSTRALIA

Prof. Jean-Claude Margueron: Ecole Pratique des Hautes Etudes, IVe Section, Sciences historiques et philologiques, 45-47, rue des Ecoles, 75005 Paris, FRANCE

Mrs Claudia Sagona: Department of Classics and Archaeology, The University of Melbourne, Parkville, Victoria 3052, AUSTRALIA

Ms Rachael Sparks: Department of Archaeology, A14, University of Sydney, Sydney, NSW, 2006, AUSTRALIA

"THE HIGHLAND SHEEP ARE SWEETER…"

BY

Charles BURNEY

Cultural interactions can be unwelcome and violent; they can be agreed and mutually profitable; or they can be subtle, slow and barely perceptible. In the ancient Near East, as elsewhere, these can be investigated from different angles. Some decades ago the emphasis was predominantly on typology, particularly of pottery.[1] Subsequently certain traditional models, such as those involving migration, have been démodés. Typology could indeed be quite a dreary business, though whether that can justify its abandonment is another matter. As the first announcement of this gathering implied, other disciplines beyond archaeology need to be brought into play, if anything like a rounded reconstruction of past cultures is to be achieved. Historians, linguists, anthropologists and students of art and religion can all contribute. Indeed the archaeologist may find himself supplying the mortar, as it were, to bond these bricks together.

Historians and linguists can assist the archaeologists only back to a certain stage in time. For the latter it is the challenge of investigating the components of early languages or proto-languages which provides the road to unravelling past conundra, whether it be the quest for the *Urheimat* of the Proto-Indo-Europeans[2] or the effort to determine the relationship of Hurrian with Urartian,[3] to name but two examples. The archaeologist as prehistorian can push back the chronological limits of socio-economic interpretations or models, and is of course perfectly entitled to do so, provided that the basic data are never lost to sight. Once models begin to be constructed on a foundation of other models, then it is time to ring the alarm bells. Discussion of discussions needs strict discipline, restraint and brevity. I shall try hard to practise what I preach!

AS	*Anatolian Studies*
BAR	*British Archaeological Reports*, International Series
JIES	*Journal of Indo-European Studies*
ARAB	D.D. LUCKENBILL, *Ancient Records of Assyria and Babylonia I-II*, Chicago 1926-27
RA	*Revue d'Assyriologie*
UKN	G.A. MELIKISHVILI, *Urartskie Klinoobraznye Nadpisi* (=Urartian Cuneiform Inscriptions), Moscow 1960

[1] e.g. A.L. PERKINS, *The Comparative Archeology of Early Mesopotamia*, Chicago 1949.

[2] J.P. MALLORY, "A short history of the Indo-European problem", *JIES*, 1 (1973), pp. 21-65.

[3] I.M. DIAKONOFF, *Hurro-Urartian as an Eastern Caucasian Language*, Munich 1985; John A.C. GREPPIN & S.A. STAROSTIN, "The make-up of the Armenian unclassified substratum", *When Worlds Collide — Indo-Europeans and Pre-Indo-Europeans*, ed. T.L. MARKEY & J.A.C. GREPPIN, Ann Arbor 1990, pp. 203-210.

Man is indeed an economical animal; and it is perfectly reasonable that the topic of trade has been at the forefront of most discussions of cultural interaction in the ancient Near East. In this context may from time to time be found surviving records which cast far more light on human endeavour and frailty than ever can be seen in the bombastic annals of Assyrian and other kings, concerned with propaganda and their place in posterity. The Old Assyrian trading network, centred on Kültepe (Kanesh), is a case in point.[4] No other corpus of written records affords such intimate light on the cultural interaction between highlands and lowlands, in this case between central Anatolia and Assyria. Detailed as the annals of some of the Assyrian kings may be, they cast light principally on the Late Assyrian period. The economic evidence available in the Old Assyrian and Old Babylonian archives is not, however, paralleled by comparable business records in the early first millennium B.C., although the brief reports from Assyrian agents can be informative on the state of affairs in neighbouring states, notably Urartu.[5]

In trying to determine the cultural interactions between the highland zone of eastern Anatolia, Trans-Caucasia and north-western Iran and the lowlands of Mesopotamia and Syria from prehistoric to early historic times, i.e. through the Bronze Age and down to the rise of the Persian empire, one is at once faced by a gaping void. For all but the last three centuries or so of these three millennia, from mid-fourth to mid-first millennium B.C., there are virtually no written records within the whole zone eventually to become the kingdom of Urartu (Van).[6] Moreover, archaeology fails us, for there is a remarkable dearth of data over most of this terrain.

From the exploitation of obsidian sources in the seventh and sixth millennia B.C. to the fall of Urartu and the establishment of the Persian empire the highland scene is only fitfully illuminated by light from the south. Cultural interactions have of course long been sought along the lines of penetration by southern merchants from the Mesopotamian cities, followed in time by military demonstrations or serious campaigns. The implication has been that this amounted to exploitation of the mineral and other resources of the highland zone by the more sophisticated southerners. There is of course much to commend this view, even if it has led to such extremes as the late Henri Frankfort's emphasis on all regions outside Mesopotamia as "peripheral", a view in part supported by Biblical scholars.[7] If large cities are seen as essential prerequisites for a developed culture — too wide a topic to debate here — then this traditional approach is doubtless justifiable. It goes some way, for example, to explain the dearth

---

[4] Among the extensive literature may be mentioned: P. GARELLI, *Les Assyriens en Cappadoce*, Paris 1963; K.R. VEENHOF, *Aspects of Old Assyrian Trade and its Terminology*, Leiden 1972.

[5] Leroy WATERMAN, *Royal Correspondence of the Assyrian Empire*, Ann Arbor 1930, letter no. 144 (rebellion), no. 146 (defeat of Urartian army by Cimmerians); no. 444 (five Urartian governors); and other index entries under 'Urartu'.

[6] Except for the Yoncalu (Malazgirt) inscription of Tiglath-Pileser I (*ARAB* I, 270).

[7] H. FRANKFORT, *Art and Architecture of the Ancient Orient*, Harmondsworth 1954.

of material remains from the centuries preceding the rise of the kingdom of Van (Urartu) during the ninth century B.C. The great fortresses built around Lake Van and subsequently further afield towards the frontiers present no problem, for they were built, it is suggested, simply in response to the threat posed by Assyria, anxious to extend her territories and to acquire ever more material wealth in the form of booty. It is rather vaguely assumed that the Assyrians were there because of the demand for iron on the Mesopotamian market. Horses, cattle and sheep provided a welcome bonus.

But is this orthodoxy really tenable? Highland communities live closer to the landscape than their urban neighbours in the plain; and that landscape can better be exploited for local advantage in terms of security. Modern archaeologists are doubly handicapped in their attempts to reconstruct the Early Bronze Age (Early Trans-Caucasian / Kura-Araks) culture and its successors, in the natural environment of the fourth to first millennia B.C.: first, they seldom spend much, if any, time in Van or Erzurum, in Muş or Malatya, in Yerevan or Tabriz during the winter months; second, it is harder for them than for travellers a century ago, such as Lynch, to find contemporary evidence to recreate the habitations and agrarian technology of prehistoric times.[8] Indeed it would not be easy today to take all the photographs of village life taken in Kayalidere in 1965-66, thanks to the inexorable advance of bulldozer, concrete mixer and lorry, not to mention the impact of radio, television and the *Gastarbeiter* syndrome. As for the natural environment, pollen and varve data from sediments in Lake Van have contributed to a picture of maximum forest cover in the mid-second millennium B.C.[9] This process must have begun at least by the time of the general climatic amelioration which reached its climax in the mid-fourth millennium B.C. What connection this may have had with the emergence of the long-lasting and widespread Early Trans-Caucasian (ETC) culture at about the same time one can but speculate. Others may think that too cautious! Pressure of population is not necessarily too facile an explanation for the rapid expansion in the ETC I period (later fourth millennium B.C.).

One possible factor behind the drive south-westward from Trans-Caucasia, towards first the Elazığ plain (ETC I) and then across the upper Euphrates to the Malatya region, including Arslantepe (ETC II), could have been the great development of metallurgy around the Ergani deposits of copper. As I pointed out elsewhere, Arslantepe can be seen as a classic "gateway" site, in this case from Mesopotamia and north Syria in the Late Uruk period into the highland zone, rapidly coming under the umbrella of the ETC cultural traditions.[10] Excavated remains of metallurgical workshops —

---

[8] H.F.B. LYNCH, *Armenia — Travels and Studies II*, London 1901, pp. 123-124 and *passim*.
[9] E.T. DEGENS & F. KURTMAN (edd.), *The Geology of Lake Van* (Maden Tetkik ve Arama Enstitüsü Yayinlarindan no. 169), Ankara 1978, p. 122.
[10] C. BURNEY, "Arslantepe as a gateway to the highlands: a note on Periods VIA-VID", *Between the Rivers and Over the Mountains* (Alba Palmieri Memorial Volume, ed. M. FRANGIPANE *et al.*, Rome 1993, pp. 311-317).

notably at Norşuntepe, Tepecik and Arslantepe — have provided material for experiments to clarify the technology available to the coppersmiths of the later fourth and third millennia B.C.[11] Percentages of arsenic, antimony and other metals have been recorded, and the clear conclusion is that arsenic is often present in percentages too high to be anything other than the product of deliberate alloying by the smelters. Such advances made possible the use of the sulphide coppers and thus the exploitation of the richer chalcopyritic deposits. It would be of significant help in our search for cultural interactions between the so-called Fertile Crescent and the highland zone to the north and north-east if it were feasible to locate many datable mine workings. In fact, however, as shown by a recent study,[12] only a minority of ancient mine workings can be dated with assurance to the Early Bronze Age: of 32 mineral deposits in the Caucasus region, only two have unquestionable traces of Early Bronze Age workings; three others are indicated as Early Bronze Age with a question-mark. Of other workings, described as of Middle or Late Bronze Age date, only one is of unquestioned date (Late Bronze Age). Unfortunately the evidence for the technological advances needed for production of deliberate copper-arsenic alloys is so far lacking in eastern Anatolia and Trans-Caucasia, i.e. in most of the ETC cultural zone outside the Elaziğ-Malatya region, unique in its accessibility for the Mesopotamian and north Syrian merchants.

It is therefore quite impossible — and all the more so in the absence of written records — to identify those who worked these copper and arsenic deposits, let alone other minerals. The weight of probability surely suggests that miners and metalsmiths were of one and the same stock, whatever their precise ethno-linguistic affinities. Neither Sumerians nor Semites seem likely to have played a direct part. Their contribution was to provide a far larger market than could ever have been available within the bounds of the highland zone, even if one takes that as extending beyond ETC limits, into central Anatolia to the west and across the Iranian plateau to the east. The existence of a term for 'metal' (*haius*) in the Proto-Indo-European (PIE) language, if securely accredited, gives a *terminus post quem* for the origins of the PIE nucleus.[13] There is the possibility that this term can be translated as copper with natural admixtures or as the alloy of copper with arsenic. The implication, the linguists conclude, is that the Hittito-Luvian dialects may thus have separated from the nuclear PIE homeland by a time in the fifth or fourth millennium B.C.[14] Whether the PIE awareness of metal can be related to south-eastern Anatolia or (more probably, in my judgement)

---

[11] A. HAUPTMANN, J. LUTZ, E. PERNICKA & Ü. YALÇIN, "Zur Technologie der frühesten Kupferverhüttung im östlichen Mittelmeeraum", *ibid.*, pp. 541-572, especially for Norşuntepe.

[12] A.M. PALMIERI, K. SERTOK & E. CHERNYKH, "From Arslantepe metalwork to arsenical copper technology in eastern Anatolia", *ibid.*, pp. 573-599.

[13] I.M. DIAKONOFF, "On the original home of the speakers of Indo-European", *JIES*, 13 (1975), pp. 92-174. See pp. 114-115.

[14] *Ibid.*

to the Caucasus is another matter, too complex to be discussed now with profit. Suffice it to point out the relevance of this problem to that of the ethnic affinities of the ETC population.[15] Is it too rash to suggest the possibility of a mixture of Indo-European elements with a dominant Hurrian population, the two races sharing the cultural traditions moulded by a common natural environment? If this were so, it must have affected the cultural interactions of the ETC zone with lands beyond the Caucasus to the north. The well-documented Hurrian presence in north Syria and upper Mesopotamia during the second millennium B.C., notably at Alalakh and Nuzi, would not have been a significant factor there in the ETC period, though not to be ruled out altogether.[16]

Of the quest for metals by lowlanders in the highlands of the former ETC zone during the second millennium B.C. and the early first millennium B.C. we have merely rather meagre references in the Assyrian records, which only in the thirteenth century B.C. begin to attempt accounts of military campaigns, a significant advance in historiography.[17] Not until the reign of Shalmaneser III (859-824 B.C.) do detailed, consecutive annals relating Assyrian attacks on Urartu and its neighbours appear:[18] if such were written down in earlier reigns, few have survived, though there is a vivid record of the first four campaigns of Tiglath-Pileser I, in the late twelfth century B.C.[19] To this reign belongs the one Assyrian inscription to have survived within the heartland of Urartu, the stele set up at Yoncalu near Malazgirt, in the upper valley of the southern Euphrates (River Murat, ancient Arsanias).[20] Among the booty from this first campaign are recorded "180 bronze vessels, five copper bowls, together with (the statues of) their gods, gold and silver, the choicest of their possessions."[21] The next year "120 chariots and their yoked teams"[22] were among the booty from the northern highlands, the land of Shubarti. The next year thirty talents of bronze are mentioned, but whether in ingot form or simply by weight of items looted is not recorded. Again in the third year of Tiglath-Pileser I (c. 1111 B.C.) "120 of their armoured chariots"[23] are mentioned as captured in battle. 1,200 horses and 2,000 head of cattle were imposed as tribute, presumably annual. Later on the well-known

---

[15] C. BURNEY, "Hurrians and Proto-Indo-Europeans: the ethnic context of the Early Trans-Caucasian culture", *Anatolia and the Ancient Near East — Studies in Honor of Tahsin Özgüç*, ed. Kutlu EMRE et al., Ankara 1989, pp. 45-51.
[16] G. WILHELM, *The Hurrians* (trans. J. Barnes), Warminster 1989, pp. 17-19.
[17] *ARAB* I, 114.
[18] Most notably in the Kurkh Monolith (*ARAB* I, 594-611); H. RUSSELL, "Shalmaneser's campaign to Urartu in 856 B.C. and the historical geography of eastern Anatolia according to the Assyrian sources", *AS*, 34 (1984), pp. 171-201.
[19] *ARAB* I, 220-238.
[20] See note 6.
[21] *ARAB* I, 222.
[22] *ARAB* I, 226.
[23] *ARAB* I, 236.

reliefs from Dur-Sharrukin (Khorsabad) depict Assyrian soldiers removing items from the temple of Ḫaldi at Muṣaṣir/Ardini.

These details of plunder, especially of metalwork, are relevant to the question of the attraction of the highlands for the Assyrian kings as a source of iron and other metals. It has often been almost taken for granted that this was a major motive for Assyrian campaigns into Nairi and Urartu, even with the implication that access to the sources for purposes of mining was sought.[24] There is in fact no evidence, written or material, to support a theory such as this. Indeed it can surely be dismissed as inherently implausible, for several reasons. First, the provisioning of miners would be an ongoing task, requiring the cooperation of the local inhabitants. Second, the Assyrian army normally sustained itself by living off the land, necessitating keeping on the move. Third, the long, harsh winters, when the passes over the mountains are snowbound, would render any Assyrians left to work at iron or copper extraction hopelessly vulnerable to attack. The attraction of the highlands as a source of iron and other metals was strong; but the Assyrians — like the Vikings after them, in north-western Europe — expected to carry off chariots, tools, weapons, jewellery, vesssels of all kinds, whatever metal artifacts they could find. That was how they gained the metals they coveted. In this respect cultural interaction, at least from about the thirteenth century B.C. onwards, was normally one-sided. This does not by any means, however, imply that highland communities were by definition backward compared with their lowland enemies. It was the latter who played the role of the barbarian plundering all they could find. The regrettable lack of archaeological data on the ground to confirm these broad hints from the written records of the enemy cannot realistically be allowed to lead us to postulate an unsophisticated society with a low level of technology.

Unfortunately it is notoriously hard to date ancient mine workings, including iron workings within the territories controlled for its duration by the kingdom of Urartu. Some suggested as being of Urartian date may in fact be medieval: these lie in the highlands south of Lake Van.[25] Archaeologists have constantly to resist any temptation to attribute undated discoveries to the period in which they happen to have a specialized interest.

The relative paucity of surviving metalwork from Urartu, with exceptions such as Toprakkale, Karmir-Blur, Altintepe, Kayalidere and Giyimli, the last not so well documented, is in marked contrast with the thousands of bronzes from Luristan, to which, for lack of any local written records, it remains impossible to attach any firm ethnic label.[26] The Urartian bronzes are readily classifiable into two broad categories,

---

[24] Prentiss de Jesus, *The Development of Prehistoric Mining and Metallurgy in Anatolia*, Oxford 1980.

[25] Oktay Belli, "Ore deposits and ore mining in eastern Anatolia in the Urartian period: silver, copper and iron in Urartu", *Urartu — a Metal-Working Center in the First Millennium B.C.*, ed. K. Merhav, Jerusalem 1991, pp. 14-41.

[26] O.W. Muscarella, "The background to the Luristan bronzes", *Bronzeworking Centres of Western Asia, 1000-539 B.C.*, ed. J.E. Curtis, London 1988, pp. 33-44.

Van Loon's 'court style"[27] and the "popular" style manifested mainly on a number of belts from the Trans-Caucasian region of Urartu and from further afield, as far north as the lower Volga.[28] The mythological creatures, such as the winged horse, of this popular style owe nothing to Assyria. One has the intuitive impression that this was a reaction against the rather slavish attachment of the court at Van to Assyrian fashions, in line with the general cultural alignment of the dynasty ever since Sarduri I founded Tushpa (Van Kale): this reaction came in the seventh century B.C., when Urartu was no longer under serious threat from the south. Rather had it suffered near-mortal damage at the hands of the Cimmerians, in the reigns of Rusa I and Argishti II. Not for the first time cultural interactions with lands on either side of the Caucasus proved as significant for eastern Anatolia and north-western Iran as did those with lands to the south.

It would of course be a great cause for satisfaction if a similar dichotomy between royal or official and popular styles could be detected in textiles, always among the most widely trafficked goods, carried along the routes through and beyond the highland zone. There is no evidence of the importation of cotton into Urartu: nor was silk known until the last days of the kingdom. While bronzesmiths and ironsmiths would have formed specialized, probably exclusive guilds, in all but name, production of clothing and rugs, whether woven or knotted, surely must have helped to pass the long, bitterly cold winter months. This would in all probability have been the work of women and children. Kilims today display regional or tribal designs and motifs, whose ancestry in some cases must extend back centuries, if not millennia. The court workshops of the Late Assyrian state are known, from the abundant illustrations in the palace reliefs, to have produced both elaborately decorated (probably brocaded) cloaks or copes and regularly patterned, fringed carpets represented on threshold slabs. In Urartu there is the Adilcevaz relief, depicting a god in his "golden garment", in the Assyrianizing court sytle.[29] Much more sensational were Rudenko's discoveries of carpets and saddlecloths in the frozen kurgans of the Altai, far to the east:[30] remarkable for their preservation, they reveal the far-flung impact of Achaemenid civilization rather than any indigenous tradition. Earlier, perhaps of tenth-century B.C. manufacture, there are some details of dress to be observed in the crowded themes depicted on the gold bowl of Hasanlu, trapped in the destruction of Hasanlu IVB (c. 800 B.C.) by the troops of Menua.[31] No evidence of textiles seems to be known from the second

[27] M.N. VAN LOON, *Urartian Art*, Istanbul 1966.
[28] U. SEIDL, "Urartu as a bronzeworking centre", *op. cit.*, ed. J.E. CURTIS, pp. 169-175, with reference to the cemetery of Achm'ilov (p. 172).
[29] C.A. BURNEY & G.R.J. LAWSON, "An Urartian relief from Adilcevaz...", *AS*, 8 (1958), pp. 211-217.
[30] S.I. RUDENKO, *Frozen Tombs of Siberia — The Pazyryk Burials of Iron Age Horsemen*, (trans. M.W. Thompson) London 1970.
[31] I.J. WINTER, "The 'Hasanlu gold bowl': thirty years later", *Expedition*, 31 (1989), pp. 87-106.

millennium B.C. From the ETC culture, however, there may be hints of textile patterns in some of the incised decoration of pottery of ETC II date from Yanik Tepe, near Tabriz, although an alternative interpretation suggests wood-carving motifs.[32] Comparable decoration is discernible elsewhere, as on pottery of Khanzadian's Shengavit style.[33]

Metalwork and textiles, though not the only manufactured goods of the highland zone, were surely the most easily and widely traded, being portable and scarcely liable to damage. As such they were vehicles of cultural interaction, on present evidence entirely from south to north, at least in courtly circles in the Urartian period.

To what extent foods were traded, influencing the receiving end of the line, is highly arguable. In general terms it seems to me that the probabilities of exports of food in the ancient Near East have sometimes been much exaggerated, except perhaps in the Gulf region, where water transport could be used and where there was demand. But drink is another matter. Material evidence, in the form of grape pips, as well as much later historical references in Classical sources, suggest that viticulture originated in the highlands from Georgia to the upper Euphrates around Elazığ.[34] The ubiquitous storerooms of the major Urartian citadels invariably contain huge pithoi, whose contents — it seems beyond doubt, if only from both Assyrian and Urartian written sources, including the pictograms at Kayalidere — included wine.[35] Grapes were therefore grown for wine on a large scale under the Urartian kings, and almost certainly also much earlier. What place, if any, wine took in trade beyond the highlands is an intriguing question.

Cultural interaction by definition involves movement of personnel. Here we are considering not large-scale migration, at least not before the arrival of the Armenians from the west, but movements of baggage trains or military formations. It was in this context that one of the strongest, most significant and permanent impacts of the highlands upon the lowlands to the south may be discerned. This was the deployment of the horse. While donkeys are better attested in trading caravans, rapid dispatch of messages or decisive impact on the battlefield required horses. Their homeland has convincingly been traced as far as the Ukraine in the fifth millennium B.C.;[36] there is

---

[32] C.A. BURNEY, "Excavations at Yanik Tepe, north-west Iran", *Iraq*, 23 (1961), pp. 138-153; "Excavations at Yanik Tepe, Azerbaijan, 1961…", *Iraq*, 24 (1962), pp. 134-149.

[33] C.A. BURNEY & D.M. LANG, *The Peoples of the Hills*, London 1971, p. 59.

[34] Edward HYAMS, *Dionysus — A Social History of the Wine Vine*, London 1965; *Genesis* IX, 18-29 (drunkenness of Noah); D.M. LANG, *Armenia — Cradle of Civlization*, London 1970; C.A BURNEY & D.M. LANG, *op. cit.* (n. 33), p. 11

[35] C.A. BURNEY, "A first season ef excavations at the Urartian citadel of Kayalidere", *AS*, 16 (1966), pp. 55-111. For the pithos room and pictograms, pp. 83-90.

[36] D.W. ANTHONY, "The 'Kurgan Culture', Indo-European origins and the domestication of the horse: a reconsideration", *Current Anthropology*, 27 (1986), pp. 291-314; J.P. MALLORY, "The ritual treatment of the horse in the early kurgan tradition", *JIES*, 9 (1981), pp. 205-226; S. BOKONYI, "The earliest wave of domestic horses in east Europe", *JIES*, 6 (1978), pp. 1-16.

fourth-millennium B.C. evidence from the Elaziğ region, near the upper Euphrates.[37] The Mesopotamian world was in some respects slow to accept the horse, though there is physical evidence from Kish (c. 2700 B.C.).[38] A little earlier the horse appears, it seems, in Proto-Elamite hieroglyphs; and by mid-third millennium B.C. in Sumerian cuneiform.[39] It was of course another millennium before the chariots of Mitanni and its knightly class of *maryannu* were to make their impact in Syria and northern Mesopotamia. But, while one may accept that chariotry was introduced into the Near East by Indo-Aryan intruders, however small their number, there is no necessity to associate the early appearance of the horse with Indo-European elements infiltrating the indigenous population. Admittedly the Maikop culture, with which is associated a tomb at Klady in the Krasnodar region with murals including a row of horses,[40] can reasonably be put in an Indo-European context; and parallels with the "standards" from Alaca Hüyük suggest those tombs likewise imply an Indo-European intrusive élite in central Anatolia in the Early Bronze II period.[41] These were among many manifestations — along with the Troy II hoards, Horoztepe and Mahmutlar — of the "cultural interface" between the Near East and the world of the steppes. With the association of kurgans with Indo-European groups, the dating of Indo-European infiltration into Trans-Caucasia, while possibly as early as the ETC II period, has recently been placed by implication at around 2250 B.C., that being the date proposed for the earliest kurgans in Georgia, as with those in Azerbaijan.[42] The ethnic affinities of the Urartian ruling class were certainly not Indo-European. Equally certainly they and their successive kings were proud, enthusiastic horsemen,[43] a tradition manifested in our own times: in 1956, for example, the bride price in the district of Gürpinar, south-east of Van and including the great Urartian fortress of Çavuştepe, was the equivalent of £800 to £1,000 sterling plus a rifle and a horse. Born to the saddle, these villagers were not over fussy about the degree to which their horses were broken in, as I myself can bear witness. By contrast, the Assyrians were not very quick to make full use of the horse, cavalry appearing in their army only in the early ninth century B.C.[44] To this day the burial ritual in Ossetia includes an echo of pre-Christian horse sacrifice, reminiscent of Scythian rites: a horse in funerary panoply is led to

---

[37] S. BOKONYI, "Horses and sheep in east Europe in the Copper and Bronze Ages", *Proto-Indo-European — The Archaeology of a Linguistic Problem*, ed. S. SKOMAL & E. POLOMÉ, Washington D.C. 1987, pp. 136-144.

[38] Theya MOLLESON, "A charioteer from the Royal Cemetery", paper delivered at the fifth annual conference of the British Association for Near Eastern Archaeology, Cambridge, December 1991.

[39] I.M. DIAKONOFF, *loc. cit.* (n. 13), p. 168, note 29.

[40] A.D. REZEPKIN, "Paintings from a tomb of the Majkop culture, *JIES*, 20 (1992), pp. 59-70.

[41] J. MELLAART, "Anatolia and the Indo-Europeans", *JIES*, 9 (1981), pp. 135-149.

[42] O. DJAPARIDZE, "Über die ethnokulturelle Situation in Georgien gegen Ende des 3. Jahrtausends v. Chr.", in M. FRANGIPANE *et al.*, *op. cit.* (n. 10), pp. 475-491.

[43] *UKN* 110.

[44] *ARAB* I, 406 (Tukulti-Ninurta II).

the grave, the reins being put in the hands of the dead man, with the words "let this be your horse".[45]

On examining the most prominent achievements of Urartian civilization, the massive fortresses as well as the finely built square temples, one is faced immediately by the problem of their background and origins. Chiselmarks abound on the rock-cut ledges of Van Kale and other strongholds, suggesting but scarcely proving the use of iron rather than of bronze chisels. Buildings cannot be moved. There is no textual or other indication of the employment of foreign artisans. No comparisons with Hittite architecture bear examination. The conclusion must surely therefore be that the skills required for these public works, carefully sited for the defence of Van itself or of the local area, were already available before Sarduri I established his new dynasty at Tushpa. Remains of pre-Urartian fortresses, yet to be located, could well lie concealed beneath larger, more massively constructed Urartian fortresses. The unification of the clans — twenty-three and then sixty of which are mentioned by Tiglath-Pileser I[46] — provided the political impetus essential for recruitment of the large labour force without which the fortresses could never have been built. Here therefore is little or no hint of cultural interaction, rather of an indigenous development inspired by a political stimulus. Just for once the highlanders matched the lowlanders at their own game, abandoning their centrifugal habits of many centuries.

What of the religious traditions inherited and bequeathed by Urartu? The temples of Urartu, like the fortresses, demonstrate independent development, even if Urartian iconography exhibits overwhelming dependence on Assyrian models. It is not sentimental to stress the love of the highlanders for their homeland, its mountains and rivers and trees, the last much more widespread than today: this is apparent in the offerings made to 'lands', 'lakes' and 'mountain passes' in the Meher Kapisi rock inscription at Van;[47] and Hurrian deification of mountains is well attested. The god, moreover, emerged from the rock through the niche representing a temple door.[48] The Armenians, most of them of Urartian ancestry though adopting the Indo-European language of their conquerors, listened with rapt attention for the oracles provided by the rustling of the *sos* trees at Armavir.[49] In none of these aspects can the religion of the highlanders have owed much to the southerners in the lowlands.

Are there not ways not normally much considered by archaeologists, but rather by anthropologists, in which both new information and ancestral stories might be

---

[45] A.D. REZEPKIN, *loc. cit.* (n. 40).

[46] *ARAB* I, 236.

[47] M. SALVINI, "The historical background of the Urartian monument of Meher Kapisi", *Anatolian Iron Ages 3 — The Proceedings of the Third Anatolian Iron Ages Colloquium held at Van 6-12 August 1990*, ed. A. ÇILINGIROĞLU & D.H. FRENCH, British Institute of Archaeology at Ankara Monographs no. 16 (1994), pp. 205-210.

[48] *Ibid.*

[49] C.A. BURNEY & D.M. LANG, *op. cit.* (n. 33), p. 215.

transmitted and widely disseminated? The epics and songs of bards should not be ruled out of consideration, even if the resultant cultural interaction was essentially from one generation to the next. From distant Ugarit, it has been claimed, come the oldest surviving examples of musical notation. Admittedly matters remain unclear; but some tablets record Hurrian songs "complete with directions for musical accompaniments."[50] Assuming for the sake of argument a predominantly Hurrian population in the ETC zone and successor cultures in the territories later within Urartu, there seems no *a priori* difficulty in postulating a role for the minstrel or bard. In the early centuries A.D. drums, pipes, lyres and trumpets were played by musicians entertaining Armenian kings: these provided the accompaniment for the minstrel (*gusan*) at the royal court and at funerals.[51] If a very distant comparison be allowed, in the Iron Age in the highlands of Scotland the bard had a highly privileged status, allowing him at times to depart from his usual role of eulogizing his master to indulging in satire, evidently with impunity, with the implication of considerable political influence.[52] In preliterate times, or when literacy was restricted to a tiny minority, what more effective way of passing on news and views? Such bardic compositions would tend to be a force for conservatism and thus for cultural continuity.

Another force for conservatism was the cult of the hearth, apparently widespread if not ubiquitous in the ETC cultural zone, exemplified by decorated hearths and shrines, most vividly at Pulur (Sakyol) near Elazığ, one of the Keban Dam Project rescue excavations of 1968-1975.[53] While such a cult was characteristic of early Indo-European communities, it did not originate with Indo-Europeans.[54] It would seem that it may well have first flourished in the ETC zone, and thus have been transmitted from the Hurrian to the Proto-Indo-European (PIE) homeland, unless one chooses to follow Gamkrelidze in locating the PIE *Urheimat* in eastern Anatolia and Trans-Caucasia, with the consequent attribution of Indo-European ethnicity to the ETC culture.[55] That seems unlikely, to put it mildly. This conclusion is not undermined by accepting the theory of Indo-European penetration into Anatolia from the east, very possibly in the fourth millennium B.C., partly on the basis of textual references to the

---

[50] G. WILHELM, *op. cit.* (n. 16), pp. 65-66; S. SEGERT, "Ugaritic poetry and poetics — some preliminary observations", *Ugarit Forschungen*, 2 (1979), pp. 729-738; A.D. KILMER et al., *Sounds from Silence: Recent Discoveries in Ancient Near Eastern Music*, Berkeley 1976; and a record with side 2 giving "A Hurrian cult song from ancient Ugarit (ca. 1400 B.C.)".

[51] C.A. BURNEY & D.M. LANG, *op. cit.* (n. 33), p. 264.

[52] I. FINLAY, *Columba*, London 1979, p. 156.

[53] H.Z. KOŞAY, *Keban Project — Pulur Excavations 1968-1970*, Middle East Technical University Keban Project Publications Series III, no. 1, Ankara 1976.

[54] A. DELLA VOLPE, "From the hearth to the creation of boundaries", *JIES*, 18 (1990), pp. 157-184, especially p. 158.

[55] T. GAMKRELIDZE & V. IVANOV, "The ancient Near East and the Indo-European question and the migration of tribes speaking Indo-European dialects", *JIES*, 13 (1985), pp. 3-91. For a contrary view: I.M. DIAKONOFF, *loc. cit.* (n. 13).

sun rising from the sea, i.e. the Caspian.[56] Intruders could have passed through the ETC lands without lasting effect and relatively quickly, perhaps at a time when the ETC cultural zone was itself undergoing rapid expansion in the ETC I period.

The cult of the hearth was domestic, presided over by the *paterfamilias* and associated, it has been suggested, with formal boundaries.[57] Traces of such have not (to my knowledge, and I may be mistaken) survived in ETC contexts; but the whole evidence for this domestic cult can be taken to imply a dominant role for the family. This fits with the climatic and other environmental factors; and it could help to explain the remarkable tenacity and longevity of the ETC culture. A trend towards larger, more densely clustered houses as time passed is discernible at a number of sites, among them being ETC II Yanik Tepe, as well as a growth in the use of rectangular annexes. A steady increase in the total settled population and in the size of the typical family unit or household seems to be indicated.[58] Whether or not credence can be given to estimates of the number of inhabitants within each round house is another matter, with the suggestion that 38 square metres, the floorspace of the typical round house, sufficed for four people being presumably related to the ratio of children to adults.[59] There are no known close parallels for the cult of the hearth in subsequent periods in the highlands, though the chthonic cult indicated in Urartu by the inscribed niches of temple door form and probably also by the plain, un-inscribed stelae of Altintepe may well have had links with the cult of the hearth.[60] As for the decorated ETC hearths and shrines, their vividly abstract eyes defy precise interpretation. They speak of a world remote from the city life of Mesopotamia and Syria.

The traditional category of evidence for discussion of cultural interactions has been deliberately left almost to the end, for fear of being lured into the common approach, in which pottery — its forms, decorations, wares and distribution patterns — seems almost inevitably to predominate. Not for nothing was I accustomed on my surveys in years past to describe myself, when asked my profession, as a *çanak çömlek mühendisi* (potsherd engineer). Whether this always allayed fears about my credentials or even my sanity I am far from sure. Pottery, as with the ETC zone, can reinforce the evidence for cultural continuity, only in parts of the zone seriously breaking down in the final period (ETC III), i.e. the later third millennium B.C. This change came about in the Elaziğ-Malatya region, the most accessible to southern intrusion and economic

---

[56] G. STEINER, "The immigration of the first Indo-Europeans into Anatolia reconsidered", *JIES*, 18 (1990), pp. 185-214.
[57] A. DELLA VOLPE, "On Indo-European ceremonial and socio-political elements underlying the origin of formal boundaries", *JIES*, 20 (1992), pp. 71-122, citing Hittite, Homeric, Vedic and other data.
[58] A.G. SAGONA, "Settlement and society in late prehistoric Trans-Caucasus", in M. FRANGIPANE *et al., op. cit.* (n. 10), pp. 453-474.
[59] R. NAROLL, "Floor area and settlement population", *American Antiquity*, 27 (1962), pp. 587-589.
[60] T. ÖZGÜC, *Altintepe II*, Ankara 1969, pp. 28-33 and 73-74; Pl. XXVI-XXVII.

impact.[61] The varied repertoire of decorative motifs and designs, normally in relief or incised, makes it tempting to try to pursue parallels across the landscape.[62] One such example, affording a parallel in general "feel" rather than in precise motifs, is with the pottery of the later third millennium B.C. of the Nagyrev culture of the central Carpathian basin, i.e. central Hungary.[63] The dating is not beyond the bounds of plausibility; but handling of this pottery from Hungary would probably at once dispel such a suggestion! Back in the 1950's I was impressed by the long life and apparent conservatism of the East Anatolian Early Bronze Age culture (not yet termed by me ETC): I suggested that it might, in the central regions such as those around Van and Erzurum, have persisted into the early second millennium B.C.[64] I wonder whether this is confirmed by Dr. Sagona's very recent discoveries near Erzurum? Ceramic typology must still of course play a leading role, if only from the ubiquity of pottery, with its accessibility for archaeological surveys.

There are surely faint hints of the ways in which the highland population lived in the apparent "dark age" of the second millennium B.C. Cemeteries such as Dedeli indicate contacts with the Urmia basin to the east, for not all Urmia ware found in Turkey today was imported recently from Iran by dealers.[65] Settlements surely existed, even if hardly any have yet been located. The forest cover had reached its greatest extent.[66] Timber, the easiest building material, was abundant. Wattle-and-daub structures in summer settlements at high altitudes are evidently characteristic of the ETC culture, at least in Georgia and probably elsewhere too.[67] If such became ubiquitous in the second millennium B.C., any impression of a cultural and maybe even of a demographic void must be thoroughly misleading. How did the clans of Nairi in the twelfth century B.C. survive the harsh winters? Are we really to believe that they survived throughout the year in tents? The record of Xenophon's *Anabasis* on the Carduchoi[68] and the fate of Enver Pasha's army near Erzurum in 1915 suggest otherwise.[69]

That the population of the territories brought under Urartian control was not inconsiderable seems to be implied by the remarkable programme of irrigation

---

[61] As indicated in virtually all the excavation reports for the sites in the area of the Keban Dam Project, especially Norşuntepe and Korucutepe: this had for some time been apparent. C.A. BURNEY, "Eastern Anatolia in the Chalcolithic and Bronze Age", *AS*, 8 (1958), pp. 157-209, especially pp. 205-208; ID., "Aspects of the excavations in the Altinova, Elaziğ", *AS*, 30 (1980), pp. 157-167.

[62] A.G. SAGONA, *The Caucasian Region in the Early Bronze Age, Part iii* (BAR 214), Oxford 1984, figs. 115-124.

[63] Rosza KALICZ-SCHREIBER, "Symbolic representation on Early Bronze Age vessels", *JIES*, 18 (1990), pp. 59-107.

[64] C.A. BURNEY & D.M. LANG, *op. cit.* (n. 33), pp. 46-47.

[65] Altan ÇILINGIROĞLU, "The second millennium painted pottery tradition of the Van Lake Basin", *AS*, 35 (1985), pp. 129-139.

[66] E.T. DEGENS & F. KURTMAN, *op. cit.* (n. 9); cf. *ARAB* II, 164-165 (Sargon II).

[67] A.G. SAGONA, in M. FRANGIPANE et al., *op. cit.* (n. 10), pp. 453-474.

[68] XENOPHON, *Anabasis* IV, iii.

[69] J. BUCHAN, *Greenmantle*, for a vivid if fictional account.

engineering initiated by Menua (c. 810-786 B.C.) and continued by his successors.[70] There is no hint of dramatic climatic deterioration to explain this, in spite of the fact that the Hiung-Nu (Huns) appear to have begun their protracted migration westwards from the borders of China at about this time, perhaps owing to drought in central Asia.[71] The Assyrians were prepared on occasions to record their admiration of some of the achievements of their enemies: horse-training, wine production and storage, gardening and irrigation were noted with approval by Sargon II on his famous eighth campaign (714 B.C.);[72] and Sennacherib followed with his impressive water supply system for the greatly expanded city of Nineveh.[73]

Of course the borrowings from Assyria cannot be ignored, most obviously that of the cuneiform script for royal inscriptions, initially recorded by Sarduri I not in his native Urartian but in the Akkadian of his Assyrian foes. Yet by the eighth century B.C. if not earlier a cosmopolitan style had developed through much of the Near East, manifested clearly, for example, in the ornamentation with bronze elements of furniture: this is discernible in a number of places, notably the North-West Palace of Nimrud, Zincirli (Sam'al), Kayalidere and Toprakkale.[74] More controversial is the precise character of the trade in bronze cauldrons with riveted protomes, most probably disseminated from production centres in north Syria to Urartu, Phrygia and Cyprus, with imitations further afield.[75] Thus the whole nature of cultural interaction was changing, as the Near East (in a sense) grew smaller, though there was no return to the palace-dominated economy of the eastern Mediterranean world in the Late Bronze Age. Nevertheless, long-distance movements of skilled metalworkers had undoubtedly occurred as early as the third millennium B.C., crossing political boundaries.[76] The market for ivory was exclusive, with professional craftsmen no doubt in contact with their opposite numbers on either side of the "highland line". Against all this cosmopolitan contact, the underlying cultural substrata were of much older ancestry than the fashion-orientated tastes of the court at Van.

---

[70] C.A. BURNEY, "Urartian irrigation works", *AS*, 22 (1972), pp. 179-186.

[71] E. HUNTINGTON, *The Pulse of Asia*, Boston 1919, p. ix; T. TALBOT-RICE, *The Scythians*, Ancient Peoples and Places, London 1957, p. 43. For an up-to-date model for the factors affecting climate in and beyond central Asia — from the viewpoints of geology, geochemistry and climatology, and based largely on American fieldwork in the Himalaya and Tibet — a BBC 2 *Horizon* series programme entitled "Tibet — the Ice Mother" and shown on 9 January 1995 seems highly relevant.

[72] *ARAB* II, 158-161.

[73] *ARAB* II, 332. J. READE, "Studies in Assyrian geography: Sennacherib and the waters of Nineveh", *RA*, 72 (1978), pp. 47-72; 157-180.

[74] H. FRANKFORT, *op. cit.* (n. 7), Plates 89 (Nimrud) and 162 (Zincirli). C.A. BURNEY, *op. cit.* (n. 35), Plates XXIa, XXVa and fig. 23 (Kayalidere). R.D. BARNETT, "The excavations of the British Museum at Toprakkale near Van", *Iraq*, 12 (1950), pp. 1-43. See fig. 22.

[75] For the "anti-Urartian" view, O.W. MUSCARELLA, "The oriental origin of siren cauldron attachments", *Hesperia*, 31 (1962), pp. 317-329.

[76] T. STECH & V.C. PIGOTT, "The metals trade in southwest Asia in the third millennium B.C.", *Iraq*, 48 (1986), pp. 39-64.

If a dark age did occur, it came with the fall of Urartu to the Medes (c. 590 B.C.) and the division of the land between Armenian newcomers and Alarodian remnants of the Hurro-Urartian population, as recounted in the *Cyropedia* of Xenophon.[77] In some sense a cultural continuum of three thousand years had come to an abrupt end. As for the arts, they were not to revive until the tenth century A.D., when King Gagik of Vashpurakan built of red volcanic tuff the richly carved church on the island of Aghtamar in the south-east corner of Lake Van.

What the highlanders absorbed from the lowlands is relatively well understood, what they gave to the lowlanders less so. With their superior bureaucratic tradition to organize the shepherds, the Assyrian sheep may well have been fatter, beneficiaries of a long governmental tradition.[78] But surely the highland sheep *were* sweeter!

I can but hope that this venture into a wide swathe of territory, in seeking new insights and reconsidering old, has not been entirely in vain. To my mind at least the archaeologist has to be an optimist, and must not allow himself to sink into the mood of the psalmist, when he wrote thus:

> "O thou enemy, destructions are come to a perpetual end: even as the cities which thou hast destroyed; their memorial is perished with them."[79]

---

[77] XENOPHON, *Cyropedia* I, 5; II, 4; III, 1. C.A. BURNEY & D.M. LANG, *op. cit.* (n. 33), pp. 179-180.
[78] P.E. ZIMANSKY, *Ecology and Empire — The Structure of the Urartian State*, SAOC 41, Chicago 1985, pp. 74-94, on (Urartian) "governmental administration and the problem of centralization".
[79] *Psalm IX*, verse 6.

THE RISE OF SOCIAL COMPLEXITY IN
EAST CENTRAL ANATOLIA IN THE EARLY BRONZE AGE

BY

Liza HOPKINS

Introduction

Changing patterns of social organisation have been the subject of study since at least the late nineteenth century when evolutionary thinkers such as Tylor[1] and Morgan[2] formulated their typologies of social forms. Although the evolutionary approach was repudiated quite early in anthropology, the neo-evolutionary paradigms of White,[3] Service,[4] and Fried[5] dominated archaeological research on the topic of social change in the middle part of this century. It is only comparatively recently that alternative theories have been proposed which include multilinear and systemic approaches to development, in place of the earlier unilinear and unidirectional schemes. It is indeed somewhat ironic that the topic of complexity in social life has itself become rather complex and difficult to discuss. Such disparate societies and forms of social organisation have been labelled as complex that the term is in danger of becoming largely meaningless as a descriptive category.

In order to investigate social change in a particular situation, it is necessary to understand exactly what is meant by 'complexity'. What in fact makes a society complex? At its most basic level every society consists of a number of individuals who interact with each other in a wide variety of ways and in a number of different situations. Yet it is the way that each group culturally transforms the basic biological interactions that is of relevance when different groups are to be compared. Since these cultural transformations are so diverse, it is not possible to study every given situation as a unique example of social organisation. Nor is this desirable, particularly for archaeology which relies (consciously or unconsciously) on ethnographic analogy to understand social functioning.

---

[1] E. TYLOR, *Anthropology*, London 1881.
[2] L. MORGAN, *Ancient Society*, New York 1879.
[3] L. WHITE, *The Evolution of Culture: The Development of Civilization to the Fall of Rome*, New York 1959.
[4] E. SERVICE, *Primitive Social Organisation: an evolutionary perspective*, New York 1962; ID., *The Hunters*, Englewood Cliffs, N.J. 1966.
[5] M. FRIED, *The Evolution of Political Society*, New York 1967; ID., "On the evolution of social stratification and the state", *Culture in History: Essays in honour of Paul Radin*, ed. S. DIAMOND, New York 1981, pp. 713-731.

The neo-evolutionists solved this problem by their broad general categorisation of every extant and conceivable social configuration. These categories were based on the economic, political, religious and social organisation of societies, with complexity being used to describe those societies whose organisations most closely resembled our own. But complexity in social life is a relative rather than absolute term, and cannot be simply identified by the presence or absence of a given list of material or organisational traits. That a society is recognised to be complex merely because of an institutionalised system of leadership, redistributive economics or centralised administration, is to needlessly restrict the range of social groups which qualify as being complex. Rather than focussing on the few who participate in and benefit from the above mentioned activities, complexity can be widened to include those who are not in the mainstream of social life: the producers, outsiders, the marginalised and the transient populations. If culture is viewed as a system, then all these different groups in society can be seen as subsystems, interacting with and affecting each other. Complexity is the arrangement or organisation of all the subsystems, not merely those relating to a social elite, and may be defined as "the degree of functional differentiation among societal units or subsystems".[6]

This rather general definition may be usefully applied to particular cases to explain changes in the archaeological record. Thus remains which indicate increasing differentiation and specialisation in economic, political and religious matters may be understood in the context of the society which produced them, rather than merely slotted into a rigid category within an unilinear evolutionary framework. This is not to deny the existence of social forms which may be labelled 'tribe', 'state' etc., rather it is to suggest a more fluid and contextual understanding of those terms.[7]

Within the parameters of such a general definition of the term 'complexity' it will be useful to be a little more specific in dealing with individual cases in the archaeological record. Two particular ways of looking at subsystems which may prove to be of value in the understanding of social change are the relative heterogeneity and/or inequality[8] of population groups within a society. The relative importance of these two social divisions may be especially useful for understanding change in areas peripheral to the great so-called 'pristine' states, such as Mesopotamia. By carefully examining the archaeological record of one such peripheral region, namely East Central Anatolia in the fourth and third millennia B.C. in terms of these two variables, light will be cast both on general processes of change in social organisation and in the specific forms of behaviour which survive only as archaeological evidence.

---

[6] M. ROTHMAN, "Evolutionary typologies and cultural complexity", *Chiefdoms and Early States in the Near East: the organizational dynamics of complexity,* ed. G. STEIN & M. ROTHMAN, Madison, Wisconsin, 1994, pp. 1-10.

[7] *Ibid.,* p. 4.

[8] R. McGUIRE, "Breaking down cultural complexity: inequality and heterogeneity", *Advances in Archaeological Method and Theory,* 6 (1983), pp. 91-142.

Heterogeneity and Inequality

That complexity may be subdivided was mooted by McGuire more than 10 years ago in his paper entitled "Breaking down cultural complexity: inequality and heterogeneity".[9] He wrote then "It is becoming increasingly clear that the concept of complexity contains too much" and proposed the identification of two "potentially independent variables", that is: diversity or heterogeneity; and stratification or inequality.[10] These two variables may be considered as divisions of society along either its horizontal or vertical axis. In other words "*Heterogeneity* refers to the distributions of populations between social groups" that are essentially politically and economically equal, whereas "*Inequality* deals with the differential access to material and social resources within a society."[11] It is also a "fallacy…[to] view cultural evolution as a simple process of lock-step increases in heterogeneity and inequality."[12]

McGuire gives as his archaeological example of this model, the massive mortuary monuments of the rulers of pristine states, such as the Egyptian pyramids, which represent a situation of low heterogeneity but very high inequality.[13] He does not claim, however, that this is a fixed stage in cultural evolution, through which all societies must pass.[14] Egypt, however, was one of the so-called primary or pristine examples of state formation. Can the concepts of inequality and heterogeneity be applied also to East Central Anatolia, a region on the periphery of the pristine Mesopotamian state, and hence vulnerable to influence from that state?

Statehood

The processes which led to the formation of the first, or pristine states must have been rather different from the conditions under which secondary states emerged. At least part of the stimulus for secondary state formation must lie in the interaction between societies with radically unequal forms of organisation. This may consist of a centre-periphery relationship, where a state society is privileged as a core society, and the less highly complex society is considered to be peripheral to that state. Another way of characterising this relationship is in terms of modern economic theories of development and underdevelopment. The core-periphery model is perhaps more relevant in a case such as the Keban sites, where the core area is a pristine state, and

---

[9] *Ibid.*
[10] *Ibid.*, p. 92.
[11] *Ibid.*, p. 93.
[12] *Ibid.*, p. 110.
[13] *Ibid.*, pp. 110-114.
[14] *Ibid.*, p. 119.

therefore the only society with that level of organisation within its world-system. Inevitably all the other groups with which the state comes into contact will be non-state societies.

Perhaps the crucial variable, then, in determining whether contact stimulates a society's development into statehood, is the level of its own internal social complexity. The more highly organized the society, the more likelihood that interpolity interaction will stimulate its own step over the threshold into statehood. Thus it is that a non-state society, perhaps because of internal heterogeneity, has developed a certain inequality resulting in the presence of some kind of elite stratum in society. This group is then susceptible to the influence of foreign elites. Such a positive feedback system will drag the non-state periphery into secondary statehood. If the peripheral groups do not already have a structure of inequality, the reverse may occur, and a negative feedback system would consolidate the egalitarian system in opposition to the core state society. Such a process may not be clearly discernible archaeologically, as "the evidence in favour of such a causal relationship is essentially negative".[15]

The influence of the Uruk state on the societies of East Central Anatolia at the end of the fourth millennium was brief but significant. Since the evidence appears to demonstrate that the Uruk settlers expected co-operation from the indigenous population,[16] it may be proposed that these local communities were already sufficiently complex to be able to cope with a higher level of organisation. Such complexity may have lain in the interaction between heterogeneous population elements engaged in different economic strategies.

Heterogeneity In East Central Anatolia

Ethnography provides a particularly interesting case study here, in the interaction between pastoral nomads and sedentary peoples. Most recent work on nomadic society has stressed the importance of a sedentary population for the establishment and continued existence of a nomadic way of life.[17]

The nature of this contact between nomadic and sedentary people is open to dispute and may well vary through both space and time. The identification of a 'trade' or

---

[15] P. KOHL, "The Transcaucasian 'periphery' in the Bronze Age: a preliminary formulation", *Resources, Power and Interregional Interaction,* ed. E. SCHORTMAN & P. URBAN, New York 1992, pp. 117-137.

[16] G. ALGAZE, *The Uruk World Sytem: the Dynamics of Expansion of Early Mesopotamian Civilization,* Chicago 1993, p. 62.

[17] E.g. C. CHANG & H. KOSTER, "Beyond bones: toward an archaeology of pastoralism", *Advances in Archaeological Method and Theory,* 9 (1986), pp. 97-148, p. 101; E. GELLNER, "Tribalism and the state in the Middle East", *Tribes and State Formation in the Middle East,* ed. P. KHOURY & J. KOSTINER, Berkeley 1990, pp. 109-128, p. 111; L. ANDERSON, "Tribe and state: Libyan anomalies", *Tribes and State Formation in the Middle East,* ed. P. KHOURY & J. KOSTINER, Berkeley 1990, pp. 288-302.

'raid' relationship is perhaps a misleading attempt to rigidify a more fluid relationship. It is not in fact in the interests of either party for the other to starve in a bad season, as both have a need to gain access to the other's trade and craft products.[18] That the balance of power between groups may have shifted through time is also not unlikely.

Contact between nomads and settled people may involve: direct trade of produce including meat, cheese, hides and possibly milk and wool in exchange for grain and other vegetable products; down the line trade of items produced further afield and acquired by nomads during other times of the year; negotiations over grazing land, camping areas and access to water. Hence the pastoralists may be more or less tied to the local settled population, and contact between the two groups may be long term and relatively stable.

It is clear that in order to negotiate such deals effectively, participants must have a certain level of knowledge and information about the price of commodities, the goods required and the possibility of alternative arrangements. Thus the individuals who carry out the negotiations on behalf of each group have access to the power which comes from the control of knowledge,[19] and the *role* of the negotiator is established. While this role is not necessarily either permanent or hereditary, and hence cannot be considered to be 'chiefly', it is nonetheless important in both defining and keeping separate the different communities. It is also able to perpetuate itself as a bridge between the groups.[20]

Evidence For Nomadism

Of what relevance is this to East Central Anatolia in the Early Bronze Age? The most important site to be considered is Arslantepe, near the present day city of Malatya, while the material from the salvage excavations in the Keban reservoir basin carried out in the late 1960s and early 1970s provide a useful comparison. To begin with it is necessary to find evidence for heterogeneity in the Late Chalcolithic period, and more specifically, evidence for a nomadic element alongside the sedentary population.

The (in)visibility of nomad remains in the archaeological record is a well recognised problem.[21] At Arslantepe the presence of red-black burnished pottery alongside a

---

[18] E. Gellner, *loc. cit.* (n. 17), pp. 111-112.
[19] A. Ahmed, "Tribal and sedentary elites: a bridge between two communities", *The Desert and the Sown: Nomads in the Society*, ed. C. Nelson, Berkeley 1973, pp. 75-96, p. 87.
[20] *Ibid.*, p. 93.
[21] E.g: I. Finkelstein & A. Perevolotsky, "Processes of sedentarisation and nomadisation in the history of Sinai and the Negev", *BASOR*, 279 (1990), pp. 67-88; S. Rosen, "Invisible nomads: a rejoinder", *BASOR*, 287 (1992), pp. 87-88; R. Cribb, *Nomads in Archaeology*, Cambridge 1991, p. 68.

chaff-faced assemblage comparable to that of 'Amuq F,[22] may be indicative of the presence of groups of people from the North East of Anatolia and Trans-Caucasia. That such people may have practised pastoral nomadism has often been suggested.[23] The apparent absence of settlement sites is not compelling evidence for or against the presence of nomads, but the use of wattle and daub architecture in the EBI period suggests that nomads were already present in this area. As it is an area of very harsh winters, the extra energy input required to construct mud-brick housing would appear to be worthwhile for any permanent occupation. That these technologies had not been lost at the end of the Late Chalcolithic age is abundantly clear from the use of such materials at other sites and indeed, at Norşuntepe, alongside wattle and daub dwellings themselves. It thus seems clear that to understand the phenomenon of this new type of architecture, social and cultural factors must be considered.

It is clear that housing fulfils many more functions than merely the provision of shelter, even in extremely cold climates.[24] The house is "a social unit of space"[25] and hence the form of the house is culturally ordained. Immigrants to an area often bring their architecture with them, even if it is ecologically unsuitable, because it is familiar and fulfils a symbolic role.[26] Architecture may then be a more reliable indicator of population change than cultural items with low symbolic value such as utilitarian artefacts. Other cultural traits with deep symbolic significance may also be useful in detecting population shifts. Mortuary practice, thus far sadly lacking in East Anatolian contexts, and ritual practice should provide useful evidence of this type.

The short term residence of nomads benefits from the simpler construction technique of wattle and daub. Thus it may be suggested, that in the Late Chalcolithic period this area already contained heterogeneous population elements, with a settled component interacting seasonally with nomadic groups.

It is almost impossible at present to identify social divisions within the nomadic population — such divisions can only be inferred ethnographically. But the settlement evidence from Arslantepe reveals the existence of an administrative system in use as early as the Late Chalcolithic period, thus suggesting a further degree of social complexity. A large public building dating to this period has been uncovered, along with

---

[22] A. PALMIERI, "Eastern Anatolia and early Mesopotamian urbanization: remarks on changing relations", *Studi di Paletnologia in Onore di Salvatore M. Puglisi,* ed. M. LIVERANI, A. PALMIERI & R. PERONI, Rome 1985, pp. 191-214.

[23] E.g.: R. AMIRAN, "Yanik Tepe, Shengavit and the Khirbet Kerak Ware", *Anatolian Studies,* 15 (1965), pp. 165-167; R. WHALLON & S. KANTMAN, "Early bronze age development in the Keban reservoir, east central Turkey", *Current Anthropology,* 10 (1969), pp. 128-133; A. SAGONA, "Settlement and society in late prehistoric Trans-Caucasus", *Between the Rivers and Over the Mountains: Archaeologica anatolica et mesopotamica Alba Palmieri dedicata,* ed. M. FRANGIPANE, H. HAUPTMAN, M. LIVERANI, P. MATTHIAE & M. MELLINK, Rome 1993, pp. 453-474.

[24] A. RAPOPORT, *House form and culture,* Engelwood Cliffs, New Jersey 1969, pp. 19-20.

[25] *Ibid.,* p. 46.

[26] *Ibid.,* p. 52. Colonial Australia provides a perfect example.

some seals and mass produced bowls, all of which point to a centralised redistributive economic system.[27] That such a system may include the products of pastoralists is not unlikely, and is indeed strengthened by the analysis of animal bone from the following Late Uruk period. At this time the number of sheep bones increases while the number of pigs declined, suggesting a degree of specialisation in pastoral production.[28]

As Stein says in the introduction to his dissertation on *Pastoral Production in Complex Societies*: "The degree of specialisation in herding provides an index of regional economic integration i.e.: economic interdependence between centres and their hinterlands. Generalised pastoral strategies indicate low levels of regional economic integration while specialised, exchange oriented production strategies reflect a high degree of economic interdependence between centres and rural settlements".[29] Thus the integration of nomadic production into the economy of the sedentary population at Arslantepe is again suggested, while it is also apparent that such a system represents not only heterogeneity but at least some measure of social inequality.

The Uruk Influence

The appearance of the Late Uruk cultural complex at Arslantepe and at Tepecik, may not be a total qualitative change imposed on Anatolian sites from outside, but rather a foreign influence which built on and intensified the level of complexity already present in local culture. That the arrival of the Late Uruk people did not cause a total disruption is evidenced by the construction of a large period VIA public building directly over and incorporating the walls of a Late Chalcolithic (period VII) building at Arslantepe. It is also clear from the continued use of local ceramic types both red-black burnished and chaff-faced wares, alongside the Mesopotamian influenced grit tempered wares and a very few imported pieces.[30]

The massive public architecture and complex administrative system of the Late Uruk period suggests that the arrival of a foreign 'elite' boosted the status and importance of the local elite, at the expense of the rest of the population, intensifying an already existing social inequality rather than initiating it.

The end of the Late Uruk phase at Arslantepe seems to have occurred swiftly, and presumably in response to events occurring further south in the Uruk homeland proper. The evidence suggests that the site was burnt and abandoned by its inhabitants,

---

[27] M. FRANGIPANE & A. PALMIERI, "Urbanisation in perimesopotamian areas. The case of eastern Anatolia", *Studies in the Neolithic and Urban Revolutions,* ed. L. MANZANILLA, Mexico: B.A.R. International Series 349, 1987, pp. 295-318.

[28] *Ibid.,* p. 299.

[29] G. STEIN, *Pastoral Production in Complex Societies*, Ph.D., University of Pennsylvania 1988, p. x.

[30] M. FRANGIPANE & A. PALMIERI, "Cultural developments at Arslantepe at the beginning of the third millennium", *Origini,* 12 (1983), pp. 523-574.

rather than destroyed by incoming invaders. It appears to have been deserted for some time before being briefly resettled by people using wattle and daub architecture and red-black burnished pottery with shapes corresponding to those common in the oldest Early Trans-Caucasian repertoire.[31]

The Indigenous Response

The probable interpretation of this is that nomads who were living already in the area took advantage of a convenient and unoccupied site to build their dwellings. Although two building phases have been discerned in this period, it seems that it may not have lasted very long, as would be expected of nomadic occupation. Such small, short-term and apparently flimsy habitations may well be widely distributed over this whole region, and by their very nature lost to the archaeological view. It is only perhaps the fortuitous choice of some nomads to settle on sites which had been previously occupied and would continue to be so for several millennia, that has revealed their presence to modern researchers.

That the post-hole architects and Trans-Caucasian pottery users were indeed one and the same group can best be indicated by consideration of the homeland of the pottery, Trans-Caucasia itself. As in East Central Anatolia, the use of mud-brick architecture in Neolithic Trans-Caucasia was in part replaced at the advent of the Early Bronze Age period by wattle and daub architecture,[32] presumably here too reflecting nomadic elements in society.

Perhaps the strongest evidence for pastoralism in this period comes from the wattle and daub houses at Norşuntepe, especially those of horizons XVII and XVIII. Two of the post hole houses of these levels have small triangular annexes which were interpreted by Hauptman as barns.[33] As has been pointed out elsewhere,[34] the key identifying feature of pastoral sites is the presence of enclosures for animals. While there is unfortunately no such clear correlation between nomadism and material culture, there are some artefacts which are more clearly suited to a mobile lifestyle. The most obvious one in terms of preservation in the archaeological record of East Anatolia is the portable hearth or andiron. Although little has been written about the hearth in an archaeological context, its role, particularly in nomad dwellings has been recognised

---

[31] A. CONTI & C. PERSIANI, "When worlds collide: cultural developments in Eastern Anatolia in the Early Bronze Age", *Between the Rivers and Over the Mountains: Archaeologica anatolica et mesopotamica Alba Palmieri dedicata*, ed. M. FRANGIPANE, H. HAUPTMAN, M. LIVERANI, P. MATTHIAE & M. MELLINK, Rome 1993, p. 362.

[32] A. SAGONA, *loc. cit.* (n. 23), p. 464.

[33] H. HAUPTMAN, "Die Grabungen auf dem Norşuntepe, 1973", *Keban Project 1973 Activities*, ed. S. PEKMAN, Ankara 1979, p. 72.

[34] C. CHANG & H. KOSTER, *loc. cit.* (n. 17), p. 101.

by ethnographers.[35] Thus the similarity of hearths from the post houses of Norşuntepe XVIII with those of North East Anatolia and Trans-Caucasia[36] is further evidence for socio-cultural continuity between these two areas.

It is interesting to note that following the collapse of the Uruk system and the brief appearance of nomadic occupation, the EBII settlements of this area did not revert to the lower level of complexity that existed prior to these events. This suggests that a level of inequality in social relations had already become entrenched and contributed to ongoing social development. The EBII and III phases at Arslantepe and at the Keban sites, in particular Norşuntepe, show an ongoing occupation with mud-brick architecture, evidence for town planning in stone built terraces and defensive walls, imported pottery, and some degree of craft specialisation, as indicated by the burnt room of Arslantepe VID2, which contained a set of craftsman's tools, figurines and vases.[37] The latest EB phase on the acropolis at Norşuntepe shows an elaborately planned palace with its large pithos storeroom, living areas and workrooms. Contemporary simple domestic quarters were located on the south terrace of the mound.[38] It is unfortunate that the excavator of the site did not indicate the contents of the various areas in his reports. Thus it is now impossible to determine if the pottery in use in different areas of the settlement was of the same style, quality and function, or if the clay stamps and figurines were found only in the palace complex or in domestic quarters also. Nonetheless the division of the site into various areas or separate quarters does suggest some differentiation in access to resources like housing for different members of society.

Arslantepe, too, shows a gradual process of increasing complexity throughout the third millennium. Following the calamitous collapse of the Uruk settlement and the succeeding short lived phase of nomadic occupation, the site was rebuilt with mud-brick dwellings. The site layout and architectural style show signs of continuity through to the end of the EB period, augmented in later periods by public works such as terraces, stone defence walls, a stone lined water channel and stone staircase.[39] Plain Simple Ware pottery alongside Early Trans-Caucasian and imported wares (including 'metallic' ware, Late Reserved Slip Ware and Karababa painted ware)[40] indicate that Arslantepe did not develop in isolation in the later Early Bronze Age.

---

[35] E.g.: I. MORTENSEN, *Nomads of Luristan: history, material culture and pastoralism in Western Iran*, London 1993, p. 225; T. FAEGRE, *Tents: architecture of the nomads*, London 1979, p. 25; D. CHATTY, "The pastoral family and the truck", *When Nomads Settle: Processes of Sedentarization as Adaptation and Response*, ed. P. SALZMAN, New York 1980, pp. 80-94.

[36] H. HAUPTMAN, *loc. cit.* (n. 33), p. 72.

[37] *Ibid.*, p. 364.

[38] H. HAUPTMAN, "Die Grabungen auf dem Norsuntepe, 1971", *Keban Project 1971 Activities*, ed. S. PEKMAN, Ankara 1974, p. 96.

[39] A. CONTI & C. PERSIANI, *loc. cit.* (n. 31), pp. 364-368.

[40] *Ibid.*, p. 387.

Nomads probably also continued to occupy marginal areas around these sites, and to interact with the settled populations, but they are again all but invisible archaeologically.

Conclusion

Inequality, and heterogeneity, then, may be useful analytical concepts for talking about social complexity and social development. That is not to say, however, that they are without problems. The most basic difficulty is probably that the archaeological record does not lend itself to straightforward identification of social divisions. These can at best only be inferred from material culture, particularly the diversity which may represent heterogeneous elements within a society. Thus in the application of this model to East Central Anatolia in the Early Bronze Age, the identification of a nomadic population cannot be proved by the presence of Trans-Caucasian pottery and wattle and daub architecture, only suggested. Nor is the apparent gap in sedentary occupation between the end of the Late Uruk phase and the emergence of local secondary states fully explained. Nonetheless, identifying inequality and heterogeneity as independent variables provides another perspective on the problem of understanding the development of social complexity.

OBSIDIAN IN THE BAYBURT-ERZURUM AREA, EASTERN ANATOLIA

BY

Peter V. BRENNAN

Obsidian was a highly valued raw material from the early Neolithic through the Bronze Age primarily because it could be easily knapped into a range of sharp-edged tools. Although obsidian artefacts and waste are found at archaeological sites throughout the Mediterranean and Near East, the volcanic sequences that contain obsidian are restricted to specific types of geological environments that are relatively uncommon in this region.[1] Consequently the distribution pattern of worked obsidian can often provide insights into cultural interaction, an inherent feature of the establishment and operation of trade or exchange networks for raw materials.

For almost three decades characterisation studies of obsidian have been undertaken in an attempt to establish the composition of possible sources throughout the Mediterranean and Near East, and, using these data, to identify the origin of obsidian found at various archaeological sites. This approach has proved to be particularly useful for obsidian procured from the important Mediterranean island sources on Melos[2] and Lipari.[3] The success of such attributions however is ultimately dependent on a detailed knowledge of the geochemistry of the sources and samples. In particular, it is essential to ensure that the full range of obsidian compositions present at the source is determined.

Application of this approach in Turkey is hampered by the much greater number of known sources, the scarcity of high quality geochemical data to adequately characterise each known source, and the knowledge that there are many more obsidian sources in Turkey yet to be located. Results from the current investigations in the Bayburt Plain and Erzurum areas (fig. 1) suggest that the application of point-source models of obsidian procurement and distribution that have been successful in the Western Mediterranean may not be warranted at the present time in Eastern Anatolia.

---

[1] M.J. BLACKMAN, "Provenance studies of Middle Eastern obsidian from sites in Highland Iran", *Archaeological Chemistry — III*, ed. J.B. LAMBERT, Advances in Chemistry Series 205, Washington D.C. 1984, p. 19.

[2] P. SHELFORD, F. HODSON, M.E. COSGROVE, S.E. WARREN & C. RENFREW, "The sources and characterisation of Melian obsidian", *An Island Polity: The Archaeology of Exploitation in Melos*, ed. C. RENFREW & M. WAGSTAFF, Cambridge 1982, pp. 182-221.

[3] A.J. AMMERMAN, A. CESENA, C. POLGLASE & M. TERRANI, "Neutron Activation Analysis of obsidian from two Neolithic sites in Italy", *Journal of Archaeological Science*, 17 (1990), pp. 209-220.

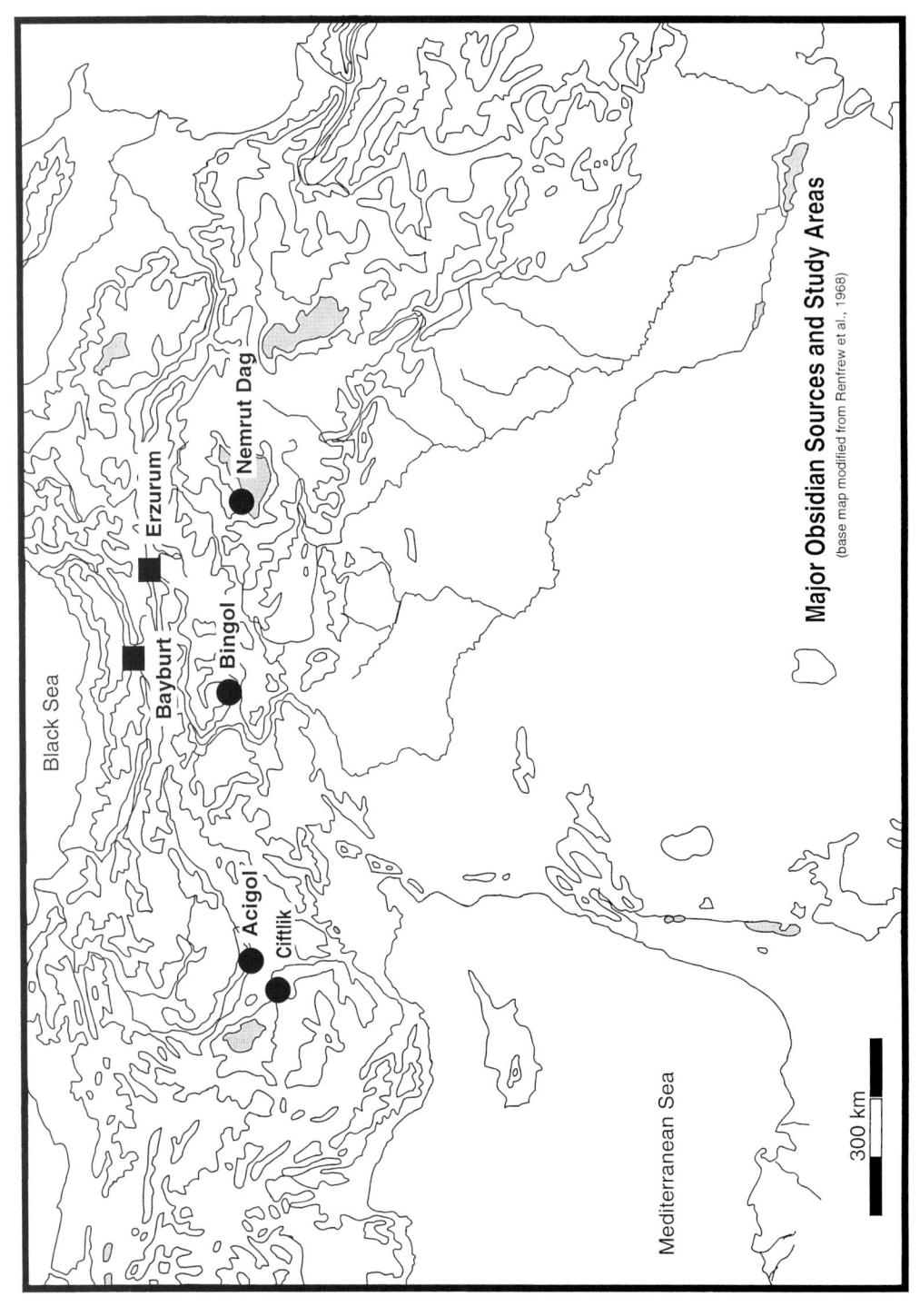

Fig. 1. Map showing the location of the major obsidian sources in Central Turkey and Eastern Anatolia (black circles), and the location of the current study areas (black rectangles).
(base map modified from Renfrew et al., 1968)

1. Geological Background

Obsidian occurs in two major zones in Turkey (fig. 1), the Central Zone containing important sources in the Çiftlik and Acigöl areas, and Eastern Anatolia where major sources occur at Lake Van, and Bingöl. Previous studies have concentrated on these sources because of their proximity to important archaeological sites in present-day Syria, Iraq, and Iran. As a result of more recent detailed mapping in Turkey it has become increasingly apparent that obsidian is much more common than originally believed, especially in Anatolia.

Eastern Anatolia is characterised by a thick volcanic sequence that ranges in age from Tertiary to Quaternary. K/Ar dating of the volcanics indicates that those in the Erzurum area are between 8.3 and 6 million years old whereas the volcanics located to the north-east, in the vicinity of Kars were formed 6.9 to 1.3 million years ago.[4] Around Erzurum the volcanic sequence includes andesitic-basaltic fissural strato-volcanoes, dacitic and rhyodacitic domes, andesitic domes, basaltic domes, and basaltic fissure volcanoes.[5] Pyroclastics and volcanoclastic sediments are also present. This sequence attains a maximum thickness of approximately 800m near Çat.[6] Of particular interest to archaeologists is the presence of layers of obsidian, and obsidian-rich tuffs throughout the area.

In the Erzurum-Çat area, reconnaissance surveys[7] have shown that obsidian occurs in significant quantities in two of the six main volcanic units, the obsidian-rich pyroclastic cones, and the basaltic fissure volcanoes. In the former, obsidian is present either as layers of orientated vitreous shards in tuffs, or as flows of obsidian up to 20cm thick.[8] The basaltic fissure volcanoes are major geologic structures, extending for more than 100km with individual ridges attaining lengths of up to 40km. The type section at Tabye Dagi is over 200m thick and contains five different basaltic lava flows with intercalated pyroclastics including obsidian-rich tuffs.[9] Given the stratigraphic thickness and lateral extent of this obsidian-bearing sequence, it is likely that numerous primary sources of obsidian are present in the Erzurum area. In addition to these primary sources, obsidian is also present in the Recent alluvium that covers much of the Erzurum Plain.[10] At the site of Pulur, to the south-west of Erzurum on

---

[4] F. INNOCENTI, R. MAZZUOLI, G. PASQUARE, F. RADICATI DI BROZOLO & L. VILLARI, "Tertiary and Quaternary volcanism of the Erzurum-Kars Area (Eastern Turkey): geochronological data and geodynamic evolution", *Journal of Volcanology and Geothermal Research*, 13 (1982), p. 228.

[5] G. PASQUARE, "Cenozoic volcanics of the Erzurum area (Turkish Armenia)", *Geologische Rundschau*, 60 (1971), p. 900.

[6] F. INNOCENTI *et al.*, *loc. cit.* (n. 4), p. 226.

[7] G. PASQUARE, *op. cit.* (n. 5), pp. 905-907.

[8] G. PASQUARE, *ibid.*, p. 905.

[9] G. PASQUARE, *ibid.*, fig. 4 for details of the type section.

[10] A. SAGONA & P. BRENNAN, "Bayburt Survey 1993", *Proceedings of the XVIth International Symposium of Anatolian Survey*, Ankara 1995, p. 307.

the Adacay River, water-worn obsidian pebbles and cobbles (the latter up to 20cm in length) are present in the river gravels adjacent to the site, while at Pasinler, to the east of Erzurum, abundant rounded obsidian cobbles occur in the bed of the Aras River.

Despite the limited amount of work that has been undertaken in Eastern Anatolia, it is apparent that there are numerous sources of obsidian present especially in the Erzurum area, none of which have yet been adequately analysed.

2. Obsidian in the Bayburt area

Field surveys in the Bayburt-Gümüshane area (fig. 2) between 1988 and 1993 have resulted in the discovery of more than one hundred new sites, that were occupied at various times between the Neolithic Period and the Middle Ages.[11] Obsidian was evident at many of these sites, as well as the site of Büyüktepe Höyük, the site excavated between 1990 and 1992.[12] Significantly obsidian does not occur in the Eocene volcanic rocks outcropping in the Bayburt Plain and Upper Kelkit Valley.[13] In an attempt to determine the source or sources of the obsidian, seven samples from the surface of sites on the Bayburt Plain (Çayiryolu Tepe 2, Kilise Tepe, Gundulak Tepe, and Ivikler Tepesi), and five samples from the stratigraphic sequence at Büyüktepe Höyük (fig. 2) were analysed by neutron activation analysis. Other than the Late Neolithic/Early Chalcolithic context for the Gundulak material, all other obsidian pieces were recovered from Early Bronze Age sites or deposits.

Eleven of the obsidian samples from the Bayburt Plain (fig. 3) have very similar geochemical compositions, and can be considered as members of the same group. The exception, one of the two analysed samples from Ivikler Tepesi, has a significantly different composition and must be considered a member of a separate group. Comparison of these results with published neutron activation analysis data[14] indicates that the Bayburt Plain obsidians are chemically distinct from the obsidian analyses from the Central Turkey, and Eastern Anatolian sources of Hotmis Dag, Göllü Dag, Hasan Dag, Nemrut Dag, and Suphan Dag (fig. 4).

[11] A. Sagona & P. Brennan, *loc. cit.* (n. 10), p. 306.
[12] See A. Sagona, E. Pemberton & I. McPhee, "Excavations at Büyüktepe Höyük, 1992: Third Preliminary Report", *Anatolian Studies,* 43 (1993), pp. 69-83, for a discussion of the excavation.
[13] There is no indication in the Explanatory Text of the Geological Map of Turkey (Trabzon Sheet) that obsidian is present in the Bayburt area. This was confirmed in discussions with staff at the Maden Tetkik ve Arama Genel Müdürlügü in May, 1993.
[14] M.J. Blackman, *loc. cit.* (n. 1), pp. 42-49.

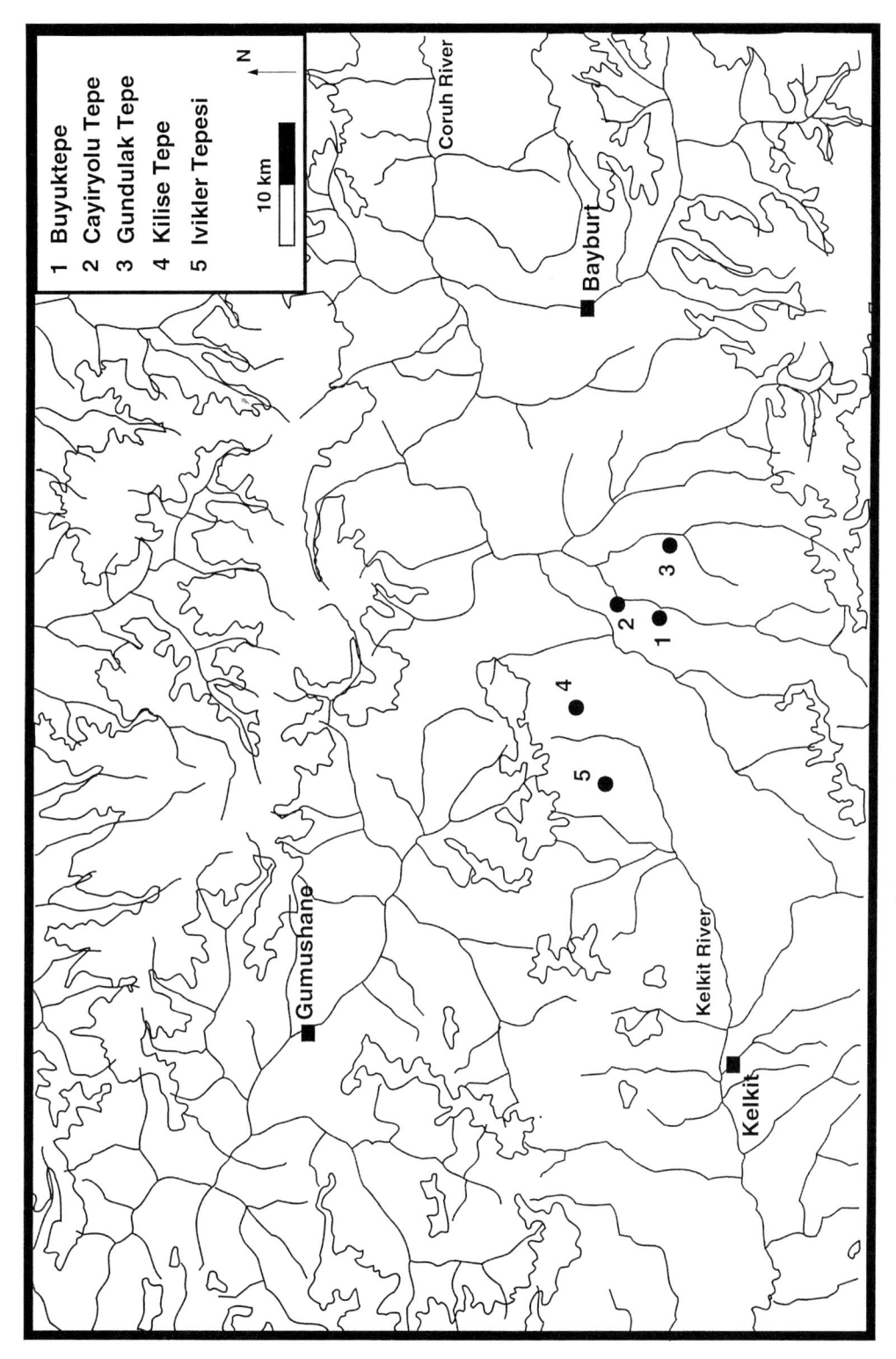

Fig. 2. Map of the Gümüshane-Bayburt area showing the location of sites from which obsidian has been analysed in the current programme.

Obsidian from the Bayburt Plain

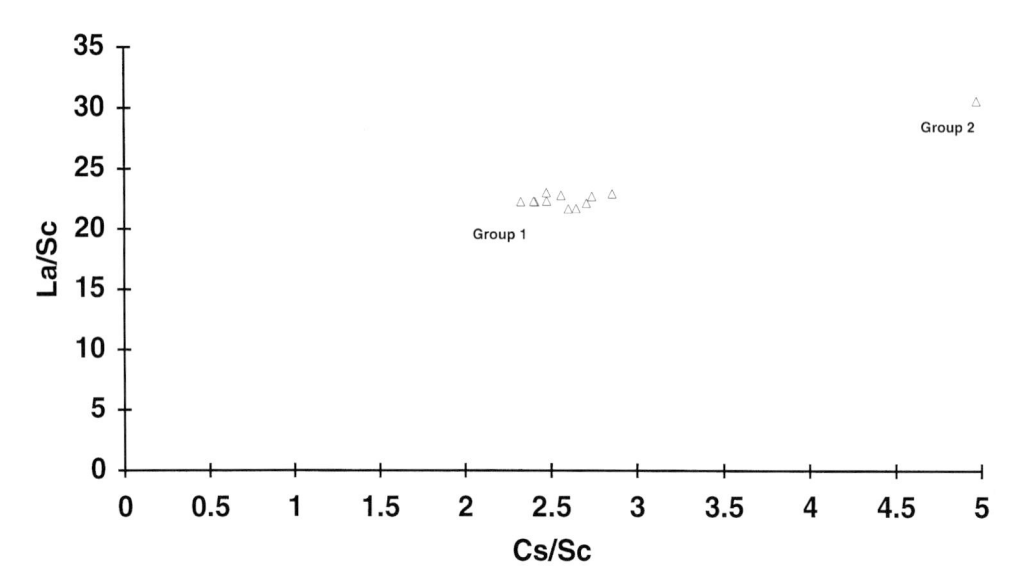

Fig. 3. A plot of Cs/Sc vs. La/Sc for twelve obsidian samples from the Bayburt Plain.

Obsidian from Central Turkey and Eastern Anatolia

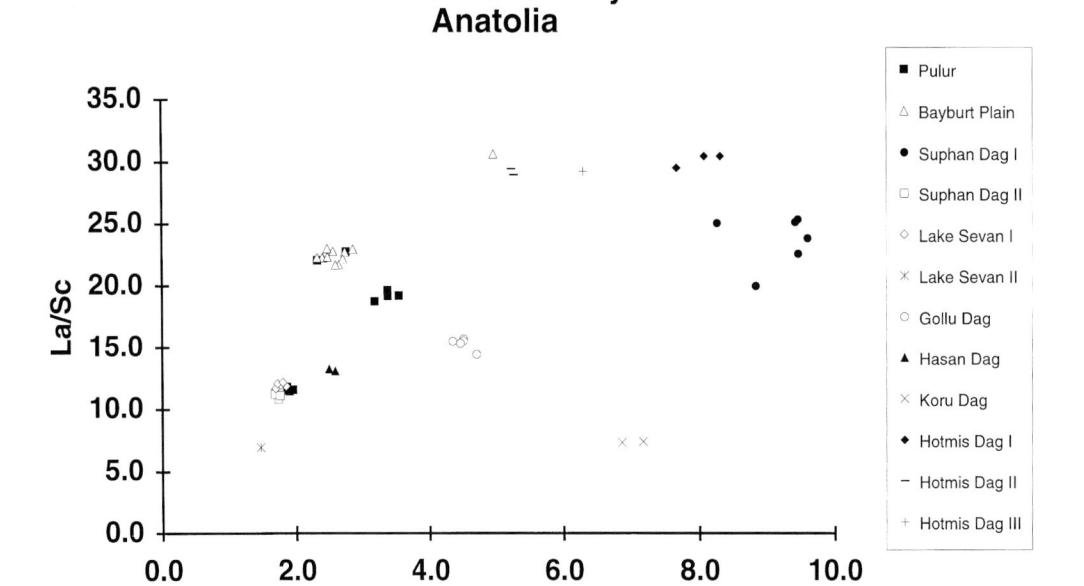

Fig. 4. A plot of Cs/Sc vs. La/Sc for obsidian samples from the Bayburt Plain, and Pulur (near Erzurum), and samples from Central Turkey and Eastern Anatolia analysed by Blackman, 1984. Samples from Nemrut Dag are not shown as they plot well outside the limits used for this figure.

3. Obsidian in the Erzurum Area

Samples of obsidian from the sites of Tepecik Koy 1, Sos Höyük, Pulur, Tepecik 2, Asiklar Höyük, Askale Höyük, Alaca Höyük, Cinis and Karaz in the Erzurum area have been analysed by neutron activation analysis. Samples were obtained from the surface of the sites, as well as the local river bed in the case of Pulur. A plot of Th vs. Rb. (fig. 5) indicates that these samples form two distinct geochemical trends. It is likely that these trends are a reflection of the distinctive geochemistry of the two different volcanic units in the area that contain obsidian, namely the obsidian-rich pyroclastic cones, and the basaltic fissure volcanoes. Further analyses are planned to test this interpretation.

Fig. 6 indicates that there are at least five discrete chemical groups among the twenty-eight samples analysed from the Erzurum area. Given the limited number of analyses, and the lack of detailed knowledge either of the location of obsidian sources or their geochemistry, it is highly likely that the number of groups will increase substantially before the current program is completed. One significant aspect of the plot is the presence of different geochemical groups at the same site, for example, the ten analysed samples of obsidian from Pulur appear to come from three geochemically distinct sources, and the four from Sos Höyük are from two distinct sources.

In general, previous research has tacitly assumed that obsidian was obtained from primary sources such as obsidian flows on or adjacent to volcanic edifices. Studies have usually concentrated on determining the composition of individual flows at known volcanic sources, and on determining the mechanism for the distribution of obsidian from these particular sources.[15] In contrast, the results of the current study indicate that, at least in some cases in Eastern Anatolia, obsidian was obtained from alluvial deposits containing material eroded from non-local primary obsidian sources. A considerable distance to the primary source is suggested at Pulur by the well-rounded appearance of the cobbles, this feature being evidence that they have undergone considerable transport in a fluvial environment. A further complication is the presence of three chemically distinct groups at Pulur. Alluvial obsidian at the site must have been derived from multiple primary obsidian outcrops further upstream.

4. Cultural Interaction

Models for obsidian exchange in the Western Mediterranean generally assume that the material was obtained from an area of very limited extent, as on Melos where each

---

[15] For example B.R. HALLAM & S.E. WARREN, "Obsidian in the Western Mediterranean: characterisation by neutron activation analysis and optical emission spectroscopy", *Proceedings of the Prehistoric Society*, 42 (1976), pp. 85-110.

Obsidian from Sites near Erzurum

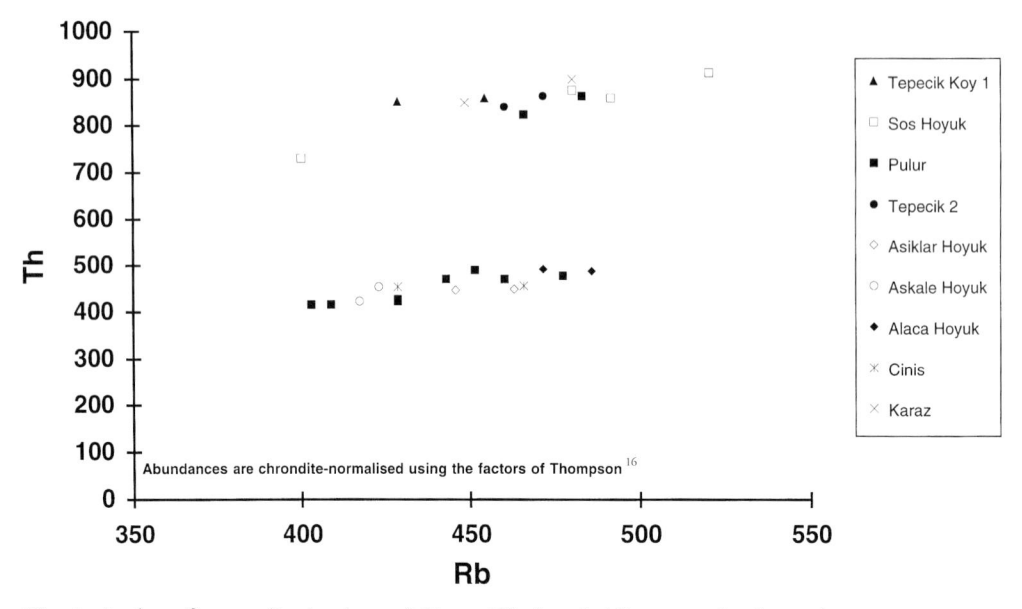

Fig. 5. A plot of normalised values of Rb vs. Th for obsidian samples from the Erzurum area.

Obsidian from Sites near Erzurum

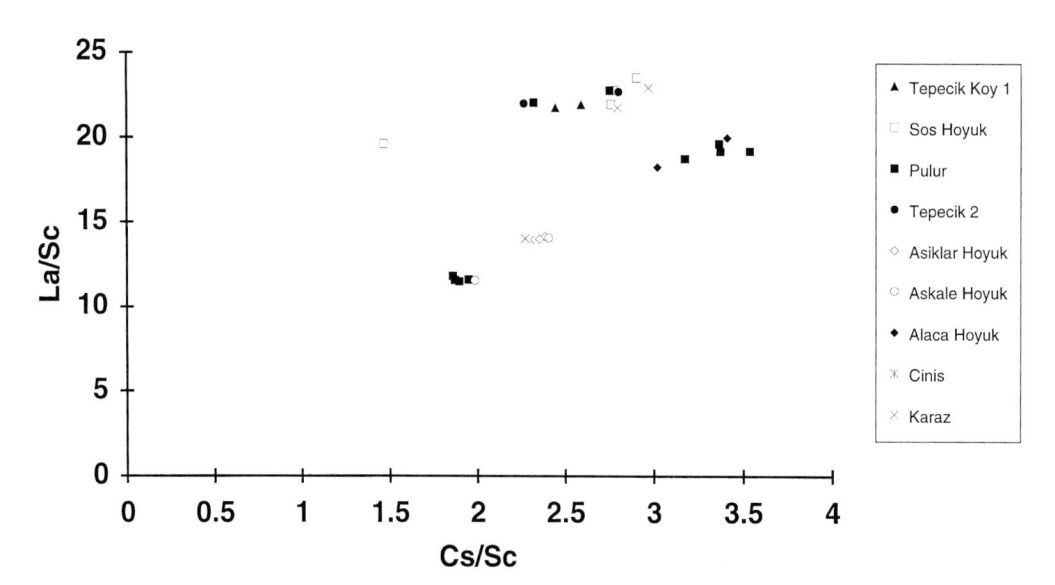

Fig. 6. A plot of Cs/Sc vs. La/Sc for obsidian samples from the Erzurum area.

[16] R.N. THOMPSON, "Magmatism of the British Tertiary Volcanic Province", *Scottish Journal of Geology*, 18 (1982), p. 105.

of the two obsidian sources occupies an area of no more than one square kilometre.[17] In the Erzurum area, it is apparent that potential primary sources, such as those in the basaltic fissure volcanoes, are much more extensive. In addition, the presence of obsidian in the Recent river gravels of both the Aras and Adacay rivers suggests that secondary sources, extending at least tens of kilometres, played an important role in obsidian supply.

This situation has important implications for the understanding of obsidian exchange in Eastern Anatolia. In the Erzurum area, obsidian was easily obtained, most likely from alluvial deposits rather than primary volcanic sources. The extensive, linear nature of the secondary sources, and the favourable terrain makes it likely that villages obtained their supplies of obsidian directly from the river gravels rather than through some exchange process. Unlike point sources, the areal extent of the alluvium would make control by any one community difficult.

Studies by Renfrew and co-workers have led to the concept of an obsidian supply zone, an area of approximately 300km surrounding the source, and an obsidian interaction zone, an area in which the sites derive at least 30% of their obsidian from that source.[18] The size of the supply zone has been thought to represent the maximum extent to which those requiring obsidian would have been prepared to walk for this raw material. Alternatively this area may have been the extent of the cultural zone in which exchange of obsidian was sufficiently efficient to provide all sites with the required amounts of obsidian.[19]

In such a model, both Erzurum and the Bayburt Plain would be located within the same supply zone. However, the abundance of obsidian at sites in both areas is significantly different with much smaller quantities, and smaller size fragments, recovered from the Bayburt Plain. If the amount observed at sites in the Erzurum area reflects the amount actually needed by village cultures, then those on the Bayburt Plain were significantly under-supplied. On this basis, cultural interaction between villages in the supply zone was probably less extensive than previously presumed.

In the case of the Bayburt Plain sites, it is apparent from the La/Sc vs. Cs/Sc plot (fig. 7) that the range of compositions exhibited by the Bayburt Group 1 and some of the samples from Pulur, Karaz, Tepecik Koy 1, Tepecik 2 and Sos Höyük coincide. This similarity may mean that one or more of these Erzurum sites supplied obsidian to sites on the Bayburt Plain. However, the absence of obsidian compositions matching those of other groups found at Pulur and Sos, and the presence of obsidian closer to the Bayburt Plains at Askale Höyük, Cinis and Alaca Höyük argue against this

---

[17] R. TORRENCE, "Monopoly or direct access? Industrial organisation at the Melos obsidian quarries", *Prehistoric Quarries and Lithic Production*, ed. J.E. ERICSON & B.A. PURDY, London 1984, p. 51.

[18] C. RENFREW, J.E. DIXON & J.R. CANN, "Further analysis of Near Eastern obsidians", *Proceedings of the Prehistoric Society*, 9 (1968), p. 329.

[19] C. RENFREW et al., *ibid*.

Obsidian from Bayburt and Erzurum

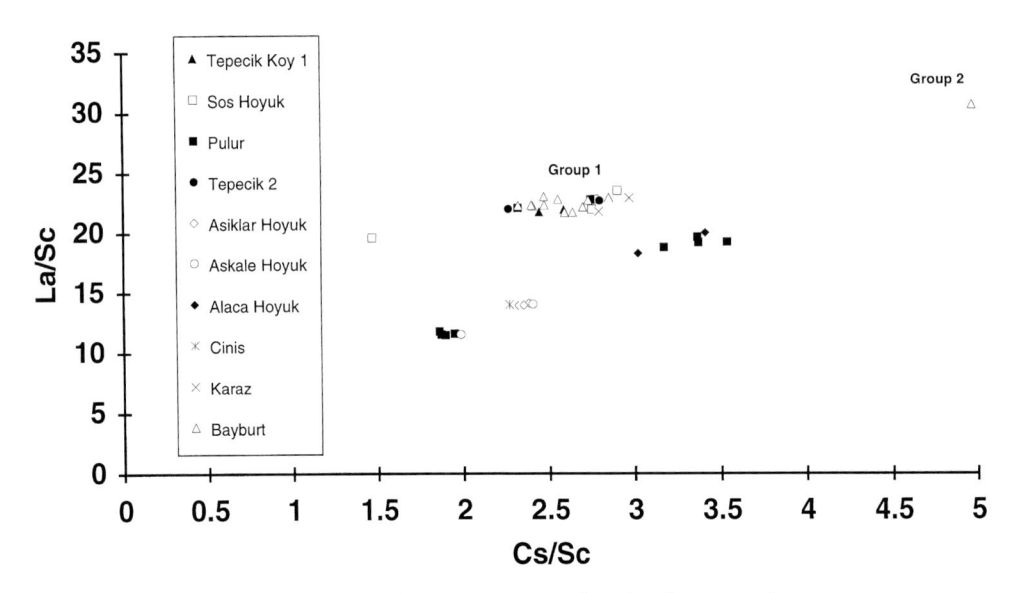

Fig. 7. A plot of Cs/Sc vs. La/Sc for obsidian samples
from the Erzurum area, and Bayburt Plains.

interpretation. A more likely scenario is that individuals or groups from the Bayburt area had access to the same primary sources, or alluvial deposits in the Erzurum area. In any event the obsidian data are consistent with relatively infrequent cultural interaction between sites in the Erzurum and Bayburt Plain. If this interpretation is valid, then current ideas about exchange mechanisms in obsidian supply zones need to be revised.

ANATOLIA AND CYPRUS IN THE THIRD MILLENNIUM B.C.E.
A SPECULATIVE MODEL OF INTERACTION[1]

BY

David FRANKEL, Jennifer M. WEBB and Christine ESLICK

The prehistory of Cyprus has traditionally been viewed in terms of long periods of relative stability and slow internal development punctuated by shorter episodes of more rapid change, often stimulated by external influences. In this paper we re-examine one of the most widely debated of these periods of change: that which marks the start of the Bronze Age. Each of the three main forms of explanation for culture change identified by Adams[2] — invention, diffusion and migration — has at some time been used to explain this transition, as internal or external forces have been variously emphasised by different scholars. In addressing the issue we will summarise earlier and current models, present a new view of the Cypriot material, assess the extent to which new technologies can be ascribed to new settlers, and consider the impact of these developments on the social fabric of both migrant and previous populations.

During the third millennium B.C.E. the Chalcolithic cultural system of Cyprus gave way to the Early Cypriot Bronze Age (EC). This, as has long been recognised, is marked by the appearance of a new array of ceramics; the development of chamber tombs; the replacement of monocellular circular or sub-rectangular buildings by rectilinear, agglomerative, multi-roomed architecture; the establishment of a copper industry; and the introduction of cattle and donkeys as elements of a secondary products revolution.

Earlier views, in which the Chalcolithic period was followed by the EC I, EC II and then EC III periods, have been shown to be too simple. Crucial to the question of cultural succession is the 'Philia Culture', which is seen as in some way intermediate between Chalcolithic and the fully developed Early Cypriot Bronze Age systems. Although considerable debate still surrounds the timing and nature of the 'Philia Culture' and its relationship to other EC material, some common understandings can be seen in more recent discussions. A broadly accepted model is of an initial Philia introduction (or development) in the Ovgos Valley, close to copper sources in the north-west foothills of the Troodos Mountains, with a later spread to the south and north coasts. In the north this spread is thought to have led to the replacement of the

---

[1] This paper is based on one given at a conference on 'Cultural Interaction in the Ancient Near East', at Melbourne University on 29-30th of September 1994. A more complete presentation of the data and argument, for publication in monograph form, is in preparation.

[2] W.Y. ADAMS, "Invasion, diffusion, evolution?", *Antiquity*, 42 (1968), pp. 194-215.

Chalcolithic by EC I as seen at Bellapais *Vounous*. This later developed into EC III (EC II is no longer used as an archaeological entity). In the south the impact is somewhat later, with some Philia material contemporary with the final phase of the Late Chalcolithic, which is now believed to have continued in this part of the island until superseded by, or evolving into, EC III. In the centre of the island Philia may have replaced the Chalcolithic at a significantly earlier time, before the development of EC III.[3]

The Philia facies of the Early Cypriot assumes particular relevance to our discussion as some Philia traits provide critical links between Cyprus and Anatolia.

Previous models of interaction

Although there is some truth in Merrillees' observation that 'Cypriote historiography, particularly the Bronze Age, has been afflicted by and suffered from an invasion syndrome',[4] a number of other explanations have been put forward for observed links between Anatolia and Cyprus. They are not all based on the same set of data, and were developed at different times, but can be seen to fall into two groups: those which involve little or no population movement, and those that see this as a significant factor.

The most widely favoured view emphasises internal developments and minimal — if any — movement of people.[5] The actual mechanisms for the introduction of new styles, technologies and animals are not often made clear, apart from a general reference to broad concepts such as 'stimulus diffusion', with trade invoked to provide an initial basis for contact. Because they are so general it is hard to formally substantiate or test these ideas. One more specific mechanism for the adoption of foreign elements without recourse to population movement links changes to the development of a more hierarchical social structure in Cyprus.[6] According to this model imports and the incorporation of foreign ideas are seen as part of the prestige-building and economic control of an emergent Cypriot elite.

---

[3] See, for example, E. HERSCHER, "Southern Cyprus and the disappearing Early Bronze Age", *Report of the Department of Antiquities, Cyprus*, 1980, p, 18 and E. PELTENBURG, "Kissonerga-Mosphilia: A major Chalcolithic site in Cyprus", *Bulletin of the American Schools of Oriental Research*, 282/3 (1991), pp. 17-35.

[4] R. MERRILLEES, "Problems in Cypriote history", *The Archaeology of Cyprus: Recent Developments*, ed. N. ROBERTSON, Park Ridge 1975, p. 36.

[5] Cf. e.g. J.R.B. STEWART, The Early Cypriote Bronze Age, *Swedish Cyprus Expedition*, vol. IV:IA (1962), p. 296; J.B. HENNESSY, "Cyprus in the Early Bronze Age", *The Cypriote Bronze Age*, ed. J.M. BIRMINGHAM, *Australian Studies in Archaeology* 1 (1973), pp. 1-9; T. WATKINS, "The Chalcolithic period in Cyprus: the background to current research", *Chalcolithic Cyprus and Western Asia*, ed. J. READE, British Museum Occasional Paper, 26 (1981), p. 19 and S. SWINY, "The Philia Culture and its foreign relations", *Acts of the International Archaeological Symposium 'Cyprus Between the Orient and Occident', Nicosia 1985*, Nicosia 1986, pp. 33-40.

[6] "Prestige, distinction, and competition: the anatomy of socioeconomic complexity in fourth to second millennium BCE", *Bulletin of the American Schools of Oriental Research*, 292 (1993), pp. 35-58.

Other explanations involve some movement of people. Following Mellaart's arguments for severe disruptions in Anatolia at the end of EB II,[7] Catling suggested that new types of material in Cyprus could be linked to the arrival of refugee groups escaping the destroyed cities of the mainland.[8] A related but significantly different explanation was favoured by Dikaios, in which the initiators of Early Cypriot culture were a sub-group of those responsible for the disruptions in Anatolia rather than displaced refugee groups.[9] The movement of Anatolians to Cyprus cannot, however, any longer be attributed simplistically to either of these processes as it now appears that changes in later EB II Anatolia were the result of a restructuring of economy, social organisation and settlement pattern rather than a more catastrophic collapse.

Mellink has recently suggested at least two phases of contact between Anatolia and Cyprus, with earlier sporadic trade, marked by a handful of Cypriot imports in EB II levels at Tarsus,[10] followed by more substantial contact.[11] She sees this as involving Anatolian (primarily Cilician) copper prospectors and miners travelling to Cyprus as part of a broadly based search for new sources of metal.

Other discussions of mid-third millennium developments in Cyprus are less concerned with the nature of external connections than with internal processes. Although an EB II Anatolian source for new technologies may lie in the background, much of their impact within the island has been discussed in socio-economic terms, especially under the rubric of the Secondary Products Revolution.[12] Newly introduced cattle and donkeys, useful as beasts of burden and for plough agriculture, allowed larger groups of people to colonise the northern fringe of the Troodos range and the central plain, areas previously uneconomic for those with a simpler, less extensive agricultural system. This spread of settlement, taking advantage of the new agricultural technology, was also promoted by the presence of mineral-rich areas in the igneous formations just south of the sedimentary soils of the plain.

Explanations for other changes, for example the transition from monocellular to multi-roomed building forms, are often incorporated within the general models of internal social evolution. It is, however, still possible to argue that many changes in

[7] J. MELLAART, "Anatolia c. 4000-2300 B.C.", *The Cambridge Ancient History* Vol. I, Cambridge 1962, p. 47.

[8] H.W. CATLING, "Cyprus in the Early Bronze Age", *The Cambridge Ancient History* Vol. I, Ch. XXVI(b), rev. ed. fasc. 43, Cambridge 1966, p. 26. Cf. also A. C. BROWN & H. W. CATLING, *Ancient Cyprus*, Oxford 1975, p. 12.

[9] P. DIKAIOS, *A Guide to the Cyprus Museum*, 3rd ed. Nicosia 1961, p. 13; ID., The Stone Age, *The Swedish Cyprus Expedition* Vol IV:IA (1962), p. 202.

[10] M. MELLINK, "Anatolian contacts with Chalcolithic Cyprus", *Bulletin of the American Schools of Oriental Research*, 282/3 (1991), pp. 167-175.

[11] Cf. E. PELTENBURG, *loc. cit.* (n.3).

[12] A.B. KNAPP, "Production, location, and integration in Bronze Age Cyprus", *Current Anthropology*, 31 (1990), pp. 147-176; ID., "Emergence, development and decline on Bronze Age Cyprus", *Development and Decline in the Mediterranean Bronze Age*, ed. C. MATHERS & S. STODDART, Sheffield Archaeological Monographs, 8 (1994), pp. 271-304.

material culture were directly introduced, although others may have evolved or developed internally from within existing systems.

Colonisation, ethnicity and technology transfer

One of the significant shifts in approaches to archaeological explanation from the 1960s onward involves a rejection of specificity in favour of general laws and processes. Older explanations for culture change, including theories of migration or colonisation, fell out of favour, and internal processes of transformation began to be preferred.[13] The decline of migration as an explanation is also closely linked to a fading belief in the validity and significance of archaeological 'cultures' as sets of material culture traits reflecting ancient ethnic groups.

The most valuable recent discussion of the processes involved in migrations in archaeology is by Anthony.[14] According to Anthony conditions favouring migration can be understood in terms of the negative stresses in the home region and the positive attractions of the destination.[15] Any application of this push-pull model must take into account several other factors. Information is especially important, as migrants are unlikely to move to areas about which they know nothing. Specialists or groups with a 'focal' subsistence strategy (i.e. one which depends on a narrow range of resources) may more readily migrate over longer distances. Those with a 'diffuse' subsistence strategy (i.e. one using diversified, less localised resources) may, in contrast, move more often but over shorter distances.[16]

The distinction between short and long distance movements is a key one, both in terms of the causal factors and social mechanisms and their relative archaeological visibility. Cumulative short distance movements, which may be explained by a 'wave of advance' model of demic diffusion[17] may be observable only at the long time-scale of millennia, and combine a variety of different types of local events. Long distance, more specific movements, which may be the result of different circumstances, are more easily recognised as individual or short-term events.[18]

Anthony recognises five mechanisms important in long-distance migration;[19] 'leapfrogging', 'migration streams', return migration, migration frequency and migration demography. The first two of these are of greatest relevance here.

---

[13] Cf., for example, W.Y. Adams, D.P. Van Gerven & R.S. Levy, "The retreat from migrationism", *Annual Review of Anthropology*, 7 (1978), p. 483.

[14] D.W. Anthony, "Migration in archaeology: the baby and the bathwater", *American Anthropologist*, 92 (1990), pp. 895-914.

[15] *Ibid.*, p. 899.

[16] *Ibid.*, p. 901.

[17] A.J. Ammerman & L.L. Cavalli-Sforza, "A population model for the diffusion of early farming in Europe", *The Explanation of Culture Change: Models in Prehistory*, ed. C. Renfrew, London 1973, pp. 343-357.

[18] Cf. D.W. Anthony, *loc. cit.* (n.14), p. 902.

[19] *Ibid.*

'Leapfrogging' — moving directly to favoured destinations — often involves advance 'scouts' who gather information on resources and social conditions. 'Migration streams', where movements are channelled along specific routes and to particular areas, are more common than a generalised wave of movements. Migration streams channel information from and assistance by first arrivals to potential and new immigrants. As initial migrant groups tend to be socially and geographically narrowly defined,[20] this common process of migration limits and structures both population and material culture. Initial innovations by earliest arrivals tend to be continued by newcomers, leading to a fairly rapid modification of artefact types from those of the place of origin (a form of artefactual founder-effect).

A critical issue in identifying migrant or colonising groups is the concept of ethnicity, defining groups of people as archaeological 'cultures' or in terms of some material markers signalling group cohesion and distinctiveness. The identification of consistently co-occurring sets of identical material items is, however, a seldom realised ideal. The rapid development of forms within a small migrant colony militates against the identification of particular items or styles. In this paper we suggest a slightly different approach. Although particular items and styles are important, we are more concerned with general aspects of behaviour, economy and especially technology. Colonisation and cultural identity are therefore explored in terms of technology transfer and the adoption of innovations.

Recent studies of the processes of adopting innovations[21] suggest that technology transfer is difficult to achieve. The successful adoption of a new technology normally requires personal contacts, especially as most technology involves much 'tacit' knowledge. The most efficient way to transfer technology is by the movement of workers who can teach new practitioners.

Diffusion of new technology within a society therefore requires an appropriate context, placing people in appropriate positions. Moreover, radical change is unlikely to occur from within a technological tradition as workers look for solutions to problems only within the tradition. Radical changes are more likely to come from without.[22]

If a generalised diffusion of knowledge and techniques is difficult, then it is possible to argue both that technology can be used as a marker of ethnicity and that the appearance of a range of new technologies — industrial and domestic — signals the presence of colonising groups from areas where those ways of making and doing things were well established.

---

[20] D.W. ANTHONY, "The bath refilled: migration in archaeology again", *American Anthropologist*, 94 (1992), p. 175.

[21] E.g. E.M. ROGERS, *Diffusion of Innovations*, 3rd ed., New York 1983 and R. LAUDAN, "Introduction", *The Nature of Technological Knowledge*, ed. R. LAUDAN, Dordrecht 1984, pp. 1-26.

[22] E.W. CONSTANT, "Communities and hierarchies: structure and the practice of science and technology, in R. LAUDAN (ed.), *op. cit.* (n. 21), pp. 27-30.

Technological innovations in third millennium Cyprus

The handful of early imports give an indication of some sporadic interaction between Cyprus and Cilicia in the first half of the third millennium.[23] Later there are few specific imports or exports. Much of our discussion is therefore based on general categories of material, rather than individual items. Following the concepts developed above, it is possible to consider this material in terms of technologies reflecting different aspects of behaviour. A more complete presentation and discussion of the data is in preparation.

Ceramic technology

Ceramics can be considered in three ways: in terms of technology, style and function. Changes in all three aspects can be identified in mid-third millennium Cyprus, and each can be linked to forms common in Anatolia.

Characteristic 'Philia' vessels form a distinctive sub-set of Red Polished Ware. Attributes such as tall cut-away spouts have long been regarded as having an Anatolian ancestry or inspiration. Bolger, for example,[24] pointed out that the closest parallels are found in south-west Anatolia. We can add to her unstratified parallels more securely dated late EB II — early EB III examples from Karataş.[25] Parallels for a wider range of shapes, notably spouted jars and juglets, bottles, amphorae and lids, can also be found in Anatolia, especially at western sites.

Mellink notes that 'few of the Cypriot pitchers and none of the later variants are literal copies of Anatolian prototypes, let alone imports'.[26] The importation is therefore of concepts of design (eg. beaked spout) and technology, especially the 'sensible use of the handle' which 'the Cypriots can only have learned from their Anatolian counterparts because the potter in the Levant was no wiser about handles than his (*sic*) colleagues in Egypt and Mesopotamia'.[27] Most such features of pottery, however, are, in Mellink's terms, 'Anatolianising, not Anatolian'.[28] They demonstrate some degree of connection,

---

[23] Cf. M.J. MELLINK, "Anatolian foreign relations of Tarsus in the Early Bronze Age", *Anatolia and the Ancient Near East: Studies in Honour of Tahsin Özgüç*, ed. K. EMRE, B. HROUDA, M. MELLINK & N. ÖZGÜÇ, Ankara 1989, pp. 319-331; EAD., "Anatolian contacts with Chalcolithic Cyprus", *Bulletin of the American Schools of Oriental Research*, 282/3 (1991), pp. 167-175; E. PELTENBURG, *loc. cit.* (n.3).

[24] D.L. BOLGER, "Early Red Polished Ware and the origin of the 'Philia' Culture", *Cypriot Ceramics: Reading the Prehistoric Record*, ed. J.A. BARLOW, D.L. BOLGER & B. KLING, Philadelphia 1991, pp. 31-32.

[25] E.g. M.J. MELLINK, "Excavations at Karataş-Semayük in Lycia, 1964", *American Journal of Archaeology*, 69 (1965), pl. 61, fig. 13-14; EAD., "Excavations at Karataş-Semayük in Lycia, 1966", *American Journal of Archaeology*, 71 (1967), pl. 82, fig. 42; EAD., "Excavations at Karataş-Semayük in Lycia, 1967", *American Journal of Archaeology*, 72 (1968), pl. 84, fig. 33.

[26] M.J. MELLINK, "Anatolian contacts with Chalcolithic Cyprus", *Bulletin of the American Schools of Oriental Research*, 282/3 (1991), pp. 172-173.

[27] *Ibid.*

[28] *Ibid.*, p. 173.

but must be understood within a broader context of technology transfer. The introduction of handles — especially those attached by use of a tenon pushed through the body of the vessel — is therefore significant, for such technological introductions imply the movement of potters, rather than of pots or concepts of design.

Bronze Age innovations in methods of decoration, such as the use of white filled incision, have also been traced to Anatolian antecedents.[29] Bolger also suggests that incised motifs characteristic of Red Polished (Philia) vessels, such as parallel chevrons and herringbone patterns without a central line, have parallels in EB I and EB II Tarsus.[30]

Metallurgy

A major development in the Bronze Age is a local Cypriot metals industry. There are less than a dozen pieces of copper known from the Chalcolithic, none of which can with any certainty be ascribed to Cypriot sources, and some of which must have been imported.[31] Philia and EC III sites have large quantities of copper artefacts. Tin-bronze appears only at the end of EC III, and then only for a restricted range of items.[32] Tin must, however, have been imported, passing through south-eastern Anatolian or Syrian ports.

The development of a local copper mining and processing industry obviously involved the introduction of a complex suite of techniques and associated knowledge. These could not have been acquired through casual contacts. New items, and older forms made in new materials, signal a range of different functional, social and symbolic needs.

Some of the Philia metal types are distinctly different from those of fully developed EC III and have clear Anatolian antecedents — most notably knives or daggers with characteristic raised and flattened midsections, flat axes with polygonal butts, poker-butt spearheads, conical-headed toggle pins and spiral rings. The best parallels for most of these are found in western and central Anatolia at the end of EB II and beginning of EB III. This contrasts with the situation at Tarsus where similar forms are less common. Within western Anatolia the best parallels at present come from the south-west, especially Karataş-Semayük, but this period is poorly represented in the archaeological record at most sites.

Textile technology

Many of the items with Anatolian parallels are associated with textile production (spinning and weaving on a warp-weighted loom), which was almost certainly a

---

[29] S. SWINY, "Excavations at Sotira Kaminoudhia", *Praktika tou Defterou Diethnous Kypriologikou Synedriou, Nicosia 20-25 April 1982*, Nicosia 1985, p. 21; D.L. BOLGER, *loc. cit.* (n. 24), p. 32.

[30] D.L. BOLGER, "Khrysiliou-*Ammos*, Nicosia-*Ayia Paraskevi* and the Philia Culture of Cyprus", *Report of the Department of Antiquities, Cyprus,* 1983, p. 73.

[31] N.H. GALE, "Metals and metallurgy in the Chalcolithic Period", *Bulletin of the American Schools of Oriental Research,* 282/3 (1991), p. 54.

[32] J. WEINSTEIN BALTHAZAR, *Copper and Bronze Working in Early Through Middle Bronze Age Cyprus*, Studies in Mediterranean Archaeology Pocket-book, 84 (1990), Jonsered.

women's activity or otherwise associated with women. It has long been suggested that at least some of the sites in western Anatolia in the EBA were producing textiles beyond their local requirements, because of the very large quantities of spindle whorls found at some sites — for example at Troy, where some 8,000 — 10,000 were found by Schliemann[33] and at Karataş.

Although small perforated stone disks or sherds may have been used in earlier times as spindle whorls, the deliberately manufactured spindle whorl signals the advent of a new approach to textile production. The biconical shape of the Philia and EC examples has clear parallels in Anatolia.

Also associated with textile production are the clay loom-weights that first appear in EC sites in Cyprus. These imply the introduction of warp-weighted looms. The 'tabby' weave noted on traces of cloth also suggests some such simple loom.[34] Although Anatolian forms of loom-weight are not identical to those of Cyprus, their general similarity of form, and undoubted equivalence of function, gives confidence to the suggestion that we are dealing with a significant change in textile production. Metal toggle pins and needles, likewise introduced in the EC period, also suggest a different approach to clothing style and manufacture.

Food preparation technology

Another area of innovation is that of food processing and preparation. In particular flat low-walled trays or pans and griddles, now known from a number of EC and MC settlements,[35] have close parallels in western and central Anatolia and at Tarsus in EB III.[36] While their precise function is uncertain (perhaps parching grain or baking flat bread), they represent a significantly different way of carrying out some culinary activities.

Unlike the items noted above, for which western Anatolian parallels are the most clear, other new domestic items associated with Bronze Age Cypriot cooking technology have eastern Anatolian prototypes. The most obvious of these are the horse-shoe shaped hobs or hearth surrounds found in EC III and MC I contexts at Marki *Alonia*.[37] These fit within a well-known form characteristic of the Early Trans-Caucasian

[33] C.W. BLEGEN, *Troy and the Trojans*, London 1963, p. 88.
[34] King, quoted in A. PIERIDOU, "Pieces of ancient cloth from Early and Middle Cypriot Periods", *Report of the Department of Antiquities, Cyprus,* 1967, p. 26.
[35] S. SWINY, *loc. cit.* (n.29), p. 37; J.E. COLEMAN *et al.*, "Cornell excavations at Alambra, 1978", *Report of the Department of Antiquities, Cyprus*, 1979, p. 163, fig. 2; D. FRANKEL & J.M. WEBB, "Excavations at Marki-*Alonia* 1993-4", *Report of the Department of Antiquities, Cyprus*, 1994, fig. 10, P. 5990.
[36] Cf. e.g. M.S. JOUKOWSKY, *Prehistoric Aphrodisias. An Account of the Excavations and Artifact Studies*, Publications d'Histoire de l'Art et d'Archéologie de l'Université Catholique de Louvain XXXIX, Archaeologia Transatlantica III, 1986, pp. 330-332, fig. 385.27, 42; S. LLOYD & J. MELLAART, *Beycesultan I. The Chalcolithic and Early Bronze Age Levels*, London 1962, fig. P.7.19, P.8.24, P.13.12-17; H. GOLDMAN, *Excavations at Gözlü Kule, Tarsus*, Vol. II, Princeton 1956, p. 158, fig. 276:667.
[37] D. FRANKEL & J.M. WEBB, "Hobs and hearths in Bronze Age Cyprus", *Opuscula Atheniensia*, 20:4 (1994), pp. 51-56.

cultures of eastern Anatolia.[38] Similar items form part of a set of imported objects associated with Khirbet Kerak Ware in the Levant and continue sporadically into the second millennium in Anatolia, for example at MB I Tarsus and Kültepe. The type could have arrived in Cyprus from Syria or as part of the same movement that brought them to Cilicia.

Agricultural technology

The introduction to Cyprus of cattle and donkeys is well attested in both faunal remains and terracotta models. In addition, the goats from the Cypriot site of Marki *Alonia* have recently been identified as a different breed from those at Chalcolithic sites,[39] notably a new strain of more productive screw-horned goats. While cattle and screw-horned goats may have been introduced from any part of the mainland, donkeys are a feature of eastern rather than western faunal assemblages.

These new animals, or new breeds, now used for traction, milk and possibly wool as well as meat and hides,[40] are part of a new agricultural technology in Cyprus, often seen as elements of the Secondary Products Revolution. They may also indicate a change in the way animals were viewed or incorporated into a Cypriot ideology.[41] A related introduction is the plough, representing a significant change in agricultural practice, both in terms of economic productivity and the structure of farm labour. The sole-ard plough represented on a model from *Vounous*, is of a type generally characteristic of western rather than eastern regions.[42]

The introduction of a specialised, new form of backed sickle blade in the Bronze Age[43] reinforces the concept that we have a package of agricultural practices, not simply the grafting on of new methods to older systems.

Architecture and building technology

It has long been recognised that there was a significant change in architecture from independent, generally circular, monocellular structures in the Chalcolithic to multi-roomed, generally rectilinear architecture in the Bronze Age.[44] The evidence from

---

[38] Cf. S. DIAMANT & J. RUTTER, "Horned objects in Anatolia and the Near East and possible connexions with Minoan 'Horns of Consecration'", *Anatolian Studies*, 19 (1969), pp. 147-177.

[39] P. CROFT, *pers. comm.* 1994.

[40] A. SHERRATT, "Plough and pastoralism: aspects of the secondary products revolution", *Pattern of the Past. Studies in Honour of David Clarke*, ed. I. HODDER, G. ISAAC & N. HAMMOND, Cambridge 1981, pp. 261-305.

[41] Cf. P.S. KESWANI, "The social context of animal husbandry in early agricultural societies: ethnographic insights and an archaeological example from Cyprus", *Journal of Anthropological Archaeology*, 13 (1994), pp. 255-277.

[42] A. SHERRATT, *loc. cit.* (n. 40), p. 267, fig. 10.7.

[43] M. SMITH, *pers. comm.* 1994.

[44] Cf. e.g. S. SWINY, "From round house to duplex: a re-assessment of prehistoric Cypriot Bronze Age society", *Early Society in Cyprus*, ed. E. PELTENBURG, Edinburgh 1989, pp. 14-31.

Alambra *Mouttes*, Sotira *Kaminoudhia* and Marki *Alonia* shows considerable variation in detail, perhaps a result of the very different settings of these sites, but there is no mistaking the complete break from earlier styles.

Most discussions of architectural change attempt to see a gradual evolution, often regarded as one response to the new Bronze Age social and economic order. However, the concepts of architectural form (and possibly the systems of social relationships that go with them)[45] are so different from earlier forms that a rapid development from one to the other is hard to explain. It is perhaps more plausible to suggest that this approach to building was introduced to the island,[46] Schaar has attempted to trace features of Cypriot housing, especially those seen at Alambra *Mouttes*, to specific Anatolian forms.[47] The variety of Bronze Age designs, however, and the generalised nature of similarities militate against such attempts to find precise parallels. Even so, the overall approach to building — multi-roomed complexes with straight walls or rectilinear rooms — was well established in Anatolia.

To this general observation we may add a related, more specific item: mould-made mud-bricks, the earliest examples of which have been identified in EC contexts at Marki *Alonia*. These make it possible to argue for an introduction not only of new architectural concepts or systems, but also of an associated building technology.

Burial customs

Jar or pithos burials are a common feature of Anatolia from the Chalcolithic onward.[48] Although only two examples have been reported from Cyprus, at Philia *Laksa tou Kasinou* (*Vasiliko*)[49] and Kissonerga *Mosphilia*,[50] this is sufficient to indicate the importation of this custom. The Philia example is of particular importance, as it provides a specific association between this burial custom and Red Polished (Philia) pottery. There are also suggestions of pithos burial in Vasilia *Kafkallia* Tomb 103.[51]

Other elements of burial customs cannot be linked directly to foreign prototypes, although the development of chamber tombs may well be connected to changes in the social order.

---

[45] Cf. K. FLANNERY, "Will the real model please stand up: comments on Saidel's round house or square", *Journal of Mediterranean Archaeology*, 6 (1993), pp. 109-117.

[46] Cf. G.R.H. WRIGHT, *Ancient Building in Cyprus*, Leiden 1992, p. 68.

[47] SCHAAR, "House form at Tarsus, Alambra and Lemba", *Report of the Department of Antiquities, Cyprus*, 1985, pp. 37-44.

[48] T.S. WHEELER, "Early Bronze Age burial customs in Western Anatolia", *American Journal of Archaeology*, 78 (1974), pp. 415-425.

[49] P. DIKAIOS, "A new chapter in the long island story of Cyprus: wartime discoveries of the earliest Copper Age", *Illustrated London News*, 2 March 1946, pp. 244-245.

[50] E. PELTENBURG, "Lemba Archaeological Project, Cyprus, 1983: preliminary report", *Levant*, 17 (1985), p. 58; ID., "Kissonerga-Mosphilia: A major Chalcolithic site in Cyprus", *Bulletin of the American Schools of Oriental Research*, 282/3 (1991), p. 31.

[51] J.R.B. STEWART, cited in J.B. HENNESSY, K.O. ERIKSSON & I.C. KEHRBERG, *Ayia Paraskevi and Vasilia. Excavations by J. R. B. Stewart*, Studies in Mediterranean Archaeology, LXXXII, Göteborg 1988, p. 29.

Other artefacts

There are a number of elements which on their own might be dismissed as minor, accidental or irrelevant, but taken together with the suite of other items, may be seen as indicative of foreign influence.

Early Bronze Age Anatolian sites all have large quantities of small, roughly made, free-standing models of animals. Such small zoomorphic figures are unknown in Chalcolithic Cyprus but appear, either as free-standing objects, components in genre-scenes or attached to pots, in EC Cyprus. Several violin-shaped anthropomorphic stone figurines in the Hadjiprodromou Collection, described by Vagnetti,[52] likewise have very close parallels in Anatolia.

Other behavioural traits

Other aspects of the cultural transition from the Chalcolithic to the Bronze Age in Cyprus involve more subtle but equally significant changes in behaviour and attitude. In particular a radical change in curate and discard strategies is becoming increasingly apparent. Both Neolithic and Chalcolithic domestic structures frequently contain a wealth of *in situ* artefactual material. Usable objects and furnishings were deliberately left behind and sealed on the house floors when structures were abandoned, remodelled or rebuilt.[53] On EC sites little, if any, *de facto* refuse remains on house floors and the pattern is radically different. This does not appear to be due simply to differing circumstances of abandonment or occupational refuse strategies, but rather to culturally determined innovations in ideological, ritual or non-cognitive behaviour.[54]

Discussion

The first observation we can make is that there was a very wide range of Anatolian or Anatolianising innovations in the Early Cypriot Bronze Age. The second is that many — if not most — elements are connected with primary food production and the domestic economy. These are not high prestige goods, special purpose or selected artefacts, but rather constitute part of a set of material representing ways of doing things, especially in a domestic context. The majority of innovations cannot simply be explained by general 'stimulus diffusion', by occasional contacts, or by the deliberate importation of prestige items. They are the result of the introduction of new

---

[52] L. VAGNETTI, "Two steatite figurines of Anatolian type in Chalcolithic Cyprus", *Report of the Department of Antiquities, Cyprus*, 1979, pp. 112-114.

[53] Cf. E. PELTENBURG, "Pattern and purpose in the prehistoric Cypriot village of Ayios Epiktitos Vrysi", *Chypre. La vie quotidienne de l'antiquité à nos jours*, Paris 1985, pp. 46-64.

[54] J.M. WEBB, "Abandonment processes and curate/discard strategies at Marki *Alonia*, Cyprus", *The Artefact*, 18 (1995), pp. 64-70.

technologies, attitudes and practices, which, as argued above, are difficult to achieve without close personal interaction and training.

Anatolian influences in ceramics, for example, must be seen in terms of technology transfer. In western Anatolia EB II pottery can be regarded as a domestic industry in the hands of women. The introduction of these new ceramic features to Cyprus suggests, therefore, the movement of (women) potters. The introduction of new functional shapes must also be linked to the broader issues of agricultural and food-processing technology and the domestic economy. It is hard to see these as diffused by some general 'stimulus' rather than by the arrival of practitioners. Other 'domestic' specialist skills (food preparation, textile production) also require training and cannot be adopted or learnt instantly, or simply by the observation of finished products.

The same applies to other technological introductions. New animals require more than the process of importation. Knowledge of animal husbandry, of feeding, breeding, care and maintenance, as well as training for milking and traction are specialised skills, hard to acquire. So too are related agricultural practices. More extensive plough rather than hoe-based agriculture must be organised, scheduled and incorporated within a different structure of individual or group activities, perhaps involving a re-allocation of duties ascribed to men and women, old and young. There are significant barriers to the adoption of this new way of doing things: they are not obviously 'better', unless a range of associated social changes also take place. The simple importation of animals, likewise, would not work unless the skills, structures and perceptions of society were appropriate. Once again, movement of farmers, as well as of material, is the most appropriate mechanism for transferring these technologies.

Metallurgy, too, requires specialised knowledge, and hence the migration of at least some knowledgeable people. The need for metals is more problematic. Copper is neither intrinsically nor functionally better than other materials for many tasks. It is, for example, softer and less efficient than stone for heavy-duty use. The replacement of stone axes and adzes by metal ones thus suggests a different *attitude* toward materials. One possibility is to see all metal artefacts as prestige items, their efficiency less important than their appearance. But this does not explain the almost complete lack of stone axes and adzes at sites such as Marki *Alonia,* which suggests a more wholesale replacement of one functional material by the other. Why then is metal adopted? Once again we may suggest migrants, bringing with them not only metallurgy as a technology, but also a *concept* of the appropriateness of metal for tools.

We would argue, therefore, that most items cannot represent a casual contact or one based on voyaging abroad in search of prestige items, or on a more generalised adoption of items and technologies by 'stimulus diffusion'. Rather they provide evidence of a transfer of a range of technologies, indicative of the movement of whole groups of people, bringing with them to their new homes skills, crafts, technologies and associated social patterns and concepts. This interpretation of the movement of people is reinforced by the implications of a very different concept of household (suggested by different forms of architecture) and of different discard/curate behaviour. A primary motivation for this colonisation may have been access to copper sources, involving the movement of people with a 'focal' technology 'leapfrogging' across to the island following initial exploratory visits. The items in this inventory do not represent a cohesive 'package' of specific items transplanted from Anatolia, but this should not be expected given the postulated rapid 'artefactual founder effect' discussed above. It could also reflect a series of movements over time, as new colonists joined a migration stream following an information flow back to the mainland.

A sequence of connections

Not all new elements come into Cyprus at the same time, or from the same areas, or necessarily reflect the movement of the same set of people. While the majority can be associated with western Anatolian traditions, some — notably the hobs and donkeys — apparently reflect an eastern origin. There may have been several, possibly successive, interactions, three of which may be summarised as follows:

1. Chalcolithic Cyprus — EB II Cilicia.

Sporadic, occasional connections are suggested by imports and exports. Small items, such as the occasional pottery vessel, or trinket, found their way into or out of Cyprus and copper (bronze) was brought into Chalcolithic Cyprus. Although evidence of this initial phase is best represented in Cilicia, it may have been sufficiently widespread to provide the background of knowledge and information necessary for later more directed connections.

2. EB II/III western Anatolia — Philia Cyprus.

Specific focal colonisation (following copper prospecting and initially directed toward mining, perhaps for export to the mainland) provided the incentive for movements to the island. Initial colonisation was of areas in the west of the island useful for copper working and associated extensive agriculture. These colonists also brought suites of other technologies, primarily of an agricultural or domestic nature. They do not form a single, cohesive package, but taken together show a distinctly different way of life from pre-existing Cypriot society.

3. EB II-III eastern Anatolia/Syria — EC Cyprus.

Some innovations may come from a culturally distinct source. These include hobs and donkeys more at home in eastern than western Anatolia. They may indicate a Cypriot link with established trade networks, perhaps connected with the spread of the Early Transcaucasian system, or even precursors of the well-known second millennium networks epitomised by the Assyrian trade with Cappadocia, in which donkey caravans carried tin (and textiles) to Anatolia. Tin is not a significant part of the Cypriot metals industry until MC III, although it does occur from EC III. Tin and donkeys may have been introduced to the island as part of a trade-based contact, perhaps in exchange for copper. But the presence of domestic items, such as the hobs, suggests some movement of people as well.

Implications for development within Cyprus

These different relationships, influences, connections or migrations lead to a more complex view of interaction between Anatolia and Cyprus in the third millennium B.C.E. At the same time they raise equally important issues for the process of technology transfer and cultural transformation within Cyprus itself. We have suggested that the Philia culture derives from a focal colonisation of the island from south-western Anatolia, stimulated by the discovery of significant copper sources, by communities bringing with them not only the new technology of metallurgy but a series of other technologies, agricultural and domestic. The number of colonists may have been relatively small. Once established on the island they would have increased in number and in extent. We must consider how this different ethnic group interacted with pre-existing Chalcolithic peoples, and how the later, presumably more unified EC III cultural system developed in different parts of the island.

Once again the critical issues concern ethnicity and technology. It is possible to argue that the original mid-third millennium colonists settled first in the north-western foothills of the Troodos range, close to major copper sources and localities where they could employ their plough-based agriculture most efficiently. These areas were less productive using hoe-agriculture than, for example, the river-valleys in the south-west and may, therefore, have had a lower population density. As the colonists had so different an economy, based on different agricultural technologies and raw materials, conflict with pre-existing people may have been minimal. Eventually, however, the concepts of, and technologies requiring, metal and cattle became dominant and we find a widespread similarity of pottery, architecture and other material and behavioural traits across much of the island. Investigation of the processes involved in the development of this EC III *koine* from the different ethnic groups of the late third millennium is another important and complex topic for future research.

EGYPTIAN STONE VESSELS IN SYRO-PALESTINE DURING THE SECOND MILLENNIUM B.C. AND THEIR IMPACT ON THE LOCAL STONE VESSEL INDUSTRY

BY

Rachael SPARKS

INTRODUCTION

In second millennium Syro-Palestine Egyptian stone vessels appear alongside locally made examples as containers for cosmetics, medicines, perfumed oils and ointments. The larger vessels were probably used for commodities such as oil, beer and wine. They are essentially luxury goods, found in contexts ranging from funerary to cultic, domestic and palatial. The Egyptian and Palestinian stone vessel industries are distinct in terms of technique and material, yet the imported examples have a considerable impact on local forms, while the Palestinian industry does not appear to have a corresponding influence on Egyptian practices.

1. MATERIALS

Stone vessels appear in a range of materials, but the most common of all are those often described as alabaster. This term has been used in the past to describe two distinct materials, gypsum and calcite. Both include white and partially translucent varieties, and may appear superficially similar, despite their distinct chemical and physical properties. In Syro-Palestine they form over 80% of the total corpus, and it is important to distinguish between them as they can play an important part in determining the origin of certain vessels. As first pointed out by Ben-Dor, one of the chief differences between the Egyptian stone vessel industry and its Palestinian counterpart is that the former chiefly used calcite, whereas the latter used only gypsum.[1]

Gypsum is composed of hydrated calcium sulphate, a fairly soft stone with a Mohs hardness of 2. It is soluble in water, often leading to severe surface weathering and poor preservation. Gypsum occurs in a number of deposits in Palestine, including one about 18 km from Beth Shan that was probably used by

---

[1] I. BEN-DOR, "Palestinian Alabaster Vases", *QDAP,* 11 (1945), pp. 94-95.
[2] I. BEN-DOR, *loc. cit.* (n. 1), pp. 95-96, see also F. BENDER, *Geology of Jordan,* Berlin 1974, p. 168.

that site in the Bronze and Iron Ages.[2] In Egypt, the only source known to have been worked in antiquity for vessels was in the Fayum, used during dynasties III-IV.[3]

Calcite is a coarsely crystalline form of calcium carbonate, with a Mohs hardness of 3 to 3.5. It can be white to white yellow in appearance; and is frequently banded with a series of translucent and opaque layers. Calcite is not known to occur in workable deposits in Syro-Palestine;[4] however there are numerous Egyptian sources, including Middle and New Kingdom quarries at Hatnub in middle Egypt.[5]

In second millennium Egypt, the majority of vessels are made out of calcite, with gypsum being extremely rare.[6] In Syro-Palestine both materials are common, with calcite vessels outnumbering gypsum ones overall, although the exact proportions vary considerably within the region. For example, at Jericho nearly all vessels are made from gypsum, while at Tell el-'Ajjul most are made out of calcite. As calcite would seem to represent the Egyptian imports, and gypsum the local products, distribution patterns should be linked to issues such as the proximity of local workshops, and degree of contact with trade routes out of Egypt.

A variety of other stone types are also used for making stone vessels, but are relatively rare in Syro-Palestine.[7] Limestone and serpentine are the next most frequent, forming roughly 2% of the total corpus each. Chlorite and steatite vessels occur occasionally in Syro-Palestine,[8] but are more popular in the northern Levant.[9] Other materials include obsidian, diorite, haematite and various porphyritic stones — but these are also rare, and some of the examples we have from Middle and Late Bronze contexts are actually survivals from the third millennium B.C.[10]

---

[3] G. CATON-THOMPSON & E.W. GARDNER, *The Desert Fayum*, London 1934, pp. 103-123; B.A. GREENE, *Ancient Egyptian Stone Vessels: Materials and Forms*, unpublished PhD thesis, University of California, Berkeley 1989, pp. 124-128; A. LUCAS & J.R. HARRIS, *Ancient Egyptian Materials and Industries*, London 1962, p. 62, with other sources mentioned p. 78.

[4] I. BEN-DOR, *loc. cit.* (n. 1), p. 95.

[5] A. LUCAS & J.R. HARRIS, *op. cit.* (n. 3), pp. 59-60; I.M.E. SHAW, in B.J. KEMP, *Amarna Reports III*, London 1986 pp. 189-212.

[6] B.A. GREENE, *op. cit.* (n. 3), p. 128 has only identified six gypsum vessels from Egypt dating from after dynasty III, all belonging to the New Kingdom. Their existence should serve as a warning against assuming all gypsum vessels will be Palestinian *per se*.

[7] The various utilitarian ground stone bowls, mortars, and heavy temple furnishings such as libation tables, frequently made out of basalts and limestones will not be considered here, as they would appear to represent a different branch of the Syro-Palestinian industry, operating independently of Egyptian products and with strong local roots.

[8] Mostly Egyptian shapes, although a tuyere from Gezer may be of local or Syrian origin (W.G. DEVER et al., *Gezer IV*, Jerusalem 1986, pl. 50.9).

[9] Particularly at Ras Shamra, where chlorite and steatite are used not only for vessels, some of which may be Minoan imports, but also for a number of tool types including whetstones, beads and spindle whorls,. Unfinished examples and seal blanks point to local production of at least some of these — see C. ELLIOTT, "The Ground Stone Industry", *Arts et Industries de la pierre*, ed. M. YON, Paris 1991, pp. 44, 57; and A. CAUBET, "Répertoire de la vaisselle de pierre, Ougarit 1929-1988", ed. M. YON, *op. cit.*, pp. 206, 215.

[10] Examples of such survivals include vessels from Kamid el-Loz (R. MIRON, *Kamid el-Loz 10. Das 'Schatzhaus' im Palastbereich. Die Funde*, Bonn 1990, pl. 24.3, fig. 16, no. 398); Beth Shan (A. ROWE, *The Four Canaanite Temples of Beth Shan*, Philadelphia 1940, pl. LIIA.6); Lachish (O. TUFNELL, *Lachish*

This scarcity of stone types other than alabaster is also seen in Egypt, marking a trend towards decreasing variety that had begun during the Old Kingdom. For example, in dynasties I to II, over 30 different stone types were used in making stone vessels; but by the Middle kingdom, there were only 14.[11] Parallel with this more limited range of options is a tendency to concentrate specifically on calcite, already evident by the IVth dynasty.[12] For example, of the 83 stone vessels and lids in the tomb of Tutankhamen, there were 70 calcite vessels to 13 in other materials, chiefly limestone and serpentine.[13] As the resources certainly existed in the Middle and New Kingdoms to mount quarrying expeditions and import raw materials and goods, we have to assume that this conservatism of type was by choice rather than economic necessity. This may relate to the relative softness of calcite as opposed to stones such as diorite or quartz, which means that it can be worked more efficiently, in terms of man-hours, while having more durability than its counterpart gypsum.[14]

2. MANUFACTURE (fig. 1)

Another feature distinguishing vessels of Palestinian origin from contemporary Egyptian ones is their method of manufacture. Used along with the criteria of material type, it is usually possible to distinguish the products of Palestinian vessel workshops from imported Egyptian pieces.

Egyptian calcite vessels have been manufactured since the predynastic period. The most distinctive stage of this process was that of hollowing out the interior of the vessel using a drill.[15] While open forms such as bowls tend to have their interiors

---

IV — The Bronze Age, Oxford 1958, pl. 26.10); and the Amman Temple (V. HANKEY, "A Late Bronze Age Temple at Amman", *Levant*, 6 [1974], fig. 1.1-2, pl. XXXIIA).

[11] B.A. GREENE, *op. cit.* (n. 3), p. 410, fig. 46.

[12] I. BEN-DOR, *loc. cit.* (n. 1), p. 93.

[13] A. LUCAS & J.R. HARRIS, *op. cit.* (n. 3), pp. 422-423 mention proportions of 76 calcite to 3 serpentine. The recent publication of this material by A. EL-KHOULI, "Stone Vessels", *Stone Vessels, Pottery, and Sealings from the Tomb of Tut'ankhamun*, ed. J. BAINES, Oxford 1994, pp. 5-35, indicates that these figures are not quite correct; he describes an additional 3 limestone vessels and 4 stoppers, two groups of unidentified 'stone' fragments and a sandstone lid.

[14] Other soft stones, such as chlorite, schist, limestone and serpentine provided alternatives, but never became as popular as calcite. The numerous local sources of calcite available in Egypt itself probably gave it the advantage over other materials, although market preference may also have been a factor.

[15] The various stages of manufacture have been discussed by J.E. QUIBELL, "Stone Vessels from the Step Pyramid", *ASAE*, 35 (1935), pp. 76-80; A. LUCAS & J.R. HARRIS, *op. cit.* (n. 3), pp. 423-425, A. EL-KHOULI, *Egyptian Stone Vessels, Predynastic Period to Dynasty III*, 1978, pp. 789-801, amongst others. Replicative experimentation has been carried out by A.J. Gwinnett and L. Gorelick ("Beads, Scarabs, and Amulets: Methods of Manufacture in Ancient Egypt", *JARCE*, 30 [1993], pp. 125-132; "Ancient Egyptian Stone-Drilling: An Experimental Perspective on a Scholarly Disagreement", *Expedition*, 25 [1983], pp. 40-47) and D. Stocks (*Industrial Technology at Kahun and Gurob: experimental manufacture and test of replica and reconstructed tools with indicted uses and effects upon artefact production*, MA Thesis, University of Manchester, 1988).

Figure 1: Manufacturing Techniques

1.1 Hieroglyphic symbol representing drill (adapted from D. STOCKS, *Industrial Technology at Kahun and Gurob*, MA Thesis, University of Manchester, 1988, fig. 32).
1.2 Egyptian craftsman drilling out a cylindrical jar (adapted from D. STOCKS, *ibid.*, fig. 39).
1.3 Reconstruction showing chisel in use on a lug-handled jar (adapted from D. EVELY, "Some Manufacturing Processes in a Knossian Stone Vase Workshop", *BSA*, 75 [1980], fig. 3).
1.4 Suggested stages of drilling out a stone vessel interior (adapted from A. EL-KHOULI, *Egyptian Stone Vessels, Predynastic Period to Dynasty III*, 1978, pl. 146).
1.5 Gypsum lug-handled jar chisel marks of varying length on interior walls — Pella XXXIIB 27.6, reg. no. 110229.

smoothed off, closed forms often show traces of this stage in the form of fine, circular lines around the interior walls,[16] and either a raised bump or depression in the centre of the base.[17] The central part of the interior was removed using a tubular drill, while undercutting the shoulders of closed forms was achieved by the use of flat, figure-of-eight shaped drill bits. Fig. 1.4 shows a suggested breakdown of these steps — taking out central cores (steps 1-2), then cutting room for the disc-shaped drill and inserting drill bits of increasing diameter (steps 3-5). Cutting the rim back to create a funnel-shaped mouth, as seen on certain shapes (alabastra and juglets in particular) was probably left till last (step 6). Occasional examples of the flat drill-bit have survived.[18] The form of the drill mechanism is known to us from a number of scenes depicting stone vessel manufacture (fig. 1.2);[19] it was also adopted into hieroglyphs, and became a determinative sign for a worker in stone (fig. 1.1).[20]

Palestinian vessels are made in a completely different fashion, with their interiors being hollowed out using flat-bladed chisels, which also tend to leave distinctive marks on the interiors of closed vessels (fig. 1.3, 1.5).[21] The resultant marks show the chisel was used both vertically and obliquely, and frequently overlap. The interior of such vessels also tend to be irregular, unlike most Egyptian examples, and the walls may vary considerably in thickness. Such marks are usually found on gypsum in Syro-Palestine, although a handful of chlorite pieces at Ras Shamra suggest that there may have been a related industry in the Northern Levant.[22] In addition, several unfinished juglets and two unfinished lug-handled jars were found at Beth Shan, attesting to the presence of workshops there from at least the latter part of the Middle Bronze Age.[23]

---

[16] I. BEN-DOR, *loc. cit.* (n. 1), p. 97. The form of these can be linked to a number of factors, including the types of abrasives used, the amount of heat and pressure generated during drilling and the hardness of the stone being worked — see L. GORELICK & A.J. GWINNETT, "Collars" in the Holes of Near Eastern Cylinder Seals", *Archeomaterials,* 3 (1989), pp. 41, 44.

[17] Resulting from removal of the drill core (P. WARREN *Minoan Stone Vases*, Cambridge 1969, p. 161).

[18] G. CATON-THOMPSON & E.W. GARDNER, *op. cit.* (n. 3), pl. LXIX.13, 16.

[19] Examples include a workshop model dating to the Middle Kingdom (A. EL-KHOULI, *op. cit.* [n. 15], pl. 147); and pictorial scenes from the XVIII Dynasty Tomb of Rekhmere (N. de G. DAVIES *The Tomb of Rekh-mi-re' at Thebes*, New York 1943, pl. LIV), and the Tomb of the Two Sculptors at Thebes (N. de G. DAVIES, *The Tomb of Two Sculptors at Thebes*, New York 1925, pl. XI). Only one type of drill mechanism is depicted in use on stone vessels, characterised by one or more weights tied to a central shaft, with an eccentric handle at the top and drill bits attached at the base of the shaft.

[20] W.M.F. PETRIE, *Stone and Metal Vases*, London 1937, p. 3; D. STOCKS *op. cit.* (n. 15), fig. 29-32.

[21] I. BEN-DOR, *loc. cit.* (n. 1), p. 97.

[22] For example A. CAUBET, *loc. cit.* (n. 9), pl V.9, X.9, RS 1-31.[001] and pl. VIII.3, RS 11.576 feature similar chisel marks. The latter is an alabastron, described by Caubet as unfinished (*loc. cit.* [n. 9], p. 209). However it displays the strongly delineated chisel marks and thick, uneven walls characteristic of gypsum vessels in Syro-Palestine, suggesting that it may be a crude local product, rather than incomplete.

[23] I. BEN-DOR, *loc. cit.* (n. 1), pp. 97-98. The juglets came from level X; the lug-handled jars are much later, from Level VI (F.W. JAMES, *The Iron Age at Beth Shan*, Philadelphia 1966, fig. 54.10), and Level III or IV, probably out of its original context (unpublished, Philadelphia University Museum P. 29-107-307).

These findings have led to the equation, which seems to generally hold true, that if a vessel is made out of gypsum and is chisel made it is of local Palestinian manufacture, whereas if it is made of harder stones and with drilled interiors, it is Egyptian. The occasional recurrence of Egyptian gypsum pieces can be discounted here, as they tend to be drill made, and none have turned up in Syro-Palestine to date.[24]

There is no good evidence that Egyptian methods of manufacturing stone vessels were ever adopted in Syro-Palestine. This is despite the fact that drill technology was certainly known in other crafts such as lapidary; and unfinished drill made objects,[25] and parts of other types of drill mechanism have been recovered.[26] It is also despite the fact that Egyptian styles and techniques were introduced in other crafts, including ceramic and silicate production at sites such as Deir el-Balah[27] and Beth Shan.[28] Although similar technology was also used for producing vessels at Atchana, in the northern Levant;[29] and in Crete,[30] it does not appear to have been introduced from those areas either.

There are at least two possible explanations for the apparent absence of this technology. Firstly, Syro-Palestine does not have sources for the types of stones favoured for vessels in this period, particularly calcite and serpentine. Therefore, even though the technology was theoretically known, it would have been economically unfeasible to base an industry entirely on raw materials which had to be imported from Egypt or elsewhere. In Crete, where raw materials were imported for its stone vessel industry,[31] they were being crafted in workshops which were already fashioning indigenous hard stones, so that the apparatus for using these imports was already in place. In Syro-Palestine, this apparatus would appear to be missing. It may also be the case that it was considered easier and more cost effective to use the chisel on soft stones rather than

---

[24] The unfinished vessels from Umm es-Sawaan appear to have been roughly worked into shape, the interior hollow pecked out and then drilled. Few examples exist from this stage of the process, although several flint drill-bits were found on site.

[25] For example, unfinished maceheads are known from Gezer and Beth Shan (R.A.S. MACALISTER, *Excavations at Gezer II*, 1912, fig. 402 p. 252; I. BEN-DOR, *loc. cit.* (n. 1), p. 97 note 3.

[26] Numerous drill caps are known, a characteristic part of the bow-driven drill that was used in the manufacture of furniture and beads; ie: Tell el-'Ajjul (W.M.F. PETRIE, *Ancient Gaza I*, London 1931, pl. LII.8, LII.17; W.M.F. PETRIE, *Ancient Gaza III*, London 1933, pl. XXVII.70), Beth Shan (A. ROWE, *op. cit.* [n. 10], pl. XXVII.33), Tell el-Far'ah (A. CHAMBON, *Tell el-Far'ah 1. L'Age du fer*, Paris 1984, pl. 77.22-24) and Megiddo (P.L.O. GUY & R.M. ENGBERG *Megiddo Tombs*, Chicago 1938, pl. 141.29).

[27] J. YELLIN, T. DOTHAN & B. GOULD, "The Provenience of Beerbottles from Deir el-Bal'ah: A Study by Neutron Activation Analysis", *IEJ*, 36 (1986), pp. 68-73.

[28] F.W. JAMES and P.E. MCGOVERN, *The Late Bronze Egyptian Garrison at Beth Shan: A Study of Levels VII and VIII*, Philadelphia 1993, pp. 161-163.

[29] Woolley excavated a vessel workshop, attributed to Level VII, which included unfinished bowls showing marks indicating the use of solid drill bits (C.L. WOOLLEY *Alalakh — An account of the Excavations at Tell Atchana in the Hatay, 1937-1949*, Oxford 1955, p. 110, pp. 292-6). An unfinished Minoan style lamp from the site shows marks characteristic of a tubular drill (C.L. WOOLLEY, *op. cit.*, p. 295, fig. 66; P. Warren, *op. cit.* [n. 17], pp. 55-56).

[30] P. WARREN, *op. cit.* (n. 17), pp. 158-161.

[31] P. WARREN, *op. cit.* (n. 17), pp. 125-126, 186, 190.

the drill. In Crete, similar soft stone industries using chisels existed alongside drill-based ones.[32]

An alternative explanation is that an egyptianising industry may exist in Syro-Palestine, but be undetectable. This would be the case if it utilised egyptian styles, materials and techniques. This scenario is very difficult to prove without actual workshop remains or debris. Against it, is the infrequency of drill cores found on sites in the region. If there was a flourishing egyptianising industry, we might also expect it to develop local resources such as limestone and basalt. This is not currently supported by the evidence; standard types of cosmetic vessels do not appear in basalt; and while limestone examples occasionally occur, it is never in sufficient quantity to suggest local production. It may be significant also that the Egyptian-style vessels found in Syro-Palestine don't seem to feature the kind of hybridisation seen in contemporary decorative arts, such as ivory working, where Egyptian motifs appear alongside orientalising ones.[33]

Therefore, it would appear that the Egyptian industry does not influence the technology of its Palestinian counterpart in any significant way. It did have a considerable impact, however, on the style and form of the local products.

3. Form

A wide variety of shapes are imported into Syro-Palestine from Egypt, ranging from simple cosmetic containers to quite elaborate zoomorphic and prestigious large scale items. The shapes found parallel those found in Egypt itself, but many types differ in popularity in the two regions, suggesting that differing patterns of local consumption were in operation.

For example, two of the most popular Egyptian cosmetic forms during the Middle Bronze Age are found only rarely in Syro-Palestine. The first of these is a small, bell shaped kohl jar in vogue from the Middle Kingdom through to the XVIIIth Dynasty (fig. 2.1).[34] While the type is imported into Syro-Palestine, only a handful of examples appear at sites such as Gezer, Megiddo, Hazor, Jericho and Lachish.[35] The shape does

---

[32] This in itself suggests that the technology was better suited to the material. For a discussion of these soft-stone industries, see P. WARREN, "A Stone Vase-Maker's Workshop in the Palace at Knossos", *BSA*, 62 (1967), pp. 195-201, and D. EVELY, "Some Manufacturing Processes in a Knossian Stone Vase Workshop", *BSA*, 75 (1980), pp. 127-138.

[33] R.D. BARNETT, *Ancient Ivories in the Middle East*, Jerusalem 1982, pl. 19a (ivory panel); F.W. JAMES & P.E. McGOVERN, *op. cit.* (n. 28), p. 179 and fig. 104.1 (basalt miniature throne).

[34] W.M.F. PETRIE, *op. cit.* (n. 20), pl. XXIX.674-8, XXX.680-2, 687-737, XXXI.738-746. According to Petrie, *op. cit.* (n. 20), p. 11, this shape was replaced by various types of kohl tube sometime during the reign of Tuthmosis III.

[35] R.A.S. MACALISTER, *The Excavation of Gezer III*, London 1912, pl. CXCVI.18, CCXIII.12, 14; G. LOUD, *Megiddo II, Season of 1935-1939*, Chicago 1948, pl. 258.8; Y. YADIN, *Hazor I,* Jerusalem

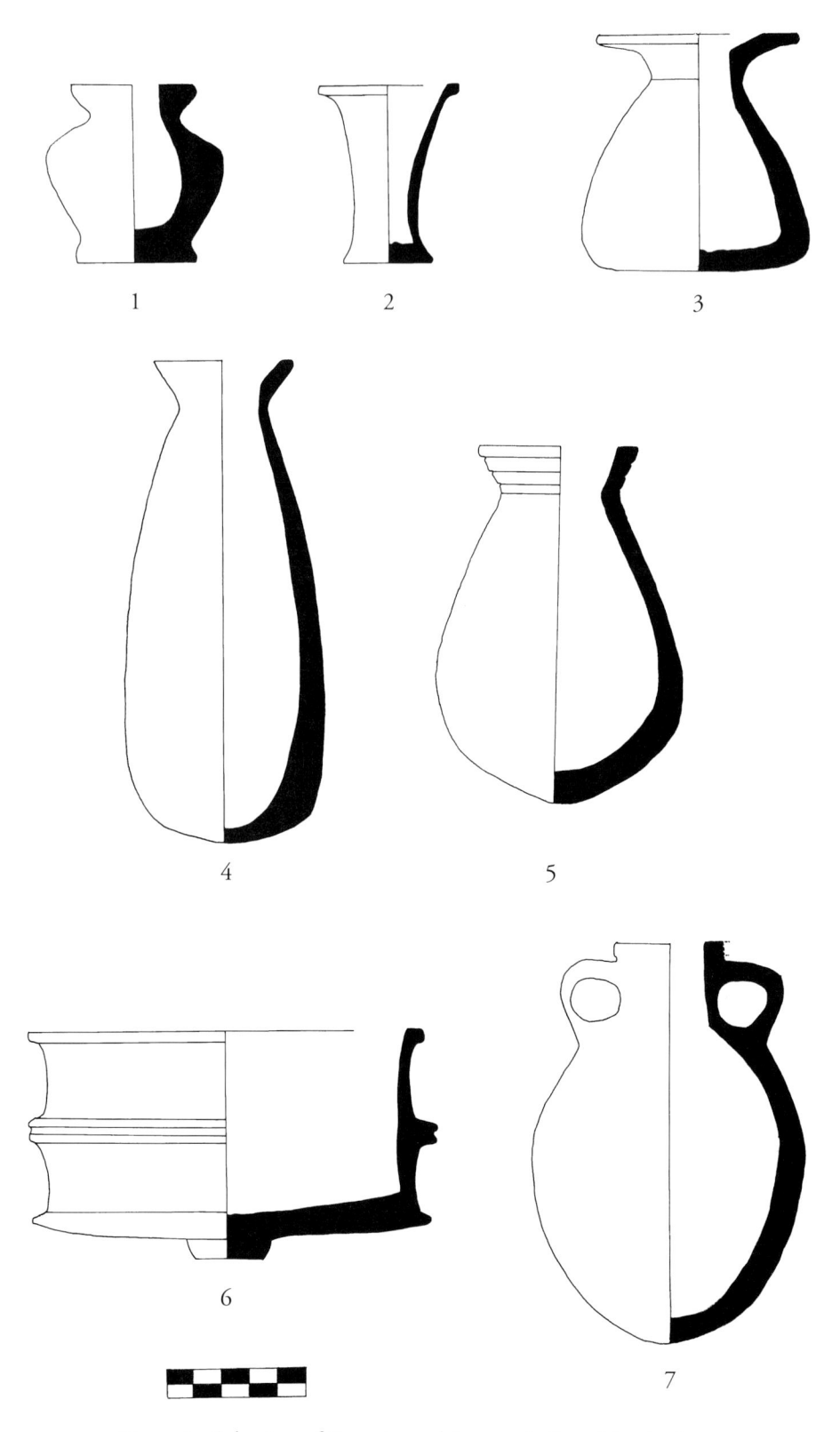

Figure 2: Selection of Egyptian calcite vessels found in the Levant

2.1 Lachish tomb 216.
2.2 Atchana AT/38/240.
2.3 Tell el-'Ajjul Area JA, Level 885.
2.4 Tell el-'Ajjul, Area E, level 457.
2.5 Lachish, 100 Ho.
2.6 Ras Shamra tomb XXV, no. 37.
2.7 Lachish tomb 508.

not appear to have taken on in the region, either because locals did not consider the contents desirable, or because some other form was serving the same function.[36] The exception to this rule is Tell el-'Ajjul, where some 31 examples were found.[37] This can be explained by the proximity of the site to Egypt, and its position as the largest city in Southern Palestine, probably to be equated with the Sharuhen of Egyptian records.

The second form is a cylindrical jar with flat base and simple concave sides (fig. 2.2). In Egypt, it occurs from the Early Dynastic period and lasts into the New Kingdom, with model versions often appearing in foundation deposits.[38] In Syro-Palestine, there are only a handful of examples of this form throughout the whole second millennium; and unlike the bell jar, these are not concentrated at any particular site.[39] As one would expect from their infrequency, bell jars and this type of cylindrical jar have little impact on Syro-Palestinian workshops and do not appear in local materials.

On the other hand, there are some forms which appear to have an equal, if not greater popularity in Syro-Palestine than in Egypt. As these appear to be of egyptian manufacture, this might suggest that at least some of the workshops in Egypt were geared towards exportation — or be an argument in favour of egyptianising workshops in the region. In keeping with the popularity of these types, these forms were also copied by local workshops.

For example, the alabastron is extremely successful in Syro-Palestine throughout the Middle Bronze Age, but less so in Egypt, where the shape originates.[40] It occurs in three forms: with a drop shaped body and everted rim (fig. 2.4); a version of this with a grooved neck (fig. 2.5); and with a conical body and flattened base (fig. 2.3). The grooved neck type is quite rare in Syro-Palestine; but the other forms are common and are copied into local repertoires. At the end of the Middle Bronze, a new version

---

1958, pl. CXLII.13; J. GARSTANG, "Jericho Reports I-III", *AAA*, 20 (1933), pl. XLI.5; O. TUFNELL, *op. cit.* (n. 10), pl. 26.37.

[36] Residues from a jar of this type from Tomb 216 at Lachish were analysed as containing manganese dioxide, an ingredient used in kohl (O. TUFNELL, *op. cit.* [n. 10], p. 85). Numerous Egyptian examples of this form contain black and dark grey dehydrated powders, which are also probably remains of kohl.

[37] W.M.F. PETRIE, 1931, *op. cit.* (n. 26), pl. XXV.31-33, 35-37; W.M.F. PETRIE, 1933, *op. cit.* (n. 26), pl. XXVI.7-12.

[38] For example, W.M.F. PETRIE, *op. cit.* (n. 20), pl. XXXII.802-3. The foundation deposits at the temple of Nekhbet at El-Kab included several calcite model cylindrical jars, inscribed with the cartouches of Amenhotep II, now on display in the British Museum, BM 32533-6.

[39] Jericho (K.M. KENYON, *Excavations at Jericho II*, London 1965, fig. 100.3, 154.12); Khirbet Kufin (R.H. SMITH, *Excavations in the Cemetery of Khirbet Kufin, Palestine*, London 1962, pl. XVII.34, 36); Tell el-'Ajjul (W.M.F. PETRIE, 1931, *op. cit.* [n. 26], pl. XXV.5).

[40] Earliest examples in Egypt date to the XII Dynasty (W.M.F. PETRIE, *op. cit.* [n. 20], p. 10, pl. XXIX.658), while in Palestine it doesn't appear until the second half of MBII (C. CLAMER, "A Calcite Vase", *'Atiqot*, 12 [1977], p. 72). The ridged neck variety is confined to the Middle Kingdom (B.A. GREENE, *op. cit.* [n. 3], p. 353; W.M.F. PETRIE, *op. cit.* [n. 20], pl. XXIX.656-7, 659-60), although the simpler drop-shaped form continues into the early XVIII Dynasty (C. CLAMER, *ibid.*). The conical alabastron was introduced in the XVIII Dynasty (W.M.F. PETRIE, *op. cit.* [n. 20], pl. XXXIV. 868-872).

60   R. SPARKS

Figure 3 Syro-Palestinian gypsum vessels

3.1 Pella, Area II tomb 89, reg. no. 100178.
3.2 Megiddo, Level VIIB, locus 1829.
3.3 Pella, unprovenanced tomb, cat. 5/912.
3.4 Beth Shan, Level XA locus 1633-4.
3.5 Pella, Area XI tomb 62, reg. no. 70752.

appears with a broad, flat topped rim. The Egyptian variety of this often has a short, offset neck. The Palestinian copies lack this neck, and also feature incised and inlaid decoration on the flat upper rim surface, something not usually seen on Egyptian stone examples (fig. 3.5, 4.1).[41] This type has a very limited distribution, perhaps centred on the North Jordan Valley.[42]

Another form with a greater popularity in Syro-Palestine than Egypt is the juglet, particularly during the Middle Bronze. The Egyptian-made examples have high shoulders, and often thickened loop handles with duck-head bases, and built-in tazza feet.[43] They also make stone versions of the Palestinian dipper juglet form.[44] Both types of juglet are not common in Egypt itself.[45] Gypsum juglets made by the Palestinian industry adopt the high shoulders of the Egyptian versions, but tend towards the flat, rather than pointed base. A sub-group from Jericho develops this form further, often featuring articulated shoulders, flat strap rather than rounded loop handles, and incised linear and herringbone designs on its outer face (fig. 3.4).[46] The Egyptian industry also uses a ceramic form — Cypriot base ring ware — as the pattern for one of its Late Bronze Age stone juglet types, also exported to Syro-Palestine. These subsequently develop into a hybrid of their original form and another common stone vessel shape of the period, the footed jar.[47] These juglets are not copied by Palestinian craftsmen, and lack the popularity of their MB counterparts, although examples appear sporadically at sites such as Kamid el-Loz, the Amman Temple, Lachish, and Tell el-'Ajjul.[48]

Another stone vessel type copied from a ceramic prototype is the pilgrim flask. These occur at numerous sites in Egypt during the New Kingdom, and are imported to Palestine (fig. 2.7). Local workshops also produced a gypsum version of the pilgrim flask, with examples found at Beth Shan and Megiddo,[49] although it could be argued

---

[41] Wooden versions of this shape do sometimes feature painted decoration on the upper rim, see J. VANDIER D'ABBADIE, *Catalogue des objets de toilette égyptiens*, Paris 1972, OT 240.

[42] To date most of the examples found have come from Pella.

[43] G. LOUD, *op. cit.* (n. 35), fig. 258.6, 261.35; W.M.F. PETRIE, 1933, *op. cit.* (n. 26), pl. XXVI.21.

[44] G. LOUD, *op. cit.* (n. 35), fig. 258.11, W.M.F. PETRIE, *Ancient Gaza IV*, London 1934, pl. XXXIX.51-54.

[45] W.M.F. PETRIE, *op. cit.* (n. 20), pl. XXVIII.557-8; R.S. MERRILLEES, "Ancient Egypt's Silent Majority: Sidmant Tomb 254", Trade and Transcendence in the Bronze Age Levant, *SIMA*, 39 (1974), fig. 16.

[46] K.M. KENYON, *Excavations at Jericho I*, 1960, fig. 171.3, 187.2, 4, 8-9, 16, 224.16; *Excavations at Jericho II*, 1965, fig. 100.6, 154.8, 171.13, 16, 179.7-8, 17-18, 20-21.

[47] W.M.F. PETRIE, *op. cit.* (n. 20), pl. XXXIII.846-859.

[48] R. MIRON, *op. cit.* (n. 10), pl. 23.1-2, 24.1-2; V. HANKEY, *loc. cit.* (n. 10), fig. 1.14, 2.15, 17-18, 27; O. TUFNELL C.H. INGE, L. HARDING, *Lachish II — The Fosse Temple*, Oxford 1940, pl. XXV.6; O. TUFNELL, *op. cit.* (n. 10), pl. 26.31; W.M.F. PETRIE, *Ancient Gaza II*, London 1932, pl. XXII.14-15, 23, 26.

[49] G. LOUD, *op. cit.* (n. 35), fig. 261.19; F.W. JAMES & P.E. MCGOVERN, *op. cit.* (n. 28), fig. 111.3-5, 113.4; F.W. JAMES, *The Iron Age at Beth Shan*, Philadelphia 1966, fig. 54.9, 57.16.

whether the stone or ceramic versions inspired these. The locally produced examples tended to lack the defined neck of both ceramic and Egyptian stone versions, and tend towards baggy, rather than spherical bodies (fig. 3.2).

One of the most popular shapes of the Late Bronze Age is the tazza, a ribbed cup or goblet with distinctive, carinated sides. In its Egyptian form, it can have a flat base, a low foot, or a trumpet shaped foot which is made separately, with a mortice in the upper part fitting a matching tenon on the underside of the bowl itself (fig. 2.6, upper portion only). The tazza is imported to Syro-Palestine in all three forms. The latter shape, with the separate foot, seems to have inspired a local version which outnumbers all three types put together, featuring this trumpet shaped foot but made in one piece out of local gypsum.[50] It does not appear to have been exported to Egypt, and the Egyptians do not produce tall stemmed one piece tazze of their own. An unusual subtype features two, instead of the more usual single midrib, and is limited to the Jordan valley (fig. 3.3).[51]

All these forms reflect the popularity of Egyptian imports into Syro-Palestine, in that they appear to have inspired local copies. However, there are a number of distinctly Egyptian features which do not get copied across to the gypsum versions. One is the occasional practice of manufacturing Egyptian vessels in several pieces, which were then glued together.[52] This technique probably developed in Egypt as a response to the difficulty of hollowing out the interiors of vessels with narrow necks and broad shoulders. Palestinian craftsmen appear to have been quite skilled at hollowing out their interiors with chisels without resorting to this approach.[53] Another Egyptian practice that developed in the New Kingdom was the tendency to make vessels with separate stands, fitting together with a mortice and tenon arrangement. This is applied to a whole range of shapes,[54] but never seems to be adopted by the Palestinian industry, even though similar trumpet shaped feet do appear.

---

[50] I. BEN-DOR, *loc. cit.* (n. 1), Type E, pp. 105-106.

[51] Found at Tell es-Sa'idiyeh T. 117 (J.B. PRITCHARD *The Cemetery at Tell es-Sa'idiyeh, Jordan*, Philadelphia 1980, fig. 21.17, 57.11), Pella (S.J. BOURKE & R.T. SPARKS "The 1963/64 DAJ Excavations at Pella in Jordan", *Trade, Contact and the Movement of People in the Eastern Mediterranean: Studies in Honour of J. Basil Hennessy*, Mediterranean Archaeology Supplementary Volume 3, Sydney 1995, cat. no. 6); Beth Shan VI Locus 1184 (I. BEN-DOR, *loc. cit.* (n. 1), p. 106, E1) and level VII locus 1087 (F.W. JAMES & P.E. MCGOVERN, *op. cit.* [n. 28], fig. 110.3).

[52] Examples occur from the Ist dynasty — see W.M.F. PETRIE, *op. cit.* (n. 20), p. 3; pl. XXVI.480.1, and for the XIIth dynasty pl. XXIV.627, 629, 632. A pilgrim flask on display in the British Museum dating to the XIX-XXth dynasties features a separately made neck, BM 32546.

[53] Vessels with small mouths and necks are common in the Palestinian repertoire, suggesting that narrow chisels must have been used; however the vessel walls rarely achieve the regularity of the Egyptian examples.

[54] W.M.F. PETRIE, *op. cit.* (n. 48), pl. XXIII.33 (tazza), A. CAUBET, *loc. cit.* (n. 9), pl. II.6. (footed jar); A. MAZAR, *Excavations at Tell Qasile, Part 2: The Philistine Sanctuary*, Qedem, 20, Jerusalem 1985, fig. 4.3 (ovoid jar with lug handles); V. HANKEY, *loc. cit.* (n. 10), fig. 1.7 (ovoid jar); Y. YADIN, *op. cit.* (n. 35), pl. CL.1; pl. CXCVI.2 (goblet).

Palestinian workshops also developed a number of shapes independently of Egypt, some of which may have been inspired by other media and differing local tastes. These include the ram's-head handled bowl,[55] and lug-handled jar (fig. 3.1). This in itself indicates that, although initially inspired by Egyptian products,[56] the Palestinian industry soon developed into a viable concern in its own right.

4. Decoration (fig. 4).

The majority of stone vessels are undecorated, probably because of the decorative quality intrinsic in the natural banding and variable colouring of the stones chosen. However there are exceptions. In the Egyptian industry, certain shapes were occasionally decorated, often choosing the less obviously banded calcites for this purpose. This decoration may be painted, incised and inlaid with colour (usually blue, black or white), or consist of added sculptural details such as zoomorphic handles. The range of motifs is fairly limited, with floral and lotus designs being quite popular. Inscriptions are also used to decorative effect, with motives placed on the neck and shoulder zones of vessels. Examples of all these types of decoration appear on vessels imported to Syro-Palestine, although they are fairly uncommon.[57]

Palestinian-made vessels are also decorated only rarely, usually by incision with black inlaid colour. The decoration is sometimes quite carelessly applied. The designs and techniques used are also used by other media, such as bone and woodworking.[58] Simple geometric designs are popular, including a dot-circle motif especially common on Middle Bronze bone inlays (fig. 4.1). Also appearing is a floral motif which may be inspired by the Egyptian designs (fig. 3.5, 4.2), and shows similarities to the punctured decoration found on tell el-Yehudiyeh wares.[59] Sculpted decoration also appears, usually in the treatment of handles, as in a class of bowl with Ram's-head shaped handles.[60] Decoration tends to be applied to zones such as on the upper rims of vessels (fig. 4.1), inside the bowl (fig. 4.2), outer handle faces (fig. 3.4), raised cordons around neck or base (fig. 4.4) and even on the underside of vessels (fig. 4.3).[61]

---

[55] R. Sparks, "A Series of Middle Bronze Age Bowls with Ram's-Head Handles From the Jordan Valley", *Mediterranean Archaeology*, 4 (1991), pp. 45-54.

[56] Note the lack of such an industry in the EB period; local workshops produce a range of bowl forms in basalt and other local materials, such as limestone; but it is not until an influx of imported calcite vessels in the Middle Bronze that the gypsum industry appears to develop.

[57] For example, G. Loud, *op. cit.* (n. 35), fig. 259.24-5, 261.28-31; R.A.S. Macalister, *op. cit.* (n. 35), pl. XXIV.1.

[58] K.M. Kenyon, *op. cit.* (n. 39), fig. 155.

[59] Cf. K.M. Kenyon, *op. cit.* (n. 39), fig. 168.27.

[60] R. Sparks, *loc. cit.* (n. 55), fig. 1-2.

[61] Seen on three gypsum vessels from Pella (Field I, Tomb 3, S.J. Bourke & R.T. Sparks, *loc. cit.* [n. 51], cat. no. 15; A. McNicoll *et al*, *Pella in Jordan 2*, Sydney 1992, pl. 61.4; unpublished, RN

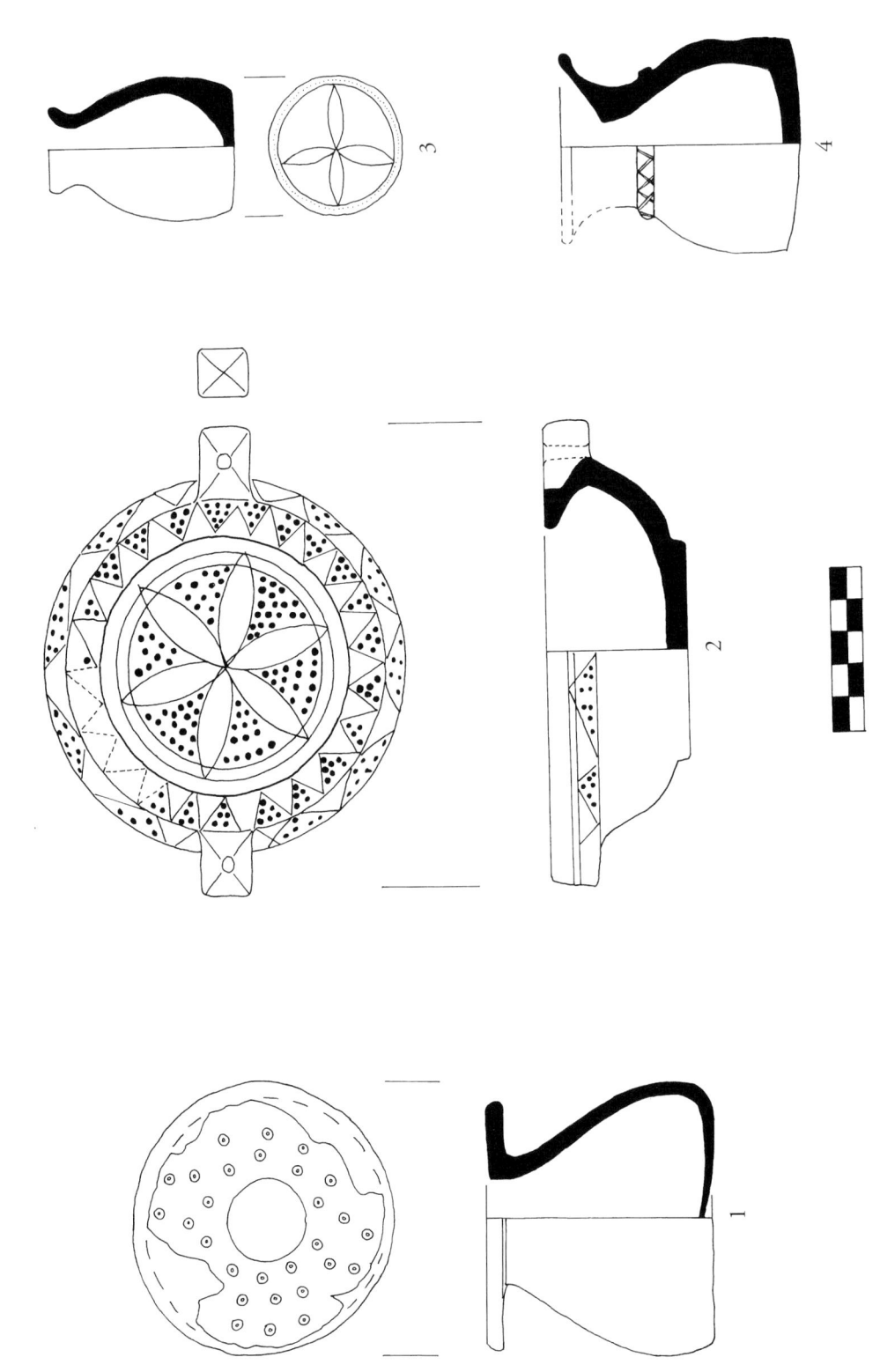

Figure 4: Syro-Palestinian decorative motifs

4.1 Pella, Area XI tomb 62, reg. no. 70864, gypsum.
4.2 Pella, Area XI tomb 20, reg. no. 32212, gypsum.
4.3 Pella, Area XI tomb 62, reg. no. 70371, gypsum.
4.4 Jericho tomb B47, reg. no. 86, gypsum.

Therefore it would appear that Egypt had a minimal impact on Palestinian decorative designs. The occasional motif may have been adapted from an Egyptian design, but generally speaking decoration shows closer links with contemporary Palestinian crafts, and is applied to different areas of the vessel.

5. Distribution

Consumption patterns of stone vessels are not uniform across Syro-Palestine. The largest sample of stone vessels found in the region occurs at Tell el-'Ajjul, the vast majority of which are Egyptian in form and manufacture, suggesting that it was a centre of either production or distribution. As one might expect, the largest concentrations of Egyptian/Egyptianising stone vessels are consistently found at major sites along the north-south trade route through Palestine. The other main centres for Egyptian imports of this kind are Lachish, Gezer, Megiddo, Hazor and Kamid el-Loz. The further north one progresses along this route, the scarcer Egyptian stone vessels become. Imports also become sporadic in settlements away from these trade lines. There would also seem to be some correlation between the size, and presumably prosperity of a settlement, and the amount of imported stone vessels occurring there. One exception to this rule is the Amman temple deposit, which contained unusually high percentages of imported stone vessels and ceramics, despite its location east of the Jordan river, away from major international trade routes.[62] However this site is exceptional.

Conversely, the largest concentrations of locally made gypsum vessels appear at sites which are off the north-south trade route, and often more peripheral to Egyptian concerns, such as Pella and Jericho. There is a definite concentration around the Jordan Valley, where at least one production centre is found at Beth Shan. Some of this local material filters through the plain of Esdraelon to Megiddo and other sites. East of the Jordan river, the majority of sites possess almost completely Palestinian repertoires, as for example at Tell es-Sa'idiyeh, Sahab and Deir 'Alla.

The position of Beth Shan during the Late Bronze Age sets it apart from these settlements east of the Jordan. As the site of an Egyptian garrison it contained a considerable Egyptian presence in the form of architects and officials. At the same time, it is curious that this presence has no apparent impact on the local gypsum industry, and that there is no noticeable increase in the amount of Egyptian stone

---

170113), two from Tell es-Sa'idiyeh T. 389 (unpublished, in the British Museum) and a basalt bowl from Kamid el-Loz (R. MIRON, *op. cit.* (n. 10), pl. 22.1, no. 399). Bases are occasionally decorated in Egypt; for example, a stand from the tomb of Tutankhamen featured a hieratic inscription on the underside of the foot (A. EL-KHOULI, *loc. cit.* [n. 13], pl. 13b).

[62] V. HANKEY, *loc. cit.* (n. 10), pp. 131-178.

vessels imported at this time, despite egyptianisation in other areas. This may be related to the position of Beth Shan on the frontier of Egypt, and the absence of raw materials to support the development of Egyptian-style stone workshops.

CONCLUSIONS

During the Middle Bronze Age Egyptian stone vessels begin to be imported into Syro-Palestine in greater quantity than before, perhaps at the same time inspiring the development of a locally based imitative industry which made use of available methods and materials. Egyptian stone vessels are imported somewhat selectively, with forms popular to Egypt occurring only sporadically in Syro-Palestine, and less common Egyptian types being imported in quantity. Local gypsum workshops copy and adapt some of these forms, while developing other types independently of Egypt. The local industry does not appear to have been damaged by an increase in foreign contact during the Late Bronze Age. Its markets also appear to have extended further inland than the Egyptian product, and remained successful well into the Iron Age when Egyptian imports decrease in quantity.

THE EGYPTIAN AND MESOPOTAMIAN CONTRIBUTIONS TO THE ORIGINS OF THE ALPHABET

BY

Brian E. COLLESS

The alphabet was once a set of two dozen picture-signs. The oldest examples that we have of these proto-alphabetic pictographs date from the seventeenth and sixteenth centuries before the current era, and are found on potsherds from the ruins of cities in Canaan,[1] that is, ancient Palestine. (See the CANAAN column of Table 1.) The largest extant collection of proto-alphabetic texts emanates from the Egyptian turquoise mines of Sinai;[2] these inscriptions were the work of Semites, who were taken there as labourers and craftsmen. (See the SINAI column of Table 1 for samples of the signs.)

The proto-alphabet was the simplest script the ancient world had known, if judged by the small number of characters it needed for putting speech down in writing (in this case, West Semitic speech). The Mesopotamian and Egyptian systems (invented around 3000 B.C.E., more than a millennium before the alphabet) required hundreds of signs to record messages. In each case the signs began as *pictograms* (or *pictographs*), which were used as *logograms* (representing whole words) and *phonograms* (or *syllabograms*, denoting a single syllable in the Sumerian and Akkadian script of Mesopotamia, and one or more syllables in the hieroglyphic writing of Egypt). The *phonograms* (*syllabograms*) were produced by the *rebus principle*, whereby the reader focusses only on the sound of the word depicted in the sign (for example, in English rebus writing, the numeral 2 could represent not only "two" but also "to" and "too", and function as a syllabogram in "2fold", "2day", and "un2"; it can also be an *ideogram* expressing duality, with "2nd" saying "second").

The Mesopotamian pictographic script soon developed into a cuneiform system; this consisted of wedge-shaped marks rapidly impressed on clay with a stylus; but these cuneiform signs (clusters of wedges) could also be laboriously chiselled on stone (the laws of Hammurabi, for example, are preserved on a diorite pillar). The Egyptian hieroglyphs were pictographs (though there was also a cursive version of Hieroglyphic, known as Hieratic); they were characteristically inscribed on papyrus with pen and ink (reed and paint); but, as befits their name hieroglyph (sacred *carving*), they were also engraved on hard surfaces (the Rosetta Stone being a celebrated example). Archaeological evidence from Syria-Palestine shows that cultural influence was exerted there

---

[1] B.E. COLLESS, "The proto-alphabetic inscriptions of Canaan", *Abr-Nahrain*, 29 (1991), pp. 18-66.
[2] B.E. COLLESS, "The proto-alphabetic inscriptions of Sinai", *Abr-Nahrain*, 28 (1990), pp. 1-52.

throughout the Bronze Age (3rd and 2nd millennia B.C.E.) by both Egypt and Mesopotamia. Egyptian inscriptions are constantly coming to light there, and also Akkadian texts on clay tablets, Akkadian having been the language of international communication. However, the inventor of the pictographic alphabet rejected the Babylonian cuneiform style, in favour of the Egyptian hieroglyphic model.

In the second millennium B.C.E., the cities of Canaan were in communication with Egypt, and were often under the Egyptian empire. The vessels that transported the cedars of Lebanon to Egypt may well have returned with cargoes of papyrus, for scribal use in such places as Byblos (Gubla, now Jibeil in Lebanon). It was in Byblos, apparently, that a "pseudo-hieroglyphic" syllabary was devised for writing West Semitic, with most of its signs being recognizable versions of Egyptian hieroglyphs;[3] this was not slavish imitation but creative borrowing. The Gublaic syllabary was presumably a predecessor of the proto-alphabet.[4] Documents on papyrus have long since disappeared, but samples of the proto-alphabetic and syllabic scripts have survived on less perishable materials, such as metal, stone, and pottery.

The invention of the proto-alphabet was simply another step in a series that culminated in the Western alphabet, as perfected by the Greeks in the eighth century B.C.E., by the addition of separate signs for vowels (see the GREECE column of Table 1). Looking backwards along the line (or digging down through the strata, archaeologically speaking) we see that the Grecian alphabet was preceded by the Phoenician alphabet, which was used throughout the first millennium B.C.E. for such West Semitic languages or dialects as Phoenician, Hebrew, Ammonite, Moabite, Edomite, and Aramaic.[5] At this stage some letters (notably W and Y) were also being used as *matres lectionis* ("reading-mothers") for indicating vowels.[6] However, this practice was eschewed by the Phoenicians.[7]

The Phoenician alphabet was a linear consonantal script: *linear*, because its signs were unrecognizable as pictures, even though they had developed out of the pictographs of the Canaanite proto-alphabet; *consonantal*, because it had no means of expressing vowels. Each sign (whether pictographic or linear) represented a particular consonant followed by any vowel or no vowel, and this West Semitic system thus appears to be a sort of syllabary, but a syllabary which was very economical in its stock of characters (an idea first formulated by I.J. Gelb).[8] However, if the term *alphabet* is

[3] M. DUNAND, *Byblia Grammata: Documents et recherches sur le développement de l'écriture en Phénicie*, Beirut 1945.
[4] G.E. MENDENHALL, *The Syllabic Inscriptions from Byblos*, Beirut 1985; B.E. COLLESS, "The Byblos syllabary and the proto-alphabet", *Abr-Nahrain*, 30 (1992), pp. 55-102; ID., "The syllabic inscriptions of Byblos: Text D", *Abr-Nahrain*, 31 (1993), pp. 1-35.
[5] J. NAVEH, *Early History of the Alphabet*, Jerusalem 1987, pp. 53-112.
[6] J. NAVEH, *op. cit.* (n. 5), pp. 76, 88-89; D.N. FREEDMAN, "The evolution of Hebrew orthography", *Studies in Hebrew and Aramaic Orthography*, Winona Lake 1992, pp. 3-10.
[7] J. NAVEH, *op. cit.* (n. 5), p. 62.
[8] I.J. GELB, *A Study of Writing*, 2nd ed., Chicago 1952.

defined as *a minimal set of signs for writing a language (whether vowels are represented or not)*, then the Canaanite pictographic script was an alphabet, the proto-alphabet, the prototype of all alphabets.

The genesis of the proto-alphabet was not a creation out of nothing, but rather out of pre-existing material. Firstly, nearly all the pictographs have counterparts in the Egyptian store of hieroglyphs (see the EGYPT column of the table of signs).

Secondly, the Byblos script (the Gublaic syllabary) had already experimented with ways of using Egyptian hieroglyphs to write a Semitic language. To this end, the acrophony principle was invoked (and perhaps even invented): thus the sign for a house stood for the first syllable of the West Semitic word for house, namely *bayitu*, hence *ba*, while the hieroglyph for a perfume jar produced a sign for *du*, from *dudu*.[9] (For examples of Gublaic syllabograms see the first sign in each row of the Phoenicia column on Table 1.)

Thirdly, the Egyptian hieroglyphic system already contained the seeds of a consonantal alphabet. The Egyptians ignored vowels in their writing, and they had signs representing trisyllabic and disyllabic words, as well as monosyllabic hieroglyphs (a sign for a word *p-r-t*, for example, could be used for any other word which had this sequence of consonants, no matter what its vowels were, and similarly a word *p-r* or *p-*). The single-consonant signs among the hieroglyphs constituted an alphabetic nucleus; and the idea that a sign could represent a consonant plus any vowel was waiting there to be combined with the acrophonic principle, to produce a Semitic alphabet. In this case, acrophony meant taking the first consonant (not the whole syllable), so that the sign representing a house (*bayitu*) denotes simply *b*, but connotes *ba, bi, bu*.

Notice, however, that many of the alphabetic signs already existed in the Byblos syllabary (for sixteen apparent cases see the first letter in each row of the PHOENICIA section of Table 1). This suggests a process of evolution or metamorphosis for the creation of the proto-alphabet: the alphabet emerged by shedding its chrysalis shell, namely two-thirds of the characters in the syllabary. Whether the proto-alphabet was a new invention or an adaptation of an earlier form remains an open question (because it is difficult to assign dates to any of the syllabic texts from Byblos, and so we can not be certain that the syllabary is older than the alphabet). Be that as it may, acrophony was still the basic principle in the proto-alphabet, and no vowels were represented in this new form of writing. In this regard, rigid application of the acrophonic principle might well be the simple explanation for the lack of vowel signs in the new-born alphabet: no West Semitic word begins with a vowel, and so no sign would be forthcoming. The words that seem to begin with a vowel, such as *'alp* "ox" (the origin of Alpha, A), actually have an initial consonant, namely the glottal stop.

[9] B.E. COLLESS, *loc. cit.* 1992 (n. 4), pp. 55-102.

When Alan Gardiner made the first breakthrough for deciphering the proto-alphabetic texts, he published his findings under the title "The Egyptian origin of the Semitic alphabet" (1916),[10] with a table of signs (akin to the one presented here) showing Egyptian hieroglyphs which seem to have been adopted for alphabetic use by Semites. The Gublaic syllabary was not known to scholars at that time, but its signary likewise appears to be based on the Egyptian system, having functioned by means of the acrophonic principle. How can we be sure that the Semitic alphabetic pictogtaphs and syllabic signs are Egyptian hieroglyphs, borrowed for new purposes? The answer lies in a number of clear cases which substantiate this instance of cultural interaction in the ancient Near East. Thus the sign for *sa* in the Gublaic syllabary, and also the letter Samek in the alphabet, is the Egyptian *djed* pillar, representing the lower part of the human spinal column, with two or three vertebrae (hieroglyph R11); here the word *samak*, from the root *smk*, "support", operates acrophonically to produce *sa* in the syllabary or *s* in the alphabet.[11] Note that a fish pictograph was an alternative sign for S in the proto-alphabetic inscriptions from Sinai and in some from Canaan. This apparently stems from *samak* "fish", a Semitic word attested in Arabic; this character eventually disappeared from the alphabet.[12]

Another example is the letter Tet (*ṭ*). Its form in the Phoenician alphabet was a cross inside a circle, and this passed over into the Greek alphabet to become Theta. Its pictograph was a cross outside a circle, at present known only from one of the Sinai inscriptions.[13] Presumably it is the Egyptian *nefer* hieroglyph (F35, "good, beautiful", the circular object being a heart, and the cross above it being perhaps a mouth and windpipe, areas where emotional responses to beauty are expressed), here standing for Semitic *ṭabu* ("good, beautiful"), though the Sinai character is on its side.[14] The corresponding sign in the Gublaic syllabary is inverted.[15] Obviously there are many uncertainties in this matter, but if all the pieces in the puzzle are equivalent, then we are observing a unique Egyptian symbol being imitated to express a similar abstract concept in Semitic speech and writing.

Similarly the well-known Egyptian sign for "life" (*'ankh*, S34), which is likewise a combination of cross and ring, and which is another anatomical specimen (apparently the bone at the top of the spine from which the spinal cord emerges), has a place in the West Semitic syllabary, but not in the proto-alphabet.[16] The sign identified by Mendenhall as *ḥi* would go with a West Semitic word for "life" (from the root

---

[10] *Journal of Egyptian Archaeology*, 3 (1916), pp. 1-16.
[11] B.E. COLLESS, *loc. cit.* 1992 (n. 4), p. 84.
[12] B.E. COLLESS, "Recent discoveries illuminating the origin of the alphabet", *Abr-Nahrain*, 26 (1988), pp. 45-47; ID., *loc. cit.* (n. 2), p. 5; ID., *loc. cit.* (n. 1), pp. 28-29.
[13] B.E. COLLESS, *loc. cit.* (n. 2), no. 23 = 351.
[14] B.E. COLLESS, *loc. cit.* (n. 12), pp. 41-42.
[15] B.E. COLLESS, *loc. cit.* 1992 (n. 4), pp. 74-75.
[16] B.E. COLLESS, *loc. cit.* 1992 (n. 4), pp. 73-74.

ḥwh/ḥyh, "to "live"). The oval at the top has opened up (presumably to distinguish it from the inverted *nefer* sign in the same syllabary). If this is a correct reading of the situation, then another mysterious Egyptian symbol has been assigned a West Semitic function in the Gublaic syllabary.

This tendency for circles and ovals to open out is also observable at other points, notably in the series ʿayin, Pe, Ṣade, Qop (see Table 1). The letters ʿayin and Pe, eye and mouth, were very similar in the beginning, but the eye became a circle (ultimately serving as the vowel o), while the mouth lost one of its lips and was rotated (like the ox-head, ʾalep, in the Phoenician alphabet). Ṣade and Qop have always been puzzling: because of their names they are widely held to be a cricket and a monkey respectively. In my view, Ṣade was originally a tied bag (hieroglyph V34), which eventually opened up and lost its circle. This proto-alphabetic sign has commonly been read as *q*,[17] but it seems clear to me that Qop would have been Qaw (a line, a cord wound on a stick, hieroglyph V24). In the early Arabian scripts, which are expanded versions of the Canaanite alphabet, the Q has the stick protruding above and below the string.[18] This is also true of the few cases we have from the Sinai inscriptions. The table of signs shows that there are two versions of the hieroglyph (V24, V25), one of which has the end of the string showing at the top, radiating diagonally. This feature is also found on the small "bilingual" stone-sphinx from Sinai, the inscribed statuette which gave Alan Gardiner the clue to decipherment (it has the name of the Egyptian goddess Hathor in hieroglyphs, and her Semitic counterpart Baʿalat in proto-alphabetic pictographs). The *q* on the sphinx has a dot for the string and two protuberances at the top (shown on the Sinai column of Table 1), as part of the word *nqy* ("my offering").[19] Without a protrusion at the top, a circle on a stem was Waw, a hook (one letter which apparently does not have an Egyptian hieroglyph behind it, as also Taw); and when Q (Qaw) lost its top piece and its identity as a cord (to become Qop), the circle of Waw opened out at the top to prevent confusion.

This was the legacy of Egypt to Canaan, and indeed to the whole world, in that the alphabet became the universal writing system. Nevertheless, important contributions from Mesopotamia must not be overlooked. Firstly, it was the Sumerian civilization which conceived the idea of writing, and the basic *rebus* principle. According to my typology of the stages in the early evolution of the alphabet (Table 2), the main steps involved three different uses of the REBUS device:

---

[17] E.g. by W.F. ALBRIGHT, *The Proto-Sinaitic Inscriptions and their Decipherment*, Harvard Theological Studies 22, London 1966; F.M. CROSS, "The origin and early evolution of the alphabet", *Eretz-Israel*, 8 (1967), pp. 8*-24*; B. SASS, *The Genesis of the Alphabet and its Development in the Second Millenium B.C.*, Wiesbaden 1988.
[18] B.E. COLLESS, *loc. cit.* (n. 2), fig. 1.
[19] B.E. COLLESS, *loc. cit.* (n. 2), pp. 13-15, no. 03 =345.

(1) the *logo-syllabic* **REBUS**, producing a logo-syllabic script (**REBUS** in Mesopotamian vocalic cuneiform script, but **R-B-S** in Egyptian consonantal, non-vocalic, hieroglyphic writing);

(2) the acrophonic *syllabic* **REBUS**, acrophonically generating a compact syllabic script (the Byblos syllabary, or the Gublaic pictographic script, comprising an economical set of signs representing open monosyllables);

(3) the acrophonic *consonantal* **REBUS**, engendering a consonantal alphabet (the proto-alphabet, the Canaanite pictographic consonantal alphabet).

Secondly, in the area of Mesopotamian influences, the Sumero-Akkadian cuneiform script was sometimes used for other Semitic languages besides the East Semitic tongues (Akkadian, Babylonian, Assyrian). Thus, around 2300 B.C.E., the scribes of ancient Ebla (in Syria) were putting their own North Semitic language, Eblaic or Eblaite, into cuneiform logo-syllabic writing. They mostly employed Sumerograms (Sumerian logograms), which were read as Eblaic words (not Sumerian or Akkadian), and this leaves us in an uninformed state about their language, except where they spelled their words out in syllabograms. Surprisingly, when they used syllabograms they tended to avoid signs for closed syllables in favour of open syllable characters (writing *ni-ka-ra-du* instead of Mesopotamian *nin-kar-du*, or *a-sa-mu-mu* for *as-sa-am-mu*, with the vowels unsounded in *ra* and *mu*, but the mute vowel corresponding to the vowel in an adjacent syllable). The result of this practice of open-syllable orthography, with dead vowels where necessary, was a reduction in the number of signs required for writing; it constitutes a compromise between the Egyptian system, with no vowels at all in its hundreds of signs, and the Mesopotamian signary, with its multitudes of vocalic syllabograms (when a hundred or less would suffice). Whether the idea of open-syllable writing originated in Ebla is not known, but it reappears in the Cretan scripts and the West Semitic syllabary (Gublaic script), all of which have a circumscribed inventory of signs. Incidentally, this concept of mute vowels may have offered additional impetus to the emergence of the consonantal alphabet, where no vowels are represented at all (a view expressed by G.E. Mendenhall).[20] However, a consonantal script was already known in the Egyptian pattern: the reader has to insert all the vowels (in every syllable), and still has to recognize the points where no vowels are sounded (at the end of closed syllables).

Thirdly, in the fourteenth century B.C.E., in the city of Ugarit or elsewhere in Syria-Palestine, another alphabet was created, out of cuneiform characters. New signs (clusters of wedges) were constructed for the purpose; it was not simply a matter of borrowing existing signs and values from the Babylonian syllabary. The cuneiform idea was combined with the alphabet form (examples on the CANAAN column of Table 1). However, it could be categorized as *semi-syllabic*, because it had separate

---

[20] *Op. cit.* (n. 4).

signs for *'a*, *'i*, and *'u*. This cuneiform alphabet functioned alongside the pictographic alphabet throughout Canaan, and its clay documents exist in vaster quantities than the proto-alphabet's meagre legacy. We would imagine, however, that the pictographic alphabet was more prevalent than the scanty remnants indicate. In any case, the cuneiform alphabet did not survive into the Iron Age (approximately after 1200 B.C.E.), while the pictographic proto-alphabet went on to conquer the whole world.

Pictorial script, like architectural decoration, quickly becomes stylized, so that sooner or later the original picture becomes undiscernible. Calligraphy can be practised for aesthetic enjoyment even with the abstract signs that evolve (witness the artistry of Arabic pencraft), but pictographic writing is certainly more picturesque. Unlike the Mesopotamians, the ancient Egyptians took care to preserve their pictographs: even though they had cursive scripts deriving from these, they kept their hieroglyphs intact alongside the new developments, namely the Hieratic and Demotic scripts. The Rosetta Stone, with the same text written in Hieroglyphic and Demotic, and a Greek version of it written in the alphabet, shows this to be true. The preservation of the Hieroglyphs by the Egyptians was possibly more for religious than aesthetic reasons, since they were hallowed, as their Greek name hieroglyphs (*sacred* carvings) implies.

In stark contrast, the pictographs of the alphabet were short-lived phenomena, and as soon as the originals had faded out of sight they were forgotten. It is to be hoped that continued excavation in the Levant will bring more proto-alphabetic inscriptions to light, whole libraries (perhaps on clay tablets like the Canaanite cuneiform alphabet and the Cretan linear scripts), and abecedaries too, so that we may contemplate with greater wonder and better understanding the original pictographs, of which our modern letters are such poor copies.

74 B.E. COLLESS

	EGYPT	SINAI	CANAAN	PHOENICIA	GREECE	
ʾ	F1 ox	ʾalp ox	Hebrew א ʾAlep	Alpha	A
B	O1 house	bayt house		Bet	Beta	B
G	T14 boomerang	gaml boomerang		Gimel	Gamma	C/G
D	O31 door	dalt door		Dalet	Delta	D
H	A28 jubilate	hll jubilate		He	Epsilon	E
W		waw hook		Waw	Upsilon	U/V
Z	[D13 eyebrow]	[zayp eyebrow]		Zayin	Zeta	Z
Ḥ	O6 mansion	ḥaṣir mansion		Ḥet	Eta	H
Ḫ	V28 hank wick	bayt thread				
Ṭ	F35 good	ṭab good		Ṭet	Theta	
Y	D36 forearm	yad hand		Yod	Iota	I
K	D46 hand	kap palm		Kap	Kappa	K
L	S39 crook	lamd goad		Lamed	Lambda	L
M	N35 water	maym water		Mem	Mu	M
N	I10 cobra	naḥš snake		Nun	Nu	N
S	K1 fish	samk fish				
	R11 column	samk support		Samek	Xi	
ʿ	D4 eye	ʿayn eye		ʿAyin	Omikron	O
P	D21 mouth	pu mouth		Pe	Pi	P
Ṣ	V33 bag	ṣirar bag		Ṣade	San	
Q	V24 cord	qaw cord, line		Qop	Qoppa	Q
R	D1 head	raʾš head		Resh	Rho	R
Š	N6 sun (raʿ)	šamš sun	šad breast?	š Šin	Sigma	S
T		taw mark BRIAN COLLESS		Taw	Tau	T

Table 1. Typology of the evolution of the alphabet.

EVOLUTION OF THE ALPHABET

Egyptian hieroglyphic script
complex consonantal logo-syllabary
pictographs (linear stylization)
logograms
phonograms: R-B-S syllabograms
determinatives
alphabetic nucleus

Mesopotamian cuneiform script
complex vocalic logo-syllabary
pictographs (cuneiform stylization)
logograms, ideograms
phonograms: REBUS syllabograms
determinatives

Gublaic pictographic script
vocalic syllabary
(cp.Sumero-Akkadian and Cretan scripts)
pictographs (Egyptian hieroglyphs)
fully acrophonic
phonograms: REBUS monosyllabograms
logograms (secondary use of signs)
determinatives
open syllable transcription (muted vowels)

Eblaic cuneiform script
complex vocalic logo-syllabary
(adaptation of Sumero-Akkadian script)
Sumerograms for North Semitic words
open syllable signs with muted vowels
(where necessary in transcription)

Canaanite pictographic alphabet
consonantal alphabet (cp. Egyptian script)
pictographs (Egyptian hieroglyphs)
fully acrophonic
phonograms: REBUS graphemes
logograms (secondary use of signs)

Canaanite cuneiform alphabet
consonantal alphabet (cp. Egyptian script)
cuneiform characters (cp. Mesopotamian)
(signs modelled on pictographic alphabet?)
not pictograms, not logograms, not rebuses
three syllabograms (ʾa, ʾi, ʾu)

Phoenician linear alphabet
consonantal alphabet
stylized pictographs (from the proto-alphabet)
non-logographic

Aramaic linear alphabet
semi-vocalic alphabet
Phoenician characters
some consonant-signs also indicate long vowels (w=u, y=i)

Greek linear alphabet
vocalic alphabet
Phoenician characters
vowel-signs constructed from unneeded consonantal signs.

Table 2.

EMAR
A SYRIAN CITY BETWEEN ANATOLIA, ASSYRIA AND BABYLONIA

BY

Jean-Claude MARGUERON

The city of Emar was situated on the right bank of the Euphrates river at the point where the river changes its course from a north/south direction leading out of Anatolia, to a south-easterly one heading towards Mesopotamia and the Arabian Gulf. An understanding of the site's location is fundamental to any appreciation of Emar's historical role. The city was located on the westernmost point of the Euphrates river where it acted as a meeting point for caravan routes coming from western countries and for river traffic coming north from Mesopotamia. It was in the optimum position to allow the unloading of the goods that were on the boats in order to transfer them to the caravans or, conversely, to transfer the goods from the caravans to the boats.

Very little is known about the origins of the city of Emar. The Ebla texts attest to its existence in the middle of the third millennium, while texts from Mari, dating to the beginning of the second millennium, show that a close relationship existed between the capital of the kingdom of the Middle Euphrates and Emar. The city is also mentioned in Ugaritic and Mitannian texts. However, although these texts prove the existence of this city, they don't tell us what it was like. The city that has been excavated is in fact a new town, founded by the Hittite kings Suppiluliuma and his son Mursili in the middle of the fourteenth century B.C. It seems that the previous city was in the process of being destroyed by a meander of the Euphrates river and that the Hittite king had decided to rebuild it.

A place has been identified where the previous town of Emar might have been located (fig. 1). While this position is not absolutely certain, it is highly probable. Traces of an ancient meander in the river can be seen on an aerial photograph (fig. 2). Following Mesopotamian tradition, the first city was placed in the valley along the river. The new city stood not far away from the old, but, following Hittite tradition, it was located on the slope of the cliff.

Excavation in the city was conducted from 1972 to 1976 in some urgency because of the creation of the lake el-Assad. The Tabqa dam was closed in July 1973 and the water reached the foot of the tell in the spring of 1974. Excavation at the site finished in 1976 because work became too dangerous on the part of the tell that remained unflooded. In 1978 we had one more season of digging at Tell Faq'ous, another Late Bronze Age site 12 km to the south. This site, a citadel that was related to the town of Emar, served to protect it from any threat coming from Mesopotamia.

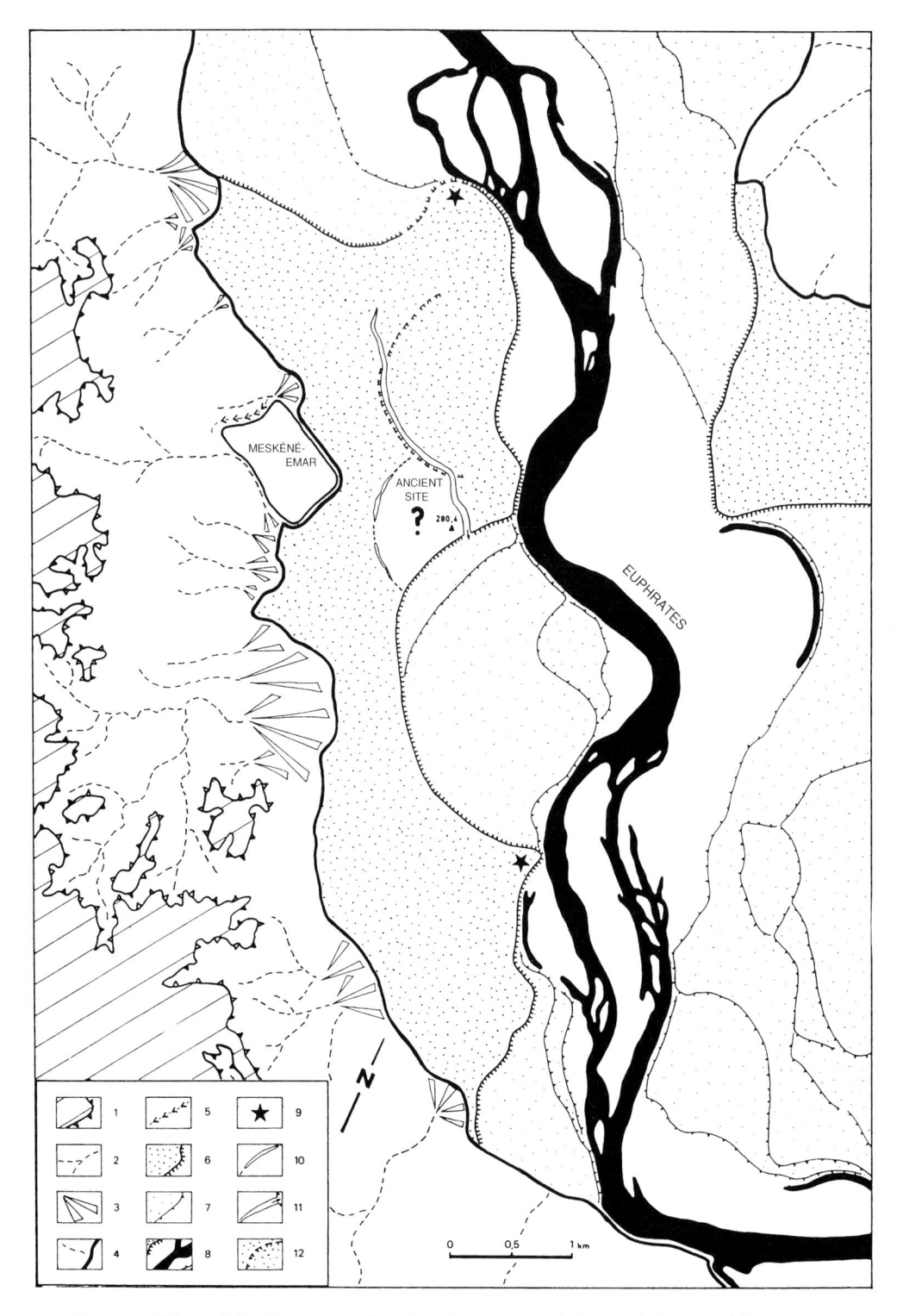

Figure 1: Map of the Emar area showing the excavated site and the possible situation of the earlier town along the Euphrates river (B. Geyer).

Figure 2: Air view showing the eastern part of the tell and the ancient meander where the site of the first city may have been.

The town that was excavated appeared peculiar, and of great interest. It was first built in the middle of the fourteenth century and destroyed at the beginning of the twelfth century. It was not rebuilt until Roman times. This city, founded by Hittite authorities, displayed some features that were typically Hittite. In fact, it was not a Syrian town, even if the majority of its inhabitants were Syrian.

Emar 's geopolitical situation is illustrated by the map of fig. 3. Close relations were maintained with Kassite Mesopotamia by means of river traffic and by the caravans that travelled alongside the river. Passage along the left bank of the river and the road along the foothills of the Taurus mountains connected Emar with the Assyrian country (in this period the Assyrian kings were practising an active policy of expansion, especially to the west). However, Emar was also connected by road and river to the region of Anatolia in the north, and so came under the domination of the Hittite empire. A road to the west linked the city with Aleppo, the Amuq plain, the Syrian coast and with Ugarit, the greatest town along the Mediterranean coast. During the Late Bronze Age, Assyrian power reached as far as the left bank of the Euphrates, while Hittite power ran along the right one. Egypt's control extended into southern Syria.

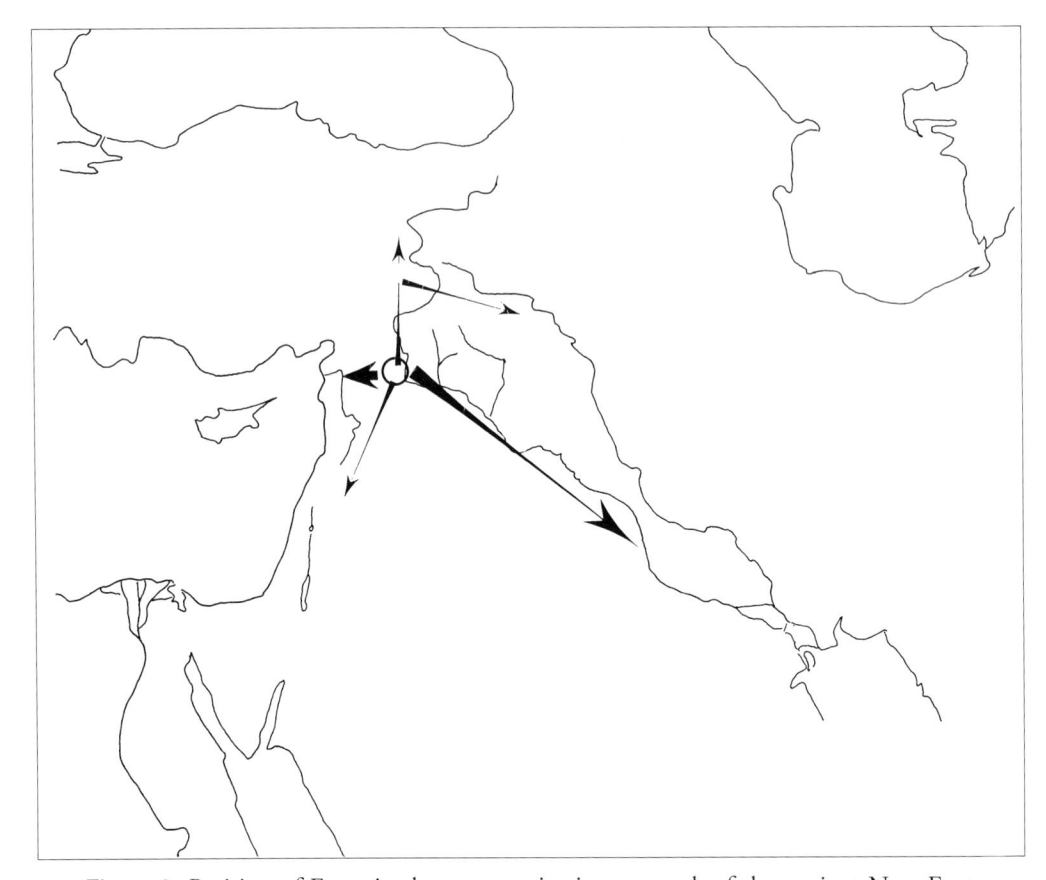

Figure 3: Position of Emar in the communication network of the ancient Near East.

Two questions deserve closer examination. Firstly, does this geopolitical situation have consequences for the new city of Emar, built by the Hittites? Secondly, can the civilization of Emar still be defined as typically Syrian, or is it a mixed one? Although it is impossible to explore here every aspect of its civilization, some of the more salient features will be outlined. The first one concerns the city itself, the second its artefacts, and the third some cultural phenomena.

The most conspicuous aspect of the newly built city is that it was not constructed in either a purely Syrian or Hittite style, despite the fact that it was erected by the Hittite power. The Hittite king planned to construct a city that catered to the habits and needs of the local Syrian people, but many aspects of the construction were nevertheless based on Hittite practices. The result was an odd mixture of features. In the Hittite fashion, the city was built on the slope of the tableland in a position that dominated the valley. Within the city a large amount of artificial structures were found, namely terraces with houses built upon them, like those of Boghaz Köy. Each block, consisting of one to three houses, was erected on a terrace (fig. 4) with main and

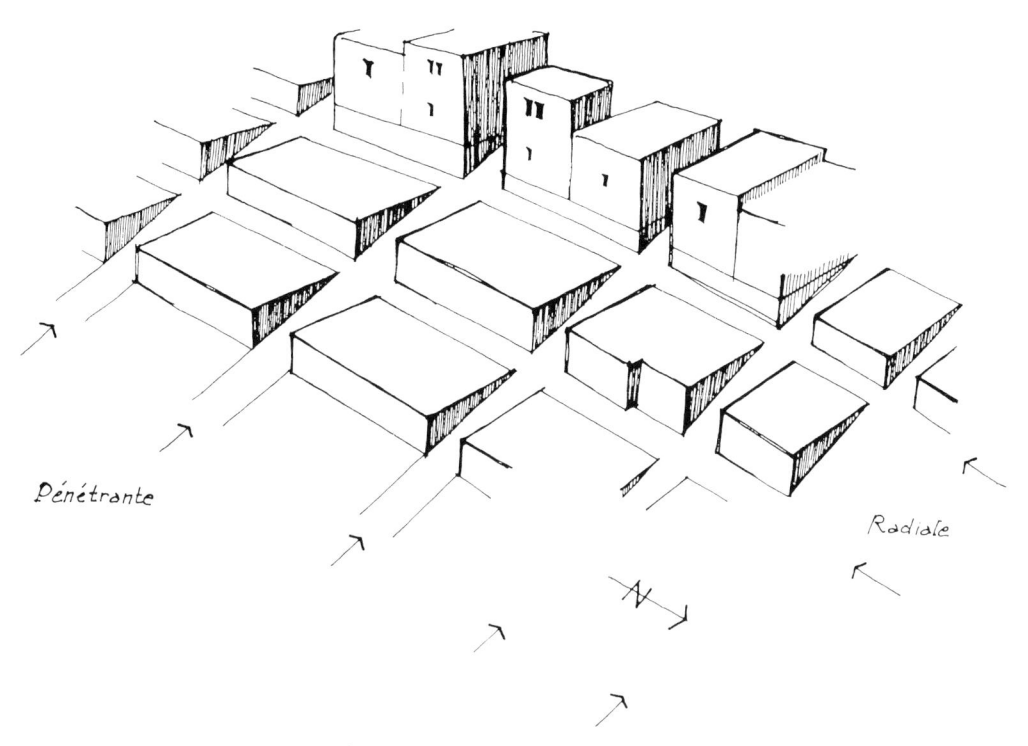

Figure 4: Reconstruction of the terrace system.

transversal streets that crossed on the slope like giant steps. The whole city was thus covered with terraces. Existing depressions were filled and rough protrusions flattened. The site was thus totally modified and, when complete, it must have resembled a giant amphitheatre dominating the valley.

The planning of the city was carried out before it was built; we found evidence that the organization of streets was designed before the erection of terraces.

One of the best examples of the topography modification program concerns the western valley (fig. 5). This valley is in fact an artificial one that was dug by the builders to define clearly the partition between the town and the plateau. With a width of 50 m, a length of 500 m and a depth of 25 m, the construction of the valley enabled the city to be independent of the surrounding plateau. The stones removed during the digging of the valley were used for the construction of the city terraces and the city-wall.

The final result can be seen on the reconstruction that I propose on fig. 6, which depicts streets of houses constructed on terraces.

The town extended for 600m-700m on its north-south side and 1 km on its east-west side. Half of the site could not be excavated because the city of Barbalissos was built upon the ruins of Emar during the Classical period. During the Islamic period this city was known as Balis and it was abandoned at the end of the Ayyoubid period.

Figure 5: The artificially excavated valley on the western side of the town.

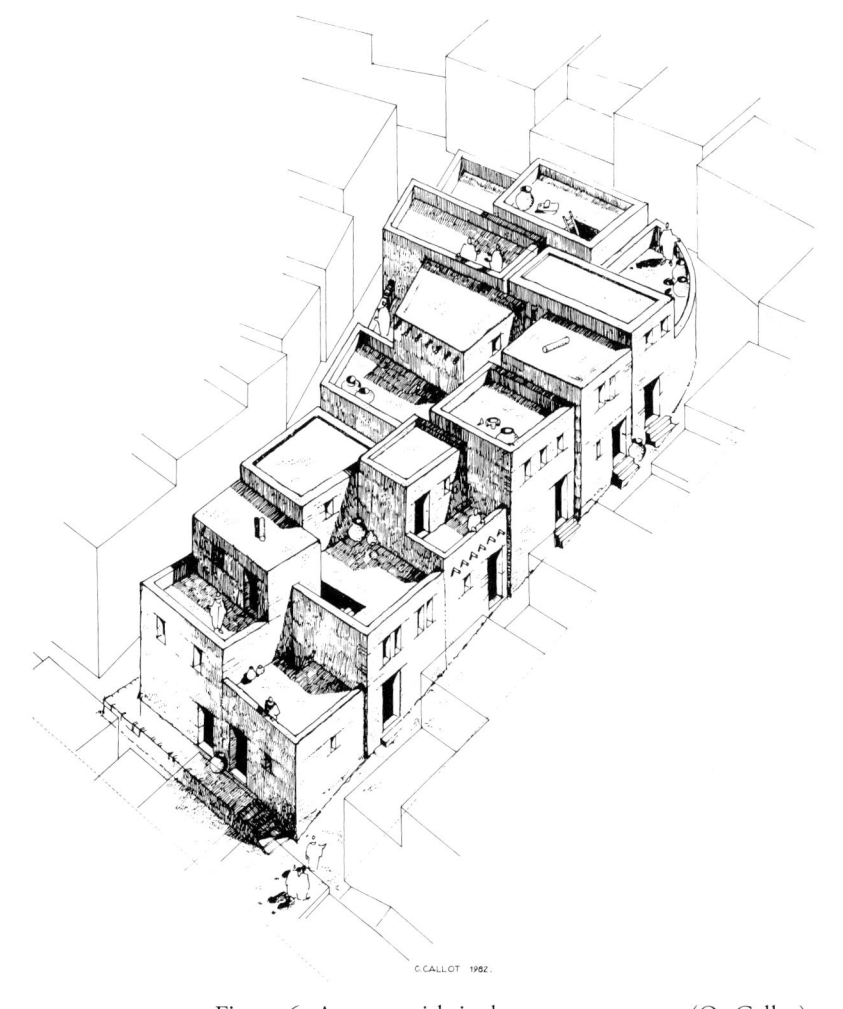

Figure 6: A street with its houses on terraces (O. Callot).

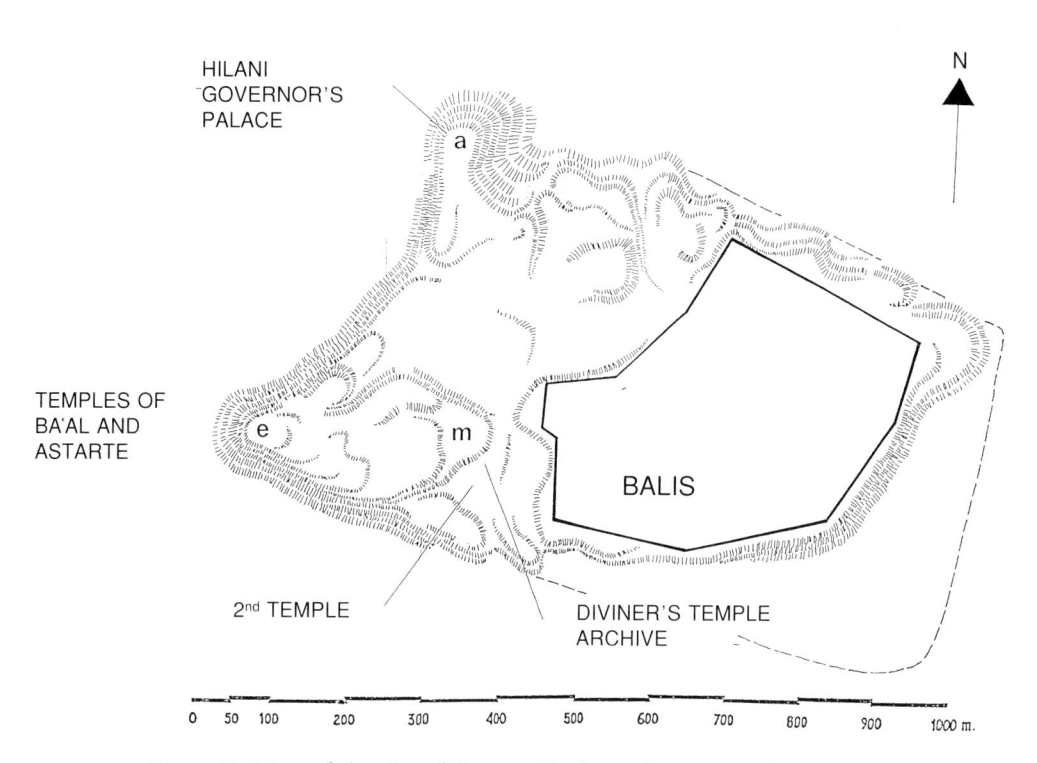

Figure 7: Map of the site of Emar with the main excavated structures.

Only the western part of the Late Bronze Age city could potentially be exhumed. It was in this area that remains from the site's main period of occupation were discovered, including some main streets, several blocks of houses, the palace and the temples.

The most outstanding monument was the palace of the local ruler (fig. 8). This structure had a wide front with a double pillared porch at its centre. Behind the porch, there were two long rooms (the second one may have been an official room) with a range of little rooms on the northern side. An upper storey was located above these long rooms. We found some evidence to suggest a connection between this monument and a group of houses set on underlying terraces on the slope of the north-west promontory which looks down the valley towards the haven and the city. This kind of palace is known in Syria during the Iron Age under the name of Hilani. The example found at Emar is one of the most ancient Hilanis which has been discovered, as it dates back to the Bronze Age. Only one other example of a Hilani has been discovered that may be older than the one found at Emar. This is the fourteenth century palace of Niqmepa at Tell Atchana which is not quite identical but does show the same principles of organization. It must be noted that, at Boghaz Köy, the foundations of a building, Building E (fig. 9), were discovered, which operate in the same way. What is clear is that this kind of structure seems to be Hittite in origin. The palace of Emar is contemporary with the palace of Niqmepa. It would be very interesting to know what

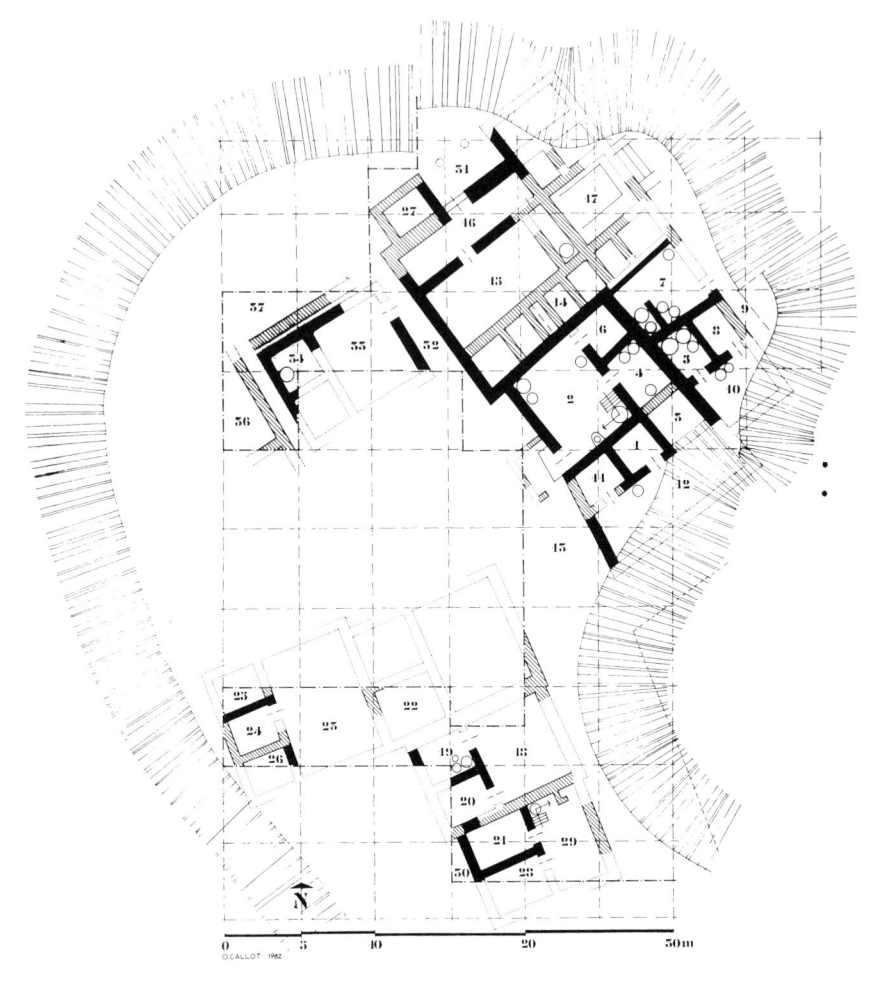

Figure 8: The Hilani and surrounding buildings.

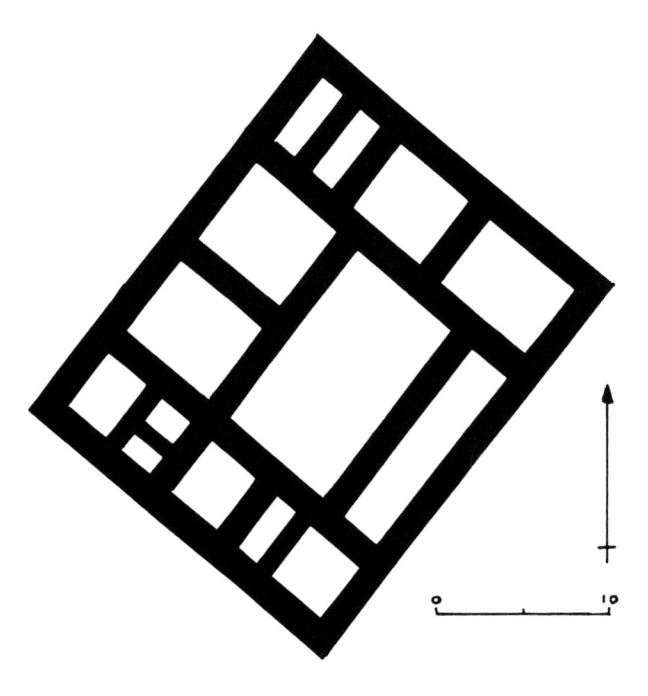

Figure 9: Plan of the foundations of building E at Boghaz Köy, a possible ancestor of the Hilani.

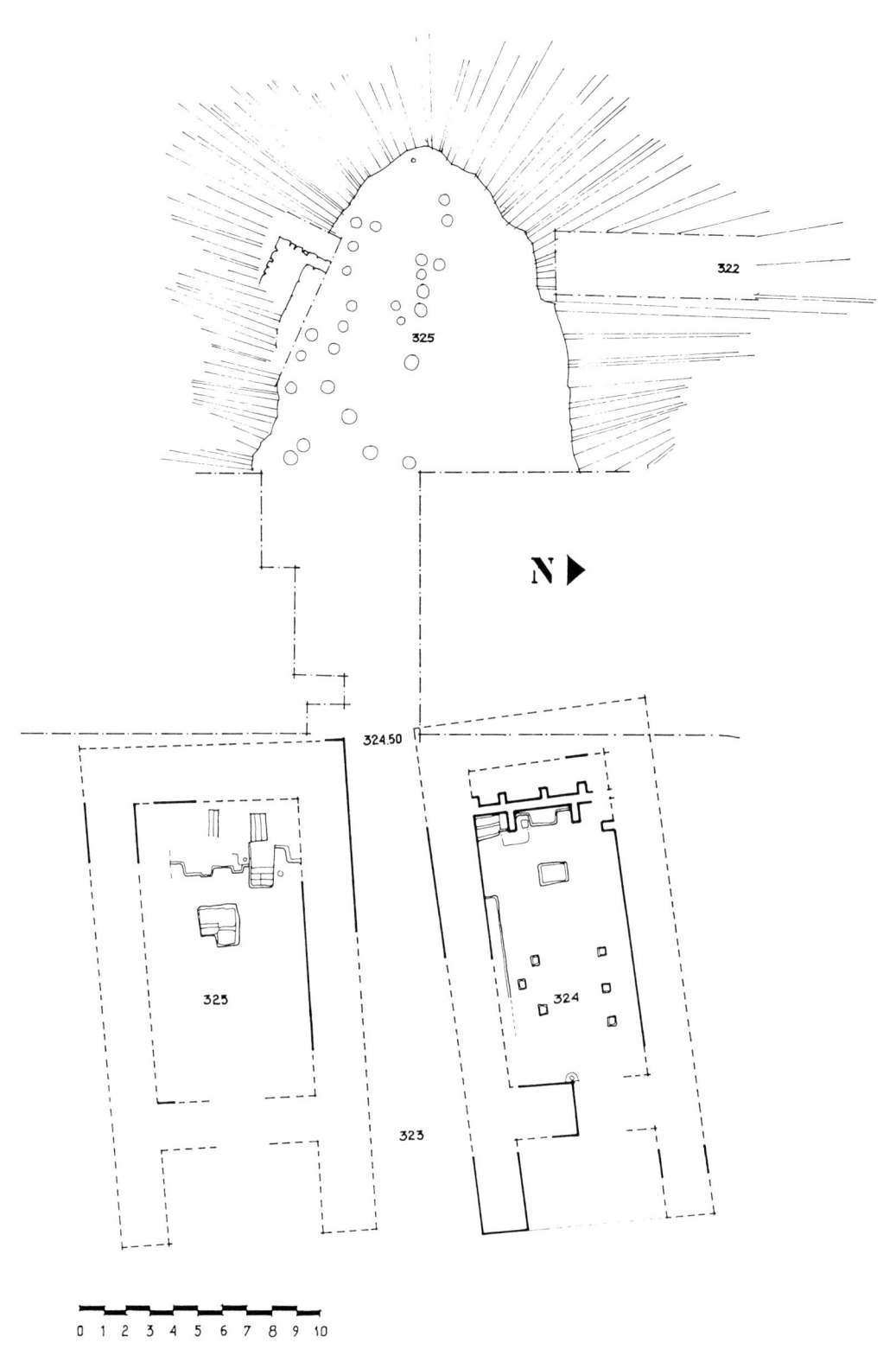

Figure 10: Temples of Baʿal and Astarte with the cultic terrace behind them.

the king of Emar had in mind when he built a Hittite structure for himself as a Syrian king. Was he expressing sentiments of servility to the foreign power or was he imitating a prestigious model?

Four temples were found at Emar. Tablets discovered in two temples located together in a single sanctuary on the top of the city revealed that they were dedicated to Ba'al and Astarte (fig. 10). A great terrace extended behind them, with an altar and a few holes in the ground, whose function is not easy to understand. The form of these temples is that of a megaron, the typical temple design known in North Syria since the fourth millennium B.C. When the Hittite king (or the local ruler) built the new city in Emar he chose the model of Boghaz Köy for the palace and kept a Syrian plan for the temples.

Another shrine, known as the Diviner's temple (fig. 11) was excavated in the town. It was similar in design to the first ones, except for its inclusion of one range of rooms on the eastern wall. A terrace for making sacrifices was located behind this temple too. The library and personal archives of a diviner were found inside the temple. He worked closely with the Hittite king and played an important role in the functioning of the city. We learn from the tablets found in the archives that the diviner communicated directly with the Hittite king and that the king asked him for information about the state of the town.

The fourth temple (designated as "second temple" on fig.11) was clearly a large and important one, but the god that was worshipped in it remains unknown.

Some thirty houses were excavated, either completely or partially. The plan used most commonly on the site consisted of one big room entered directly from the street and two small rooms placed opposite the entrance (fig. 12). The only exceptions to this plan occurred when the house had to fit to the shape of the streets or of another house. This type of house looks very simple but it must be borne in mind that only the first level has been preserved; the houses originally would have had upper floors. Figure 4 shows an example of what the town may have looked like based on this kind of house plan. Where can this plan have originated from - Syria or Anatolia? Similar examples have been found at Kanesh, at Tell Atchana and in Palestine.

In summary it seems that the city of Emar was built with a Hittite palace, Syrian temples and Syro-anatolian houses.

Emar was rich in artefacts, but poor in art products. A common type of artefact found at Emar was the ceramic model house, of which thirty examples, either in the shape of a tower or of a stepped house, were found. These models have been frequently discovered in the area of lake el-Assad, but their function is not evident.

Another type of artefact were the figurines, most of which were typically Syrian in form. A collection of bronze Syrian figurines were found in the temple of Ba'al (fig. 13). Among the terracotta figurines there were a lot of Syrian shapes and also some others with features that may be Hittite, as was to be expected.

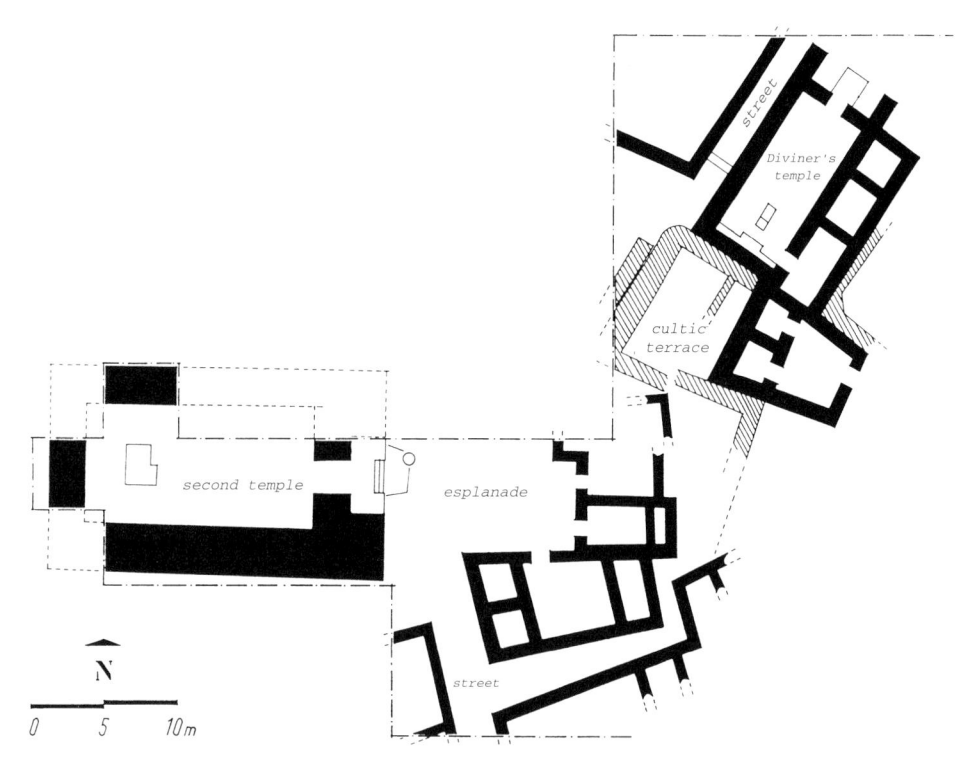

Figure 11: The Diviner's temple and the "second temple".

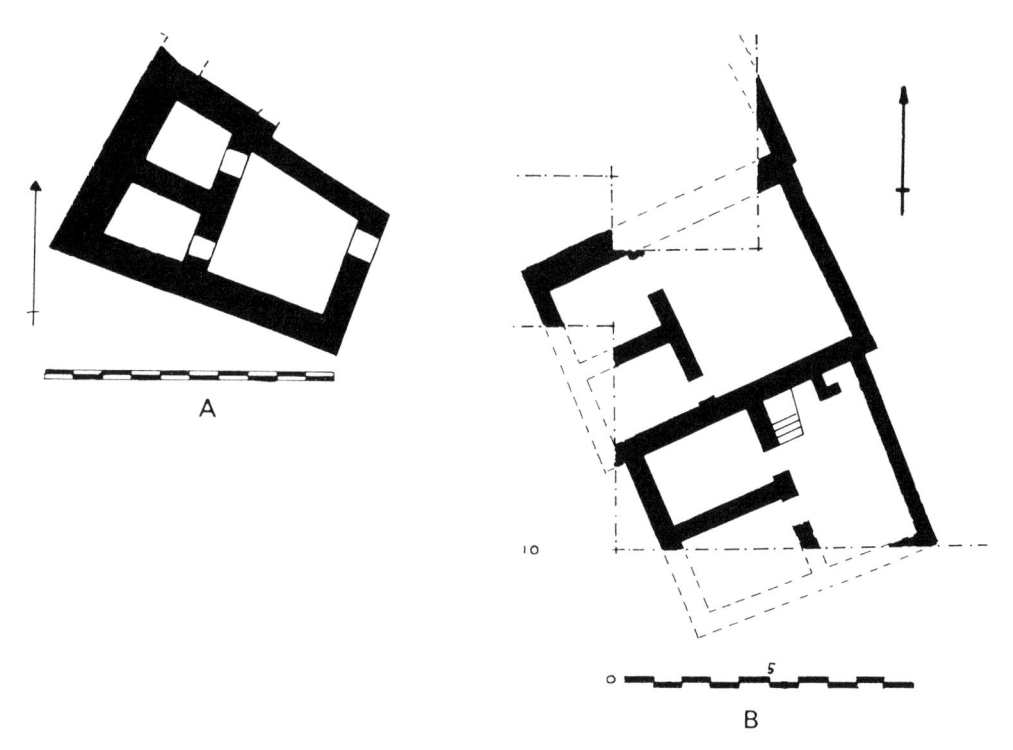

Figure 12: House plans of Emar.

Figure 13: Bronze figurine of the bull of Ba'al found in the southern temple.

Glazed ceramics were also common on the site. They were found abundantly both in the temples and in the palace. Such ceramic types were used during the second millennium in areas ranging from Egypt to Mesopotamia. Even if the Syrians seem to have specialized in the production of glazed ceramics, one cannot state definitely that Emar was a centre of their production, as most of these pots came from monumental buildings and not from workshops.

Yet another type of artefact that need to be mentioned are cylinder seals. No actual cylinder was discovered at Emar, but more than four hundred impressions on tablets have been found. Some are in the traditional Mitannian style, others are Assyrian, Babylonian, Hittite and Syrian. Altogether a very mixed lot.

Finally we shall mention a sculptured horn (fig. 14) found in the great temple. Although it is not an exceptional artwork, it reveals a provincial art similar to that found in the palace at Ugarit, but it is not quite so finely executed.

Nearly five hundred cuneiform tablets were found at Emar, some in the palace, others in the temples, in private houses, and a large amount in the Diviner's temple. Their language and their form are Syrian, sometimes Mitannian; a lot are Hurrian and one

Figure 14: Drawing of the carved horn (O. Callot).

is Hittite. They concern daily life and economics; some are letters and many come from the library of the diviner, which was a scriptorium, that is to say a room where the diviner taught young students. This room has revealed traditional texts from Babylonia, mythical and canonical ones, and many hepatoscopic documents. Emar was also the place where the diviner's practices, that originated in Babylonia, passed from the Syro-Babylonian area to the Hittites, and then to Etruria. Thus Emar appears to have been an essential link in the process of cultural transmission at the end of the second millennium between Near Eastern and Mediterranean countries.

I hope this presentation has in some way helped to explain and portray the complexities of the city of Emar, a city that combined Syrian and Hittite influences, and maintained close links with Babylonia and Assyria.

ETHNIC MOVEMENTS IN THE THIRTEENTH CENTURY B.C. AS DISCERNIBLE FROM THE EMAR TEXTS[1]

BY

Murray R. ADAMTHWAITE

This study seeks to examine the text-corpus from Emar with a view to ascertaining the light they shed on ethnic composition and movements in the late thirteenth century B.C. and *apropos* the destruction of Emar itself. The archaeological analysis by the excavator, Prof. J.-C. Margueron, given elsewhere in this volume, will be assumed for the purposes of this paper. The present study will explore in particular the ethnic composition at Emar in its final phase; the contacts with other centres in the Middle-Euphrates region; and the attacks on Emar cited in the texts. This, plus a revised chronology, seeks to determine the time and the likely agents of the destruction.

In part the issue is one of chronology, since the mention of the second regnal year of the late Kassite king Melišihu/Melišipak[2] (1188 - 1174 B.C.) on one tablet (RPAE 26) from a sub-corpus from Emar has been held to fix the *terminus ad quem* for the destruction of Emar. Since this in turn is held to be attributable to the chronologically coincident invasion of the Sea Peoples who rampaged along the coast of North Syria at this time, some have drawn the conclusion that the Sea Peoples were responsible for the destruction of Emar as well. In this paper it will be argued that this conclusion is premature. The picture is on closer inspection much more complex.

---

[1] In addition to those in *CAD*, Vol. Š, the following abbreviations will be used: **AO**: Aula Orientalis; **AO1987**: D. ARNAUD, "La Syrie du moyen-Euphrate sous le protectorat hittite: contrats de droit privé", *Aula Orientalis*, 5 (1987), pp. 211-241; **AOS1**: D. ARNAUD, "Textes syriens", *Textes Syriens de l'âge du Bronze récent*, Aula Orientalis Supplementa, Vol. 1, Barcelona 1991; **ARI**: A.K. GRAYSON, *Assyrian Royal Inscriptions*, Wiesbaden 1976; **ASJ**: *Acta Sumerologica Japonica*; **AT**: D.J. WISEMAN, *The Alalakh Tablets*, London 1953; **HCCT**: Hirayama Collection of Cuneiform Tablets, A. TSUKIMOTO, *Acta Sumerologica*, 12 (1990), pp. 177-227; and 13 (1991), pp. 275-333; **RPAE**: D. ARNAUD, *Recherches au pays d'Aštata*, Emar VI/3, Paris 1986.

[2] The sign HU in this name is read either *hu* or *pak*: Brinkman and Boese opt for the latter, Arnaud for the former. For a full discussion see J.A. BRINKMAN, *ZA*, 59 (1969), pp. 238-242, esp. pp. 241-242. Since Arnaud reads Melišihu in all his writings, that will be the spelling adopted here.

1. ETHNICITY

From an onomastic study we can gain some idea of ethnic representation at Emar, and from this the overwhelming make-up is late Amorite or general West Semitic.[3] This can be seen from a sample of representative names:[4]

Zu-Aštarti	}"he/she of…"[5]
Zu-Ba'ala	}
Zu-Asdi	}
Abi-Rašap	"Rašap is my father"[6]
Dadu	"Beloved"[7]
Dagan-malik:	"Dagan rules"[8]
Pilsu-Dagan	"viewed by Dagan"[9]
Ḫinnu-Dagan	"Dagan is gracious"[10]
Ipḫur-Dagan	"Dagan gathers"[11]

At least fifty percent of the names include Dagan as their theophoric element, another twenty-five percent include Ba'al, while deities such as Rašap, Aštarti, Sîn/Šaggar, Asda, Išhara make up much of the remainder.

Another significant ethnic component at Emar are Hurrians.[12] Again, some typically Hurrian names in the texts are:

Puḫi-Šenni	"Puhi is the brother"[13]
Eḫli-Kuša	"prosperity of Kuša (the moon)"[14]
Wendib-Šarri	"The king is (on) your right"[15]

---

[3] See R. ZADOK, "Elements of Aramean Pre-History", *Ah, Assyria…: Studies in Assyrian History and Ancient Near Eastern Historiography Presented to Hayim Tadmor*, ed. M. COGAN & I. EPH'AL, Jerusalem 1991, p. 114; ID., "Notes on the west-semitic material from Tell Emar", *Annali dell'Istituto Orientale di Napoli*, 51 (1991), pp. 113-137.

[4] Cf. I.J. GELB, *Computer-Aided Analysis of Amorite*, University of Chicago Oriental Institute, 1980. See also the important study of onomastics, including some note of Emar names, in R. S. HESS, *Amarna Personal Names*, Winona Lake, 1993.

[5] E.g. RPAE 256, 33; RPAE 252, 20; AOS1 55, 11 respectively.

[6] RPAE 148, 29; AOS1 16, 41.

[7] AOS1 15, 17.

[8] RPAE 12, 24. The Dagan-ma of RPAE 131, 29 is most likely an abbreviation of Dagan-malik.

[9] RPAE 4, 26; 8, 44 *et passim*.

[10] AOS1 38, 9.

[11] RPAE 5, 32.

[12] Elements as rendered in E. LAROCHE, "Glossaire de la langue hourrite", *RHA*, 1976, 1977, pp. 20-21. Cf. R. ZADOK, "On the onomastic material from Emar," *Die Welt des Orients*, (1989-1990), pp. 45-61.

[13] RPAE 181, 19.

[14] RPAE 148, 30

[15] RPAE 176, 30.

Ewri-Tešub	"Tešub is lord"[16]
Piḫa-muwa	unknown[17]
Tagi	"beautiful"[18]
Mutri-Tešub	"Tešub is …"[19]

Since Emar lay on the eastern border of Hanigalbat we would expect this; the surprising thing is not the presence of Hurrian elements but their relative scarcity, especially among the mainstream citizenry. Equally interesting are the various other elements present at Emar: Palmyrenes, Eblaites, Assyrians, even Egyptians (if the names are any indication), and of course, Hittites from the ruling city of Karkemish.

However, for the purposes here the most significant of these minorities is the Ahlamite-Aramaean group, possibly to be seen in the following examples:

(i) 7 UDU.ḪÁ ¹*Aḫ-la-mi-ú* DUMU *Ia-da*.[20] In this text involving the exchange(?) of seven sheep Zadok identifies the individual as an Ahlamite,[21] i.e. an Aramaean according to the accepted equation.

(ii) *Aḫ-la-mi-*[*i* in a broken text regarding sheep, according to Zadok[22] the same ethnic name as above.[23]

(iii) NA₄.KIŠIB *I-la-nu* DUMU *Aḫ-la-me-ú*, a text dealing with adoption and regulation of inheritance.[24]

It must be noted that these three occurrences as they stand are all proper names, since the determinative ¹ appears before two of them, whereas the third is broken at that point. For the word to be a true gentilic we would expect the determinative LÚ. For all that, the name itself may well indicate Ahlamû/Aramaean ethnicity, since Ahlamû is the Akkadian gentilic, as Zadok notes.[25] In summary, the evidence could well be indicative of Aramaean contacts, but by itself it must not be pressed.[26] Furthermore, trading contacts by Aramaeans at this time are what we would expect.

---

[16] RPAE 212, 28.
[17] *Ibid.*, 29.
[18] AO1987 11, 1, 11.
[19] RPAE 211, 19; AOS1 36, 30; 76, 19 *et passim*.
[20] RPAE 331, 1
[21] R. ZADOK, *loc. cit.* (n. 3), p. 113.
[22] *Ibid.*
[23] RPAE 322, 5.
[24] D. ARNAUD, "Tablettes de genres divers du moyen-Euphrate", *Studi Micenei ed Egeo-Anatolici*, 30 (1992), p. 211, no. 9, 38-39.
[25] R. ZADOK *loc. cit.* (n. 3), p. 104. Note how Ahlamû is used as a common noun rather than as a gentilic in the Annals of Tiglath-Pileser I. See *ARI*, 13 & n. 70.
[26] Liverani notes that a name denotes more usually something cultural rather than strict ethnicity. See his "L'élément hourrite dans la Syrie du Nord (c. 1350-1200)", *RHA*, 36 (1978), p. 150.

Possibly also indicative of Aramaean presence is the occurrence of the West Semitic title LÚ *na-si-ku* in a text of unknown provenance but believed on good evidence to have come from Emar.[27] According to this text the official is in charge of labour on a canal project, but the title itself is known from texts of the neo-Assyrian era as that of a sheikh or chief, usually of an Aramaean.[28] However, since the title also appears in the Old Babylonian period of a supervisor of field work, this occurrence from the Middle Assyrian period (i.e. the twelfth century B.C., that of the Emar texts) seems more closely related to the Old Babylonian usage than the later Aramaean usage.

2. An Attack by Aramaeans on Qaṭna.

These occurrences aside, there is little doubt that the relayed report in text RPAE 263 from a certain Šini-Ṣuri is that of an Aramaean incursion. He informs his Hittite overlord, the LÚ.UGULA.KALAM.MA in Emar, that two Aḫlamû ("Araméens" for Arnaud) from Sūḫi have reported that the LÚ *sakin* KUR.*Sūḫi* with chariots and troops (!) had laid siege to and pillaged Qaṭna. While the text designates the messengers as Aḫlamû and not the troops, since they both come from Suhu well-known from other Middle Assyrian texts as an Aḫlamû stronghold (see below), it seems reasonable to extend the designation to the troops as well. This is most significant for this study, leaving aside at present the identity of Qaṭna, since Aramaean attacks on cities elsewhere is strong analogical evidence of an attack by them on Emar itself. That the attackers are Aramaean is probable, since the transition from the gentilic *Aḫlamû* to the Aramaic *nisbe*, *Aramu*, is attested.[29]

However, though this equation has been challenged,[30] the terms are nevertheless closely related and certainly in later neo-Assyrian times Aḫlamû is used in clear reference to Aramaean by both the settled Assyrian and Babylonian peoples, as Brinkman observes.[31] By the same token, by that time it is a fossilized term. Hence, whether it is valid, or anachronistic, of Arnaud simply to translate *Aḫ-la-mu-ú* by "Araméens" in RPAE 263 (without note!) is a moot point. Probably we should rest content by accepting the assumed close historical relation between the two in these early times.

As to the identity of Qaṭna in RPAE 263, for Arnaud this is the Syrian city of that name, the modern Mishrife, but G. Bunnens raises the possibility that it could be

---

[27] As published by M. SIGRIST, *JCS*, 34 (1982), No. 1, 5, p. 246. Discussion in R. ZADOK, *loc. cit.* (n. 3), p. 114.

[28] As noted by J.A. BRINKMAN, *A Political History of Post-Kassite Babylonia, 1158-722 B.C.*, Rome 1968, p. 274 and n. 1767.

[29] As cited by R. ZADOK, *loc. cit.* (n. 3), pp. 104-105.

[30] S. MOSCATI, "The 'Aramaean Ahlamu'", *JSS*, 4 (1959), pp. 303-307. A. MILLARD, in *Peoples of Old Testament Times*, ed. D.J. WISEMAN, London 1973, p. 135, concurs with Moscati.

[31] J. BRINKMAN, *op. cit.*, (n. 28), pp. 277-278 and n. 1799, wherein he replies to Moscati.

Qatni, a shortened form of the Qattunan known from the Mari texts and situated in the Habur region.[32] The advantage of this location is that it does not involve travel for long distances over desert, almost certainly through Palmyra, well beyond their own region. It must be observed here, however, that for others looking at this text this issue does not constitute a problem. Thus Durand simply comments, "L'expédition depuis le Suhi contre Qatna montre que l'on franchit le désert entre Palmyre et l'Euphrate normalement à cette époque".[33]

Bunnens also reasons that the context points to an eastern location, and from that quarter the news comes.

For all this, however, the Qatna in North Syria remains the more likely location for the following reasons:

(i) The letter is addressed by a subordinate to the Hittite LÚ.UGULA, the ambassador-at-large to the vassal states for the oversight of Hittite rule. In this capacity an attack on a major Syrian city would be of the utmost concern to him, whereas an attack on a faraway location in Assyrian territory, out of his jurisdiction, as Qatni was, would be nothing more than mildly interesting news at most. More likely such news would please the Hittite overlord, since this would mean the discomfiture of their Assyrian enemies. On the contrary, the tone of agitation in the report, in particular about the booty which the Aramaeans took (*mi-nu-me-[e šal-l]a-tu₄ ša iš-[lu-]lu-ni*), and the fact that Šini-ṣuri makes his report in the normal course of his travels along the Euphrates (see point iii below), combine to make this a report about matters within the overlord's jurisdiction.

(ii) Contiguous with this, texts from both Emar and Tell Munbaqa (Ekalte) respectively attest the presence of men from Qadesh (Kinza),[34] Palmyra (Tadmir),[35] and Qatna? (*Qa-ta-[..*).[36] There can be no objection in principle to movements of Ahlamû-Aramaeans in the direction envisaged. The classic texts from Tiglath-Pileser I (see below) indicate that the Aramaeans were a mobile people.

(iii) With respect to the alleged eastern locality it is difficult to see what the context supplies in that regard. That context indicates that the Ahlamû come from Suhi, their homeland, as will be shown below. Thus the mention of Suhi in connection with the Ahlamû is little more than a truism. Apart from Suhi the only other place mentioned is Šatappi (if we accept Arnaud's restoration in line 13), to where Šini-ṣūrī reports that he has gone. This is a town clearly linked with Emar, as seen from a number of texts in the official corpus. For example, there is a contract for the sale of four children of Šatappi, each of whom has a foot impression made (three of which have been recovered), coming from the Diviners' Temple at

---

[32] G. BUNNENS, "Emar on the Euphrates in the 13th Century B.C.", *Abr-Nahrain*, 27 (1989), p. 34.
[33] J-M. DURAND, review of RPAE, *RA*, 84 (1990), p. 78.
[34] RPAE 277, 5.
[35] RPAE 21, 15-18.
[36] W. MAYER, "Die Tontafelfunde von Tall Munbaqa 1988", *MDOG*, 122 (1990), p. 47.

Emar;[37] then the king of Šatappi participates with the king of Emar in the ritual of the installation of the NIN.DINGIR priestess at Emar.[38] Thus Šatappi is most likely in the general vicinity of Emar, even though its modern location has not been identified.

The further significance of this is twofold:
(i) the leader is the LÚ *sà-kìn*.
(ii) his origin is from Suhu.

These will be discussed in turn:

(i) The leader of the attack is "the prefect" of Suhu, with his organized militia, as noted. This term LÚ *sà-kìn* occurs at Alalah as LÚ *sà-ki-ni*,[39] though in most texts where this term occurs it is usually followed by a GN, the form is LÚ GAR-*kín ša* KUR-*ti* GN. Thus it occurs in Ras Shamra and Amarna texts.[40] The noteworthy contrast here is that in the text under discussion the leader of the Aramaean attack is not a king, whereas according to RPAE 42, 11 the "king" of the Hurrians led the attack on Emar (LUGAL ERIM.MEŠ KUR *Hur-ri*). Durand speculates that he would have been little more than a tribal chieftain by this time.[41] The explanation probably lies on the Hurrian part in nostalgia for their former glory, while *sākinu* for the Ahlamû leader reflects his real title and status: both a tribal chieftain (as with Durand) and a military prefect[42] leading a concerted attack on a major population centre.

(ii) As to the the "land of Suhu" (KUR *Sú-ú-hi*), according to his annals from the fourth year on, Tiglath-Pileser pursued the Ahlamû-Aramaeans "from the edge of the land of Suhu to Karkemish".[43] Indeed, there are several references to Suhu, to Anat of Suhu, and to the region of Mt. Bishri further upstream from Suhu. In all it is clear that Suhu was not only a population centre for Ahlamu-Aramaeans but their homeland, and in turn a hotbed for their forays against cities both west and east of the Euphrates. Thus, from its own perspective, letter 263 corroborates these military raids from Suhu, although we should note the apparent military organisation involved in their deployment: chariots and infantry. This could well have been a decisive factor in Aramaean success.

In summary, what remains to be observed is that if a stronghold like Qatna could be pillaged, *a fortiori* Emar, closer to the Aramaean homeland, was likewise vulnerable from the same source. Equally, whatever the location of Qatna, Aramaean attacks and

---

[37] RPAE 217-220. Note the appearance of the name of Laheia, the current LÚ.UGULA.KALAM.MA for both Šatappi and Emar in RPAE 220, 3.

[38] RPAE 369, 16-17; 55-58.

[39] D. J. Wiseman *JCS*, 8 (1954), p. 17.

[40] *CAD*, Vol. S, 76-77.

[41] Durand, comments *apropos* Text 42 in *loc. cit.* (n. 33), p. 183. Durand renders the phrase as "chef de bandes armées". See also *NABU*, 1989/53.

[42] See M. Dietrich, O. Loretz, & J. Sanmartin, "Zur ugaritischen Lexikographie", *UF*, 6 (1974), p. 41.

[43] As in *ARI*, 13-14; 21.

incursions were by this time a significant factor and this evidence must figure in any account of the historical situation. The point here is that an Aramaean attack on Tell Mishrife is more significant for Emar and the Middle Euphrates than a similar attack on a more easterly location.

3. Emar and its Vicinity: Whose Control?

While Emar itself clearly lies within the Hittite domain, when we turn to the commercial and other contacts Emar has with its neighbours, largely along the Euphrates, we may note the following sites, also known from elsewhere:

Aštata: occurs with the URU determinative, not KUR. Likewise at Alalah. Hence it is a town, as well as a region.[44]

Ekalte: read *I-kal-tá* in RPAE 7,2 and AOS1 96, 16 instead of Arnaud's *I-rib-da*.[45]

URU *Ta-ad-mi-ir*: Palmyra[46]

Anabi: Attested in AO1987-11 but could be read as Ana with -bi as a Hurrian genitive suffix. That this is a city in the Hurrian zone is seen from both the Hurrian and Hittite names in the text.[47]

Ebla: known from the third millennium B.C.[48]

Tuttul: Attested in two texts,[49] the one from the Japanese collection being the more interesting as it attests a disembarkation from a boat at Tuttul, whence a woman's son entered servitude to a certain Dagan-bani. The transaction appears to have all the elements of normality other than the famine cited at the outset of the text. There is no hint of dealings with a foreign administration like that of Assyria. On the contrary, the town seems to have still been within the Hittite domain. The texts from Tell Biʿa (Tuttul) are unfortunately of limited use in this connection, since they date from an earlier period, that of Yasmah-Addu.[49] In Subaru, however, we do encounter the presence of Assyrians. Likewise *Šuwadikani*, or *Šadikani* (not *šu-pi-ṭi ka-ri*, as Arnaud reads),[50] a city in the Habur region under Assyrian control, has an Assyrian population, judging from the names attested in this text.

---

[44] RPAE 19, 11-12; *AT* 89,3, cf. G. Bunnens, *loc. cit.* (n. 32), pp. 24-25.
[45] As noted by W. Mayer in *UF*, 24 (1992), p. 268, n. 11. Note here that Tell Munbaqa is, in fact, Ekalte, and not Uri, as Mayer shows in *loc. cit.* (n. 36), pp. 49-50.
[46] RPAE 21, 16-18.
[47] AO1987 11,1.
[48] RPAE 254, 1
[49] Respectively RPAE 274, 2: "Dagan of Tuttul"; and *ASJ*, 10 (1988), text E, pp. 166-168.
[50] RPAE 127, 2. Cf. J.-M. Durand, "Suffète fantôme à Emar", *NABU*, 1989/53.

Suhu: home of the Ahlamû/Aramaeans, as noted above. This was under neither Hittite nor Assyrian control.

Hence a tentative conclusion is that Emar had quite free contacts with cities to the south and west, and more importantly, to the east and south-east, even to cities under Assyrian control. Meanwhile, Tuttul and other more nearby towns betray no evidence of Assyrian control. All this lends support to the proposition that the western Jezireh constituted a "hole" in Assyrian administration of Hanigalbat. This stands to reason from a geographical perspective: the region is very desolate and Assyrian interests lay elsewhere. Within this hole tribal people, bandits, freebooters and the like could launch attacks. From certain texts in the Emar corpus this is precisely what we find. To these we now turn.

4. The Hurrian attack and its chronological implications

While the texts from the official excavation and others scattered in various journals remained the only published material up to 1989, the text No. 42 from the archive of the twin temples of Ba'al was the only one which mentioned this attack during the reign of Pilsu-Dagan. However, since the publication of the Hirayama Collection, plus the further textual material of Arnaud himself, we have at least three references to this event, one of which uses it as a chronological benchmark. A discussion of the texts is relevant before examination of the historical implications.

(a) Sources

1. RPAE 42

Since the initial notice of this text by D. Arnaud,[51] and the full text and translation in *Recherches au pays d'Aštata, Emar VI.3*,[52] several other discussions of this text have appeared as follows: Durand;[53] Zaccagnini;[54] Tsukimoto;[55] Dietrich.[56]
As Zaccagnini notes, the orthography of the tablet is poor despite the "signature" of the scribe Ea-mudammiq in three places on the tablet, corresponding to the three inscriptions.[57] Most likely it is, as he observes, a school text copied inexpertly under

---

[51] D. Arnaud, "Catalogue des textes cunéiformes trouvés au cours des trois premières campagnes à Meskéné Qadime ouest", *AAAS*, 25 (1975), p. 92; ID., "Les textes suméro-accadiens: un florilège", *Meskéné - Emar: dix ans de travaux: 1972 - 1982*, ed. D. Beyer, Paris 1982, p. 44.

[52] RPAE 42.

[53] J.-M. Durand, review of RPAE, *RA*, 83 (1989), pp. 183-184.

[54] C. Zaccagnini, *Orientalia*, 59 (1990), pp. 518-520.

[55] A. Tsukimoto, *ASJ*, 12 (1990), pp. 191-192.

[56] M. Dietrich, "Die akkadischen Texte der Archive und Bibliotheken von Emar", *UF*, 22 (1990), pp. 33-35.

[57] *Loc. cit.*, (n. 54), p. 518.

the supervision of this scribe, hence ŠU ¹ᵈE-a-SIG₅ DUB.ŠAR in lines 7, 19 and 23 should be read as "by the agency (hand) of Ea-mudammiq". At two crucial points the poor orthography has either misled the earlier editors or is genuinely capable of diverse readings. Having regard to these difficulties, the relevant part of the text reads as follows:

    ¹*Pí-su*-ᵈKUR DUMU ᵈIŠKUR-*ka-bar*
    LUGAL URU *E-mar* LUGAL ERIM.MEŠ KUR *Ḫur*¹-*ri*
10. URU *E-mar i-la-mi-in*²
    ù ᵈ*Pí-su*-ᵈKUR³ IGI-2-*šu*
    a-na ᵈU *i-ṣi-ma ù* ᵈU
    *eg-re-ti*⁴ MUŠEN GI *ša* ŠA-*šu*
    i-di-na-su ù ERIM.MEŠ *ḫu-ra-du*
15. *ša* ŠA-*šu ù* BÀD-*šu* TÉŠ-*ba nak-ra-šu*⁵
    im-ḫa-aṣ U URU *E-mar ú-ba-li-iṭ*
    GAL GUŠKIN 30 KI.LA.BI *a-na* ᵈU
    be-lí-šu a-na NAM-TI-LA ZI-*[š]u*
    IN.NA.AN.BA ŠU ¹ᵈEa-S[IG₅ DUB.ŠA]R

Notes on the Text

1. Arnaud originally read here *Ki-ri* (RPAE 42,9). No sooner was it formally published than Arnaud himself raised doubts about the reading.[58] Durand[59] proposed the reading *ḫur*, as Arnaud had suggested, since in the Emar orthography, KI and HUR are generally very close. Zaccagnini, accepting this reading, drew attention to a similar phrase in the Idrimi inscription: LUGAL ERIN.MEŠ *Ḫur-ri*ᵏⁱ *ú-na-kir-an-ni*. (l.44). Tsukimoto assumes the reading *ḫur* in his transliteration of the portion in connection with a similar passage in HCCT 7 (see below), while Dietrich includes a discussion of the poorly executed sign. However, an examination of the tablet itself reveals that the sign sequence is LUGAL ERIN.MEŠ KUR *Ḫur-ri*. The penultimate sign in line 9 is 𒉽 which is indeed much more akin to an imperfectly formed HUR than KI, which in the same tablet is written consistently as 𒆠 or 𒆠 or 𒆠, usually with two horizontals, i.e. rather like DI, as Dietrich appropriately remarks. The final confirmation of this reading comes with the later-published texts where the same invasion is mentioned, and the sign HUR in the name *Ḫur-ri* is clear, formed thus: 𒄯. The line thus mentions a "king" of the Hurrians, leading an assault on Emar.

2. While the reading of the signs is clear, the verb constitutes a problem: a zustand verb, *lemēnu*, with a causative meaning. Zaccagnini proposes *ú-la-mi-in*.[60] Durand's

---

[58] See D. ARNAUD in *Hethitica*, 8 (1987), p. 11 and n.14.
[59] *Loc. cit.* (n. 53), p. 183.
[60] *Loc. cit.* (n. 54), p. 519, n.6.

translation, "*le roi des tribus hourrites (et) la ville d'Emar étaient en mauvais termes*",[61] is grammatically fitting but the context seems to require a meaning like "acted wickedly". However, this need not be so; an extended meaning of the present durative (so Dietrich) to yield "were (mutually) hostile" suits the flow of the short narrative well enough.[62] There is no need to invoke a "forme IV" as with Durand.

3. The evidence that Pisi/u-Dagan is a phonetic, or at least an orthographic variant of Pilsu-Dagan is quite conclusive.[63] The text published by Tsukimoto (HCCT 1) lists as the primary witness Elli, DUMU *Pí-sí-*^{d}*Da-gan* and bears the seal now identified as the royal seal. This can be none other than the king Pilsu-Dagan, father of Elli. Both Durand and Tsukimoto see a phonetic shift from -*ls* to -*ss*-, the former by appeal to analogous evidence from Mari, and a discussion by von Soden. The sign BI should be read likewise as *pí*. Thus "Bisu-Dagan" is a phantom king.

4. Clearly in the light of immediate and broader contexts a variation of *egirrû*: "oracular utterance". The following logogram denotes the familiar bird-oracle as for example known at Mari, e.g. in the "dream of Ayala" as translated by Dossin, *i-na iṣṣūrāt* [MUŠEN] [*h*]*u-r*[*i-i*]*m wa-ar-ka-sà ap-ru-ús-ma*.[64] Durand's rereading, *iq-ri ti-iš-gi*… has little to commend it. Both Zaccagnini and Dietrich support Arnaud at this point. Dietrich has drawn attention to a similar theme in the Idrimi inscription MUŠEN.HI.A *ú-za-ki*.. "I caused a bird to fly…(in the seventh year Tešub turned his face to me)".[65] The remainder of line 13 has given rise to diverse readings and renderings. A straightforward reading of the signs, clear from both the photograph and the cuneiform transcription, is as indicated. The reconstructions of neither Durand (above) nor Zaccagnini (*ik-ri-bi*$_{4}$[BAD] *el-qí*) are convincing. The normal logographic reading of GI: *šalāmu* makes good sense, as Dietrich adopts, and which is followed here.

5. Line 15 is particularly difficult, not least as the signs are obscure in both the photograph and the transcription. The photograph would appear to yield the following:

The best understanding of this sequence is close to that of Durand:
TÉŠ-*ba nak-ra-šu*: "…together (and) his enemy (he struck)".

---

[61] *Loc. cit.* (n. 53), p. 183.

[62] *Loc. cit.* (n. 56), p. 34 and n. 33.

[63] The discussions of this issue are already quite extensive since Arnaud's initial reading in *Syria*, 52 (1975), pp. 89-90. See J.-M. DURAND, *loc. cit.* (n. 53), p. 184, and n. 79, wherein he raises the possibility that the two names refer to the same person; M. DIETRICH, *loc. cit.* (n. 56), pp. 34-35; A. TSUKIMOTO, *loc. cit.* (n. 55), p. 180, commenting on HCCT 1, 25; F. M. FALES, "Notes on the Royal Family of Emar", *Marchands, diplomates et empereurs*, ed. D. CHARPIN & F. JOANNES, Paris 1991, pp. 81-90, N.B. n. 22, wherein his path to the same conclusion as above is via orthography. Arnaud himself in 1982 still saw two different individuals, see *loc.cit.* (n. 51), pp. 43, 44.

[64] G. DOSSIN, "Tablettes de Mari", *RA*, 69 (1975), no. 2, 14-15 (Le songe d'Ayala, republished as *ARM* XXVI 229). See also the Hittite bird-oracle procedure reproduced in G. WILHELM, *The Hurrians*, Warminster 1989, pp. 69-70.

[65] *Loc. cit.* (n. 56), referring to lines 28-30 in the Idrimi inscription.

From the above discussions, the translation of lines 8-19 would result as follows:

"Pilsu-Dagan, son of Ba'al-kabar,
king of the city of Emar — The king of the Hurrian troops
and Emar were (mutually) hostile.
Then Pi(l)su-Dagan raised
his two eyes to Ba'al, and Ba'al
(by means of) a bird-oracle gave him
the prosperity which he desired. Then his
choice *ḫurādu*-troops, and his garrison (troops)
together struck his enemy and he thus saved
the city of Emar —
has presented a gold cup weighing 30 šiqlu
to Ba'al his lord for the preservation of his life."

2. HCCT 7

Tsukimoto has published, *inter alia*, a text which mentions the same Hurrian attack. The relevant section of this text reads as follows:

A.ŠÀ *ša píl-su*[d] *da-gan* LUGAL-*ri*
i-nu-ma ERIM[meš] *Ḫur-ri*
30. BÀD [URU]*E-mar*[ki] *il-mi*
ù [1]*maš-ru-ḫé* LÚ.MAŠ.ŠU.GÍD.GÍD
ša LUGAL-*ri ù* URU[ki]
ù ba-ru-tu₄-šu ik-šu-du₄-ma
ù píl-su [d]*dagan* LUGAL-*ru*
35. A.ŠÀ *an-ni-um*
a-na NÍG.BA *qí-iš-ti-šu*

"A field belonging to Pilsu-Dagan, the king.
When the Hurrian troops
surrounded the citadel/city-wall of Emar
then Mašruhe, the diviner
of the king and the city,
- his divination came true.
So Pilsu-Dagan the king
has given this field to him
as a present.

This section is quite legible from the tablet and there are no major problems of orthography or translation. The content dovetails neatly with the information from RPAE 42, viz. the siege itself and the diviner, here named, who gave a favourable prognostication on the outcome to the king.

3. AOS1 9, 21-2

Confirmatory evidence comes from the newly-published texts from Arnaud,[66] as follows:

i-na KÚR.KÚR KALA-*ti ša Hur-ri*
: BÀD *il-mi-ma*

"— during the ferocious war when the Hurrians laid siege to the citadel —"

Here there is no question regarding the reading *Hur-ri* (l.21), despite the generally poor orthography of the tablet. Hence it yields correlative confirmation of the same reading in RPAE 42, 9.

The reference to the Hurrian invasion in AOS1 9 occurs in a text which attests "Pilsu-Dagan, king" as the primary witness, followed by members of his family. This agrees with the evidence of RPAE 42 and HCCT 7, both of which cite Pilsu-Dagan as king. It seems a fair conclusion that all three references are to the same event.

The last reference above also mentions the "citadel" or "rampart" (BÀD) which was the target of the Hurrian siege. Archaeological investigation of Tell Meskéné has sought to identify the defensive structure of the ancient town and this rampart in particular.[67] Attention finally focussed on an artificial ravine which separated this plateau from the surrounding landscape, i.e. Area Y down to Area H on the western side of the tell. Margueron is in little doubt that this is part of the "rampart" or "citadel" which constituted the main defence system.[68] Worth noting here is the reference to *kirṣitu i-na* BÀD *wa-ti-ir* in AOS1 14, 6.

The steep slope of the tell at this and several other points around the western side, even allowing for erosion to have mitigated the slope, provides at least a partial explanation of why the attack failed during Pilsu-Dagan's reign.

(b) Historical discussion[69]

The obvious problem which arises here is that by the late thirteenth century the Assyrians were well and truly in charge of the Hanigalbat region. How could Hurrian warriors operate in this way when under the Assyrian administration after the Hurrian war of 1239 B.C. their leaders, and many others, were deported to Assyria, their land

---

[66] Here designated AOS1. See n. 1.
[67] See J.-C. MARGUERON, "Quatre campagnes de fouilles à Emar (1972-1974): un bilan provisoire", *Syria*, 52 (1975), p. 67; ID., "Rapport préliminaire sur les 3e, 4e, 5e et 6e campagnes de fouilles à Meskéné-Emar", *AAAS*, 32 (1982), p. 239 in reference to a rampart in Area R.
[68] Personal communication from Prof. Margueron.
[69] The discussion which follows is indebted to A. HARRAK, *Assyria and Hanigalbat*, New York 1987, in particular pp. 162-284.

placed under Assyrian military rule through *huradu*-troops and subjected to *ilku* service? Assyrian rule under Tukulti-Ninurta I reinstated the network of local officials in the local residences or palaces already built under Shalmaneser I. Whatever local insurgency by the Hurrians there may have been now remained restricted to the northern mountain areas of Katmuhu, Kashiari, Paphu and Alzu. Then came his defeat of Babylon, 1233 B.C. Harrak concludes: "at this time Assyria became the policeman of the entire river (Euphrates)".[70] Further evidence comes from the site of Tell Fray, on the eastern bank of the Euphrates approximately 30 km downstream from Emar, where texts dated initially to the fourteenth century B.C. more plausibly date to the thirteenth, to the reigns of Shalmaneser I and Tukulti-Ninurta I respectively. Though the question cannot be finally settled, this data, Harrak argues, places Tell Fray in the expansionist plans of the Assyrian monarchs.[71] Hence Hurrian insurgency this far south on the Euphrates in the late thirteenth century does constitute a problem.

However, the evidence of Hurrian attack during the reign of Pilsu-Dagan of Emar (which synchronizes with Tukulti-Ninurta I, though space forbids the argumentation for this conclusion) is as it is, and this must be matched with the evidence which Harrak collates. There are two ways of reconciling the data. One way is to follow Zadok and conclude that Assyrian control of the western Jezireh was ineffective,[72] leaving the Hurrians with free rein. An alternative scenario would envisage a degree of traditional Assyrian control such that traditional Hurrian enmities against the middle-Euphratean towns were exploited by the Assyrians for their own ends, especially useful to control the western frontier, while Tukulti-Ninurta I punished the Hurrian pockets of resistance in the northern mountains. For their part, the Hurrians may well have had old scores to settle.

The recent discussion by R. Zadok[73] in his investigations of Aramaean origins, and the contributions of H. Sader and T.L. McClellan[74] have shed further light on the issue. With the abolition of Hanigalbat as a buffer state between Hatti and Assyria, argues Zadok, and the deportation of the inhabitants of a number of provincial centres to Assyria a population vacuum (or semi-vacuum) resulted, into which West Semitic semi-nomads moved. Archaeological evidence from the Jezireh region (between the Habur and the Eastern Euphrates) indicates a decline of occupation in the Late Bronze II to Iron I era, immediately after the period in question. Both Sader and McLellan confirm this picture.[75]

---

[70] *Ibid.*, p. 257. Consider here that Tukulti-Ninurta's great battle for the Hanigalbat region was at Nihriya in the North-west. See I. SINGER, "The Battle of Nihriya and the End of the Hittite Empire", *ZA*, 75 (1985), pp. 100-123.

[71] A. HARRAK, *op. cit.* (n. 69), pp. 175-178.

[72] *Loc. cit.* (n. 3), p. 112.

[73] *Loc. cit.* (n. 3).

[74] Respectively, H. SADER, "The 12th Century B.C. in Syria; The Problem of the Rise of the Aramaeans"; T.L. MCCLELLAN, "Twelfth Century B.C. Syria: Comments on H. Sader's Paper", *The Crisis Years: The 12th Century B.C.*, ed. W.W. WARD & M.S. JOUKOWSKY, Dubuque, Iowa, 1992, pp. 157-173.

[75] *Ibid.*, pp. 160-161 & 167-169.

Zadok ventures that the new Assyrian provincial administration of the former Hanigalbat exercised less control over these semi-nomads than had the Hurrian rule, since the latter hegemony ranged over nomad territory both east and west of the Euphrates.[76] By contrast, Assyria did not control the western region until much later, and control of western Jezireh even in Tukulti-Ninurta's time was less than effective. Probably this was due to the domestic strife in Assyria proper resulting from the latter's conquest of Babylonia and the ensuing tensions, internal and external, which occupied the latter half of his reign and culminated in his assassination. Yet in precisely these western and southern regions lay the concentrations of semi-nomads according to the evidence Zadok cites, but very few if any further east. Within this administrative hiatus semi-nomadic tribes could launch their attacks.

It is therefore suggested that the attenuated nature of Assyrian administration in the western Jezireh makes room for Hurrian and other semi-nomadic incursions against settlements in North Syria, especially along the Euphrates. Whatever the merits of this hypothesis, a final solution of this mystery must, of course, await further evidence from Emar or elsewhere.

5. Another Attack, or the Same Attack under a Different Term?

Two other references, tantalizing by their brevity and enigma, deserve discussion:

a) AOS1 25, 2-3

>   i-na MU ERIM.MEŠ *ṭár-wu*
>   URU.KI *la-mì*
>   "in the year when hordes (?) of troops
>   besieged the city."

At least two questions arise from this enigmatic dating formula, viz. who are the *ṭarwu* troops, and is this the same invasion as that attested above?

b) AOS1 44, 32-3.

>   *i-na* MU KALA.GA *ša* ERIM.MEŠ *ṭár-wu*
>   URU *E-mar il-mi-ma*
>   "in the year of distress when hordes (?) of troops
>   besieged the city of Emar."

While there seems to be little doubt that this refers to the same event as in (a), it sheds no further light on the enigmatic *ṭarwu*. To this problem we now turn. In all, there are four options:

[76] *Loc. cit.* (n. 3), pp. 111-112.

(i) That of Arnaud, who interprets it as a *qatl*-theme noun related to an Arabic root *ṭrw* "to come from afar, come unexpectedly", hence by extension, "bandits".[77] Neither Akkadian nor Ugaritic, nor Hebrew, are of any assistance with such a root. Ugaritic lists a root *ṭry*, but this is probably irrelevant.[78] Meanwhile, resorting to Arabic roots can be hazardous for second millennium B.C. texts,[79] and, even if allowed, the extended meaning from the root which Arnaud suggests is tenuous.

(ii) Another approach is to treat *ṭarwu* as a proper name, either of an ethnic group or as a geographical name. A problem with the latter is the lack of a determinative in both references, in contrast to the presence of KUR with the *Hur-ri* in RPAE 42,9, and the normal use of URU with Emar and other city names in these and other texts. While this point may not be decisive, as seen in the lack of a determinative with *Hur-ri* in HCCT 7 and AOS1 9 above, nevertheless the fairly consistent use of a determinative elsewhere is an important consideration. One other consideration, however, is the question of identity and possible mention elsewhere in roughly contemporary texts. To date, no such ethnic group or geographical name as *ṭarwu* is attested anywhere in the second millennium. While this again is not decisive, it is still strong presumptive evidence against any identification as a proper name.

Be this as it may, the identification of *ṭarwu* as an ethnic name remains a serious option, despite the lack of a parallel mention in other texts.

(iii) Yet another suggestion, possibly the least likely but worth a mention, is to see *ṭár-wu* as an abbreviation or contraction of the Hurrian word *taršuwani*: "humanity"[80] thus ERIM.MEŠ.*ṭár-wu/a* would mean "troops of men". If this is adopted, the invaders could thereby be identified with the Hurrians, though not necessarily with the invasion during the reign of Pilsu-Dagan. However, the lacunae required by *tar-<šu>wa-<ni>* constitute a serious difficulty in both texts nos. 25 and 44.

(iv) The final suggestion is that we must conclude that it is another Emarite common noun of which we are ignorant. This is basically Arnaud's position, albeit without the Arabic "explanations".

All in all, despite the difficulties, the explanation as an ethnic proper name is probably the best on available information. For the sake of discussion, this one will be adopted below.

The question now remaining is the one already raised, viz. whether the *ṭarwu* raid is to be identified with that of the Hurrians in the reign of Pilsu-Dagan or whether it is later, perhaps during the time of the last king, Elli. One fruitful line of inquiry to

---

[77] AOS1 11.
[78] See in UT 62, 42.
[79] Cf. by analogy the futile attempt to derive a meaning "strong", "strengthen" for the ancient Semitic *mrr* family on the basis of Arabic etymology. See D. PARDEE, "The Semitic Root *mrr* and the Etymology of Ugaritic *mr(r)//brk*", *UF*, 10 (1978), pp. 270-273. Noteworthy in this connection is Arnaud's rendering of this very word in RPAE 253, 6, viz. *u-ma-ri-ir-šu-nu*, as "a confirmé"!
[80] E. LAROCHE, *RHA*, (1977), p. 258.

help answer this question is a prosopographic study of the many names in the texts in order to obtain synchronisms. However, even a detailed sample of this type of study is outside the scope of this short article.[81] Suffice it to assert that such lines of evidence converge to suggest the possibility that two *different* incursions of *ṭarwu*-troops are mentioned, one in the early tablet 44, another in the later tablet 25. The latter *may* be identical with the Hurrian attack of RPAE 42, but that identification is neither necessary nor even likely.

In summary, a more likely scenario would be as follows:

Event	Reign
ṭarwu-troops attack Emar (AOS1 44)	Abbanu.
Hurrians attack according to RPAE 42, HCCT 7, AOS1 9	Pilsu-Dagan
ṭarwu-troops attack "the town" (URU), AOS1 25	Elli.

If this sequence of attacks has support from the texts, we need only note that there must have been one further attack, this time successful, i.e. the one which spelt the destruction of Emar. To anticipate the point to be argued below, this event took place at some time late in the thirteenth century B.C., forty years at least *before* the date Arnaud designates on the basis of the dated tablet RPAE 26, which cites the second year of Melišihu of Babylon. Such a date would, of course, rule out any agency by the "Sea Peoples".

6. The Dated Tablet: a Terminal Point for Emar?

At this point the issue of this regnal date on RPAE 26, and the corpus of seven texts in which it appears,[82] must be discussed at length. Both Bierbrier[83] and Boese[84], following Arnaud's date (1187 B.C.),[85] have used it both as indicating the time of Emar's destruction, and in turn to correlate this date with the invasions of the "Sea Peoples" in North Syria, which brought the final end of Ugarit and the fall of the Hittite empire.

However, an inspection of this corpus as a whole, plus a consideration of the above argumentation, requires a re-assessment. Were it not for this dated tablet, a prosopographic

---

[81] See my forthcoming thesis on the Emar texts wherein a full explanation will be given on this point. In summary, the argument is that (i) all texts belong to the mid to late 13th century B.C., i.e. the reign of Ini-Tešub to the early part of the reign of Talmi-Tešub of Carchemish, but not later, and (ii) the *terminus ad quem* of the extant corpus is the final destruction of the site.

[82] RPAE 23-29.

[83] *JEA*, 64 (1978), pp. 136-137.

[84] *UF*, 14 (1982), p. 18.

[85] As in D. Arnaud, *loc. cit.* (n. 63), pp. 88-89 and n. 1.

study and exploration of synchronisms would be fairly conclusive: the entire corpus belongs to the mid to late thirteenth century B.C.[86] The synchronisms arising from a prosopographic study support this, while nothing so far in the occasional publications of tablets contradicts this. To cite one important fact: Talmi-Tešub "king of Carchemish" is attested in a recently published tablet in the Hirayama collection in which the case of "an Emarite wife" is heard before Kunti-Tešub, the DUMU.LUGAL.[87] This king belongs to the latter part of the thirteenth century and so far this is his only mention in the Emar corpus, though the name of his son Kunti-Tešub is also attested in RPAE 267, 1-2. However, the successor and son of Talmi-Tešub, Kuzi-Tešub (not to be confused with Kunti-Tešub[88]), is not attested as king of Karkemish in the Emar texts. A fair conclusion is that Talmi-Tešub's reign forms a *terminus ad quem* for Emar's existence, and thus synchronizes with the reign of Elli, the last king of Emar.

Elli's father Pilsu-Dagan, for his part, clearly belongs to the later reign of Ini-Tešub[89], and the Hurrian attack probably belongs to a later time in that reign. That the Emar archives continue up to the town's destruction seems to be fairly conclusive in the light of Margueron's observation that the epigraphic and other objects occurred only in burnt areas.[90]

The following points should be made regarding this sub-corpus and tablet 26 in particular:

1. In this small corpus of seven texts, there are no less than three date references (RPAE 24; 26; 28), compared with the less than ten percent of such references for all the remaining texts of the Emar provenance. The most interesting feature of this small corpus is that these dates are all in the standard month names of the Babylonian calendar, thus:

RPAE 24, 6	ITI.GAN.GAN.È:	month of Kislim
RPAE 26, 9	ITI.KIN.2.KÁM:	second month of Elul
RPAE 28, 23	ITI.KÁM ša Ta-aš-ri-ṭi	month of Tašrit
	[U]$_4$.16.KÁM:	16th [da]y

---

[86] This will be fully explained in my forthcoming thesis as intimated above, n. 81.

[87] First noted in A. TSUKIMOTO, "Eine neue Urkunde des Tili-Šarruma, Sohn des Königs von Karkemiš", *ASJ*, 6 (1984), p. 68. Now published in full by A. TSUKIMOTO in *ASJ*, 14 (1992), pp. 294-297 as HCCT 46.

[88] As argued by J.D. HAWKINS, "Kuzi-Tešub and the 'Great Kings' of Karkamis", *AnSt*, 38 (1988), p. 99 and n. 1.

[89] Ini-Teshub had quite a long reign during the mid thirteenth century B.C. From RPAE 90 Laheia, the royal overlord, is contemporary with a Belu-malik, one of the royal scribes for Pilsu-Dagan (RPAE 125; 137; 180; 183), while on the other hand he is contemporary with Baʿal-malik, a third generation member of the diviner-dynasty of Iadi-Baʿla (RPAE 217), which in turn provides our link with Ini-Teshub (RPAE 201; 202).

[90] J.-C. MARGUERON, *loc. cit.* 1975 (n. 67), p. 69.

Nowhere else in the mass of texts from the Emar region is there any attested use of the Babylonian calendar. Certain scribes of the earlier period used the local Emar calendar and eponym system, but never the Babylonian calendar. Was there a deliberate change from one to the other in the later history of Emar? There seems to have been an adoption of a Babylonian-type formula for designation of years by certain events, but these are, of course, local events.[91] Only in tablet 26 do we have dating by Babylonian regnal year.

2. The second feature of this corpus is the preponderance of Babylonian and Kassite names. Thus we meet with Raïndu (from *ra'imtum*) who, with her husband, runs the business enterprise which these tablets attest. In addition, we encounter Amel-Adad, Ahi-mukin-apli, Sîn-apla-iddin, Nadin-gula, Sîn-uṣur, Nabunni, Ulamburiaš, Eriba-Marduk and Šamaš-rabû. Names of this type do occur elsewhere. Thus we do find, for example, Milki-Ea-šarri (146,29); Ari-Ea-šarru(69,2); Marduk (75,4,10, abbreviated?), but they must be sifted from the mass of local Emarite, plus the occasional Hittite and Hurrian names. What remain are rare occurrences.

3. The third factor, or set thereof, worthy of note are the physical features of this tablet corpus. They can be listed as follows:

(i) Their size is generally smaller than the remainder of the corpus, and in the case of tablet 27 much less (4 × 4 cm), while the shape, while rectangular, is sometimes higher than wide, sometimes vice-versa. The obverse is generally flat, with a slight rounding on the reverse.

(ii) The colour is on the whole, light grey-brown, often with small black blotches or spots, sometimes not at all blackened. In all, they betray little or no evidence of having been burnt, a remarkable phenomenon considering that the whole surrounding area had been completely and thoroughly burnt.[92] Thus tablets from the palace building (the *hilani*), which were found in an intact jar, were nevertheless heavily blackened by burning.[93] Similarly, another corpus of tablets, apparently from a private archive in Area C, viz. nos 30 - 33, is likewise badly burnt.

Clearly, in the light of these phenomena, the origin and *raison d'être* of the corpus requires explanation, since they would appear to attest a Babylonian trading business, having dealings with several Babylonian personnel; and operating according to the Babylonian calendar. Text no. 27 relates that six donkeys belonging to an Eriba-Marduk have sunk (presumably into the river), and the human survivors have as a result entered into slavery (É EN-*šu i-ru-bu*) to compensate for the loss.[94]

While it is known that Emar was a major trading centre from Old Babylonian times, few trading documents have turned up, either in the official excavations or in

---

[91] As, for example, in RPAE 15, 35-36.
[92] Cf. J.-C. Margueron's graphic description in *loc. cit.* (n. 42), p. 69.
[93] J.-C. MARGUERON, "Rapport préliminaire sur les deux premières campagnes de fouille à Meskéné-Emar", *AAAS*, 25 (1975), pp. 77, and 83, fig.6. ID., *loc. cit.* (n. 67), pp. 60, and 76, fig. 9.
[94] See discussion in G. BUNNENS, *loc. cit.* (n. 32), pp. 34-35.

the many pirated texts. This may be either an accident of discovery, or may well and more likely indicate that the Late Bronze Age Emar on its new site had declined as a trading junction. In the latter case, the house where these documents were found would thereby represent either an exception to this general picture of decline, or, as will now be argued, a later intrusion out of chronological context with the Emar community.

Discussion here leads us to the archaeology of the place of discovery. Regrettably, in the articles and preliminary reports so far published, detailed information regarding the stratigraphy and precise locus of these tablets is difficult to obtain. From what information is available, however, the following facts emerge:

a) According to the interesting observation of Margueron, in burnt areas of the site much epigraphic and ceramic material was found, whereas very little of either was found in unburnt areas.[95] As observed above, the reasonable conclusion from this is that the archives continue to the time of destruction, and rules out the suggestion of Dalley and Teissier that the archive represents merely a three generation period somewhere within the period of occupation.[96]

b) the fire which destroyed the burnt areas was of particular intensity, such that faience and other melted material has formed a mass so hard that a pick could hardly dent it.[97]

c) the tablets in question were apparently found near the threshold of a house in the general vicinity of the palace (Area A) on an earthen floor ("sur un sol") and in association with a broken jar embossed with nude female figurines.[98] The house in question was one of two in side-by-side configuration. Presumably the tablets were found *in* a layer of ash (from the destruction)[99], though the 1982 report is not precise about this. If this is the case, then why do the tablets in question betray no visible evidence of fire? Furthermore, questions arise about the relation of the tablets to the house. Had they originated from either of the two houses, or the palace area in general? If the former, did they show evidence of having fallen in the conflagration from either a shelf or from an upper storey of either house? Hence conclusions from the evidence of the preliminary reports must remain tentative. All that needs to be observed is that a case can be made for alleging that the tablets are in some way intrusive.

While Margueron may be correct to conclude from observation (a) that there may have been a partial abandonment of the town before the final destruction, it could equally be true that Dietrich's speculation is correct that the site continued in a small way as an Assyrian relay station for military and trade purposes.[100] This is plausible in

---

[95] *Loc. cit.* 1975 (n. 67), p. 69.
[96] As in S. DALLEY and B. TEISSIER "Tablets from the vicinity of Emar and elsewhere", *Iraq*, 54 (1992), p. 84.
[97] *Loc. cit.* 1975 (n. 67), p. 69.
[98] J.-C. MARGUERON, *loc. cit.* 1982 (n. 67), p. 234.
[99] This is concluded by connecting the report in *loc. cit.* 1975 (n. 67) with that of *loc. cit.* 1982 (n. 67), i.e. that epigraphic material came from burnt areas, and the tablets in question were no exception.
[100] *Loc. cit.* (n. 32), p. 27.

the light of the Babylonian connection indicated above, since we know that Tukulti-Ninurta I conquered Babylon, captured and deposed Kashtiliashu (IV), c. 1230 B.C., and instituted rule from Assyria over Southern Mesopotamia at the same time as Assyria held hegemony over Hanigalbat to the left bank of the Euphrates.

In the first case, that of prior partial abandonment, it would be more plausible to maintain that the tablets should be found *in* rather than *on* the ash (which we should bear in mind that the report does not mention), and should be burned themselves. Neither, however, was or is the case. By contrast, this small and unique corpus of tablets is better explained as reflecting a small scale Assyrian occupation on a nearby unburnt section. Alternatively, the fact that it was not found in any obvious storage area or archive may well indicate transportation in antiquity from some other location. To repeat, whatever the ultimate explanation, there is room for the conclusion that archaeologically the corpus is anomalous and intrusive, and thus should not be used to conclude a destruction of the entire site in or shortly after the second year of Melišihu of Babylon. At most, the corpus gives a *terminus ad quem* for the house where it was found.

7. Agents of Destruction: Possible Candidates.

Proceeding from this negative conclusion, some possible scenarios as to the real agent(s) of Emar's demise must now be considered. Those who reject the "Sea Peoples" hypothesis tend to see the destruction as resulting from the general ferment of tribal groups at the end of the Late Bronze Age, in turn brought on by the decline of imperial power, in particular that of the Hittites.[101] Thus Arnaud has published one text which designates such groups as *Umman-gayu*,[102] but later suggests that the Phrygians or *Mušku*, mentioned in inscriptions of Tiglath-Pileser I, may have been responsible.[103] Regarding this latter suggestion, they too appear to be too late to have had anything to do with Emar's destruction, unless their settlement in Northern Mesopotamia is seen as gradual over the thirteenth century B.C., and/or that they are to be equated with the *ṭarwu* as discussed above. However, the *Mušku* are properly a twelfth century phenomenon, coming after the destruction of Emar.[104] The Aramaeans have likewise been held responsible, as suggested in passing by both G. Bunnens and I. Singer.[105]

---

[101] So A. Harrak *op. cit.* (n. 69); I. Singer, "Dating the End of the Hittite Empire", *Hethitica*, 8 (1987), p. 418; H. Sader, *loc. cit.* (n. 74), p. 160; T. L. McClellan, *loc. cit.* (n. 74), pp. 167-170.

[102] D. Arnaud *Annuaire de l'Ecole pratique des Hautes Etudes*, 90 (1981-82), pp. 210-211 (unavailable to me at the time of writing).

[103] D. Arnaud, *loc. cit.* (n. 51) p. 43.

[104] See G. Wilhelm, *op. cit.* (n. 64), p. 41.

[105] Respectively, G. Bunnens, "I Filistei e le invasioni dei Popoli del Mare", *Le origini dei Greci*, ed. D. Musti, Bari 1985, pp. 241-242; I. Singer, *loc. cit.* (n. 101), pp. 418-419.

This latter suggestion is more plausible, and is indeed the thesis of this paper. To summarise we now return to the evidence cited at the outset of this article in order to highlight the basic conclusions.

In summary, the texts attest Hurrian enmity and attacks, plus evidence of Aramaean incursions elsewhere. It is reasonable to suppose, on one scenario, that either Hurrians or Aramaeans were responsible for Emar's destruction, or even both, but without any subsequent occupation by either of them. The other candidates are the enigmatic *ṭarwu*, as seen from the evidence cited above, if indeed they are to be seen as a distinct group. This leads to the following possibilities regarding the *ṭarwu*:

1. The *ṭarwu* are Aramaeans, and the attacks mentioned in AOS1 25 & 44 are those of Aramaean tribes from the south and south east.
2. The *ṭarwu* are the Hurrians under another name, as one of the above proposals suggests. On this hypothesis these attacks are identical to that mentioned in AOS1 9; RPAE 42; HCCT 7, or additional thereto.
3. The *ṭarwu* are a tribe in their own right, and the term should be treated as a proper name, as also suggested above. On this view Emar was attacked by two, or possibly three different groups: Hurrians, Aramaeans, and *ṭarwu*.[106]

Despite the difficulties involved, the view which seems to have the most evidence for it from the texts is the third option, i.e. that Emar was the target for attack from three sources: the *ṭarwu*, the Hurrians and the Aramaeans. The first enemy is evidenced by the new texts AOS1 25 & 44; the Hurrians are attested by RPAE 42, where the admittedly difficult verb *i-la-mi-in* in RPAE 42, 10 we have rendered "mutually hostile", following the lead from Dietrich, and by HCCT 7. Whatever the precise details of the translation of RPAE 42, the implication from this is that enmity against Emar on the part of the Hurrians had a history, possibly a long one. The evidence for the third enemy is admittedly more inferential, but in conjunction with the later evidence of Ahlamû/Aramaean activity in the time of Tiglath-Pileser I the report of the Aramaean attack preserved in RPAE 263 puts their incursions back into the thirteenth century.

The upshot of this evidence is that at least one, possibly two, attacks came from the Hurrians, and at least two or possibly three came from the *ṭarwu*. The suggestion here is that after these attacks all failed, then came the better equipped and better organized Aramaeans, possibly in coalition with some or all of these other forces, and this time

---

[106] Mention must also be made of the suggestion of Marguerite Yon that the *ṭárwu* are possibly the Sea Peoples themselves. However, she does not even consider that the term may be a proper name. See Marguerite Yon, "The End of the Kingdom of Ugarit", in W.W. WARD & M.S. JOUKOWSKY *op. cit.* (n. 74), p. 117.

the attack was successful. This last attack naturally went unrecorded, since it resulted in the sack of Emar, at least of the palaces and the temples. In conclusion, the picture is similar to that postulated by Albright two decades ago:

"The original speakers of Aramaic were nomads of mixed origin, who began settling down on the fringes of the Syrian Desert in the third quarter of the second millennium. They may then have headed a confederation of tribes which took advantage of the collapse of the Hittite and Egyptian empires, followed by the break-up of the Assyrian empire of Tukulti-Ninurta I, to invade en masse already tilled lands."[107]

Apart from the postulate of "mixed origin" the new texts serve to inject some fresh detail into this general picture, even if some of the conclusions of necessity remain speculative.

---

[107] W.F. ALBRIGHT, "Syria, the Philistines, and Phoenicia", in *CAH*, II, 2, 3rd ed., 1975, p. 532.

SYRO-ANATOLIAN INFLUENCE ON NEO-ASSYRIAN TOWN PLANNING

BY

Guy BUNNENS

The pattern of cultural interaction generated by the Assyrian conquest of the Neo-Hittite and Aramaean kingdoms should not be viewed as a one-way process in which the Assyrians were imposing their own view of the world, together with economic exploitation and political domination, on the countries they subdued. They were also receptive to western ideas and concepts which they incorporated into their own culture. Not long ago Irene Winter made a comprehensive review of such cultural borrowings.[1] They extended from iconographic motifs to gardens reproducing western landscapes, flora and fauna.

Not the least prominent among these borrowings were architectural features. The Assyrian custom of lining walls with carved orthostats or adorning gates with protecting figures had antecedents in Hittite Anatolia and the adoption of architectural forms such as that of the *bit hilani* was acknowledged by Assyrian kings. Further investigation would indicate that more features of Assyrian culture might be explained by western influence. A close examination of the urban layout of Neo-Assyrian capital cities, for example, would suggest that the general conception of these settlements might also have its roots in the West.[2]

Khorsabad, ancient Dur-Sharrukin, offers a good opportunity for the study of the main principles that underly the establishment of a Neo-Assyrian capital city. As a new foundation of Sargon II, abandoned soon after Sargon's death, it represents a site built almost entirely to one plan.

---

[1] I.J. WINTER, "Art as evidence for interaction: Relations between the Assyrian empire and North Syria," *Mesopotamien und seine Nachbarn*, ed. H. KÜHNE, H.J. NISSEN & J. RENGER, Berlin 1982, pp. 355-382.

[2] Discussions on Mesopotamian urbanism can be found in H. FRANKFORT, "Town planning in ancient Mesopotamia", *Town Planning Review*, 21 (1950), pp. 99-115; A.L. OPPENHEIM, *Ancient Mesopotamia: Portrait of a Dead Civilization*, Chicago & London 1964, pp. 109-142 (cf. ID., "Mesopotamia — land of many cities", *Middle Eastern Cities*, ed. I.M. LAPIDUS, Berkeley, Los Angeles, London 1969, pp. 3-18); P. MATTHIAE in *L'alba della civiltà*, ed. S. MOSCATI, vol. I, Turin 1976, pp. 102-139; J.-L. HUOT (ed.), *La ville neuve, une idée de l'antiquité?*, Paris 1988; J.-L. HUOT et al., *Naissance des cités*, Paris 1990; J.-C. MARGUERON, *Les Mésopotamiens*, vol. 1, Paris 1991, pp. 23-39; E.C. STONE, "The spatial organization of Mesopotamian cities", *Aula Orientalis*, 9 (1991), pp. 235-242. Plans of cities have been very conveniently collected by P. LAMP, *Cities and Planning in the Ancient Near East*, New York 1968.

Before going any further, however, it must be stressed that caution is necessary when studying the plans of ancient Near Eastern sites. Excavations have never been able to expose the entire settlement of any ancient Near Eastern site. Most often many important features, such as the street network, are not known. Moreover, in the particular case of Dur-Sharrukin, the city may not reflect the standard principles of Assyrian urbanism but only Sargon's personal ideas. As the king apparently wanted to create a new capital symbolizing a new era in the empire's history, he may have adopted a plan aiming to mark a departure from traditional urban development practices. Be that as it may, there is enough evidence to allow hypotheses to be made.

A few features of the urban layout of Dur-Sharrukin attract particular attention.[3] The settlement is almost perfectly square, with the four corners orientated to the cardinal points (fig. 1). According to the published plans, seven gates were opened in the four sides of the fortification wall (the number seven was probably not a coincidence although it must be noted that Sargon's inscriptions mention eight gates).[4] Two enclosed areas were visible on the north-west and south-west sides of the settlement, protruding outside the city-wall. These enclosed areas sheltered official — religious and administrative — buildings, but their location is surprising. One would have expected to find the official constructions in a more central position. The north-western area was the sector of the royal palace and, therefore, probably the most important one. It consisted of two distinct parts, both enclosed by the same fortification wall. The higher one, built on a platform, was the place where the royal palace stood and, next to it, a temple. This part was built astride the city fortification wall. The lower part included more palaces and also temples.

If we wanted to sum up these characteristics, we would say that the settlement was regular in size, with two official areas built, not in the middle of the site, but against, or rather astride, the city fortification wall, and that the main area consisted of several palaces and temples which were arranged in two separate sectors.

Where does this fit in the Assyrian tradition? If we consider other new, or renovated, Neo-Assyrian capital cities, Kalhu (modern Nimrud) and Nineveh are the closest in time. Kalhu was rebuilt, in the 9th century B.C., by Ashurnasirpal II who chose it as his residence.[5] The site is almost square, with straight walls on the west, north and east sides (fig. 2). Only the south side is more irregular. In the south-west corner was the main complex of buildings, the "acropolis", with palaces built by various kings, and temples. In the south-east corner was another public building, conventionally called Fort Shalmaneser. Both these complexes, built on the edge of the terrace

---

[3] See plan in G. LOUD & C.B. ALTMANN, *Khorsabad*, vol. II, Chicago 1938, pl. 69.
[4] D.D. LUCKENBILL, *Ancient Records from Assyria and Babylonia*, vol. 2, Chicago 1926, §§ 85 and 121.
[5] See plan in J. READE, "Nimrud", *Fifty Years of Mesopotamian Discoveries*, ed. J. CURTIS, London 1982, fig.75, p. 103 (after Felix Jones).

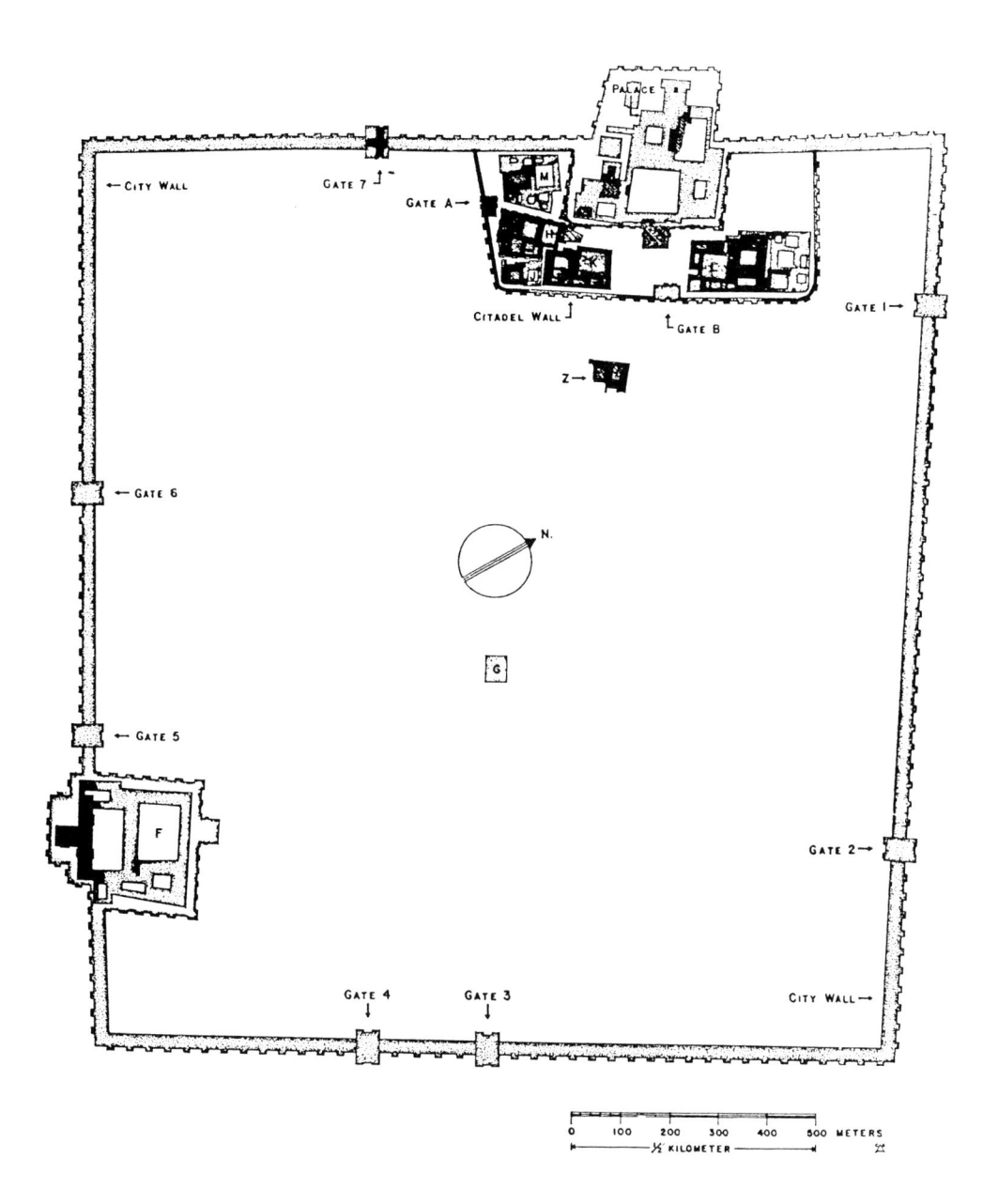

Figure 1: Plan of Khorsabad, ancient Dur-Sharrukin (from G. LOUD & C.B. ALTMANN, *Khorsabad*, vol. II, Chicago 1938, pl. 69).

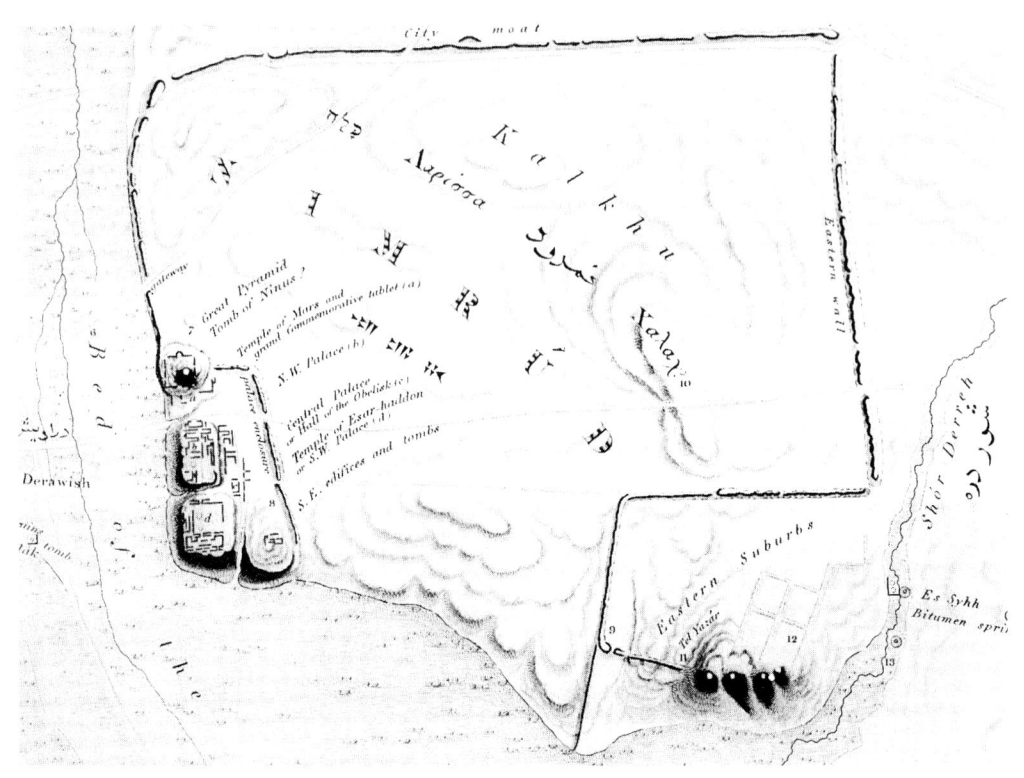

Figure 2: Plan of Nimrud, ancient Kalhu (from J. READE, "Nimrud", *Fifty Years of Mesopotamian Discoveries*, ed. J. CURTIS, London 1982, fig.75, p. 103).

overlooking the Tigris valley, seem to have been contained within the ramparts of the city. It must be noted that they were built against the ramparts and not in the middle of the settlement. It is impossible to say, however, to what extent this layout corresponded to a deliberate choice on the part of Ashurnasirpal II. The site of the two official complexes may have been selected because they offered an elevated position dominating their surroundings. Suffice it to say that the end result was quite close to the plan of Dur-Sharrukin. The main difference is probably the absence of a clear partition in the organization of the acropolis. It would seem possible, therefore, that Sargon had the model of Kalhu in mind when he devised the plan of Dur-Sharrukin.

The construction plan of Nineveh, chosen by Sennacherib as his capital city, is rather similar to that of Kalhu. It was surrounded by straight walls defining a sort of trapezoid (fig. 3).[6] Two existing mounds, Kuyunjik and Tell Nebi Yunus, were chosen as the site of official buildings. Apparently the main one, with palaces and temples,

[6] See plan in R.C. THOMPSON, "Excavations on the temple of Nabu at Nineveh," *Archaeologia*, 79 (1929), pp. 103-148 (pl. 61); J.M. RUSSELL, *Sennacherib's Palace without Rival at Nineveh*, Chicago 1991, fig. 1, p. 2 (after Felix Jones).

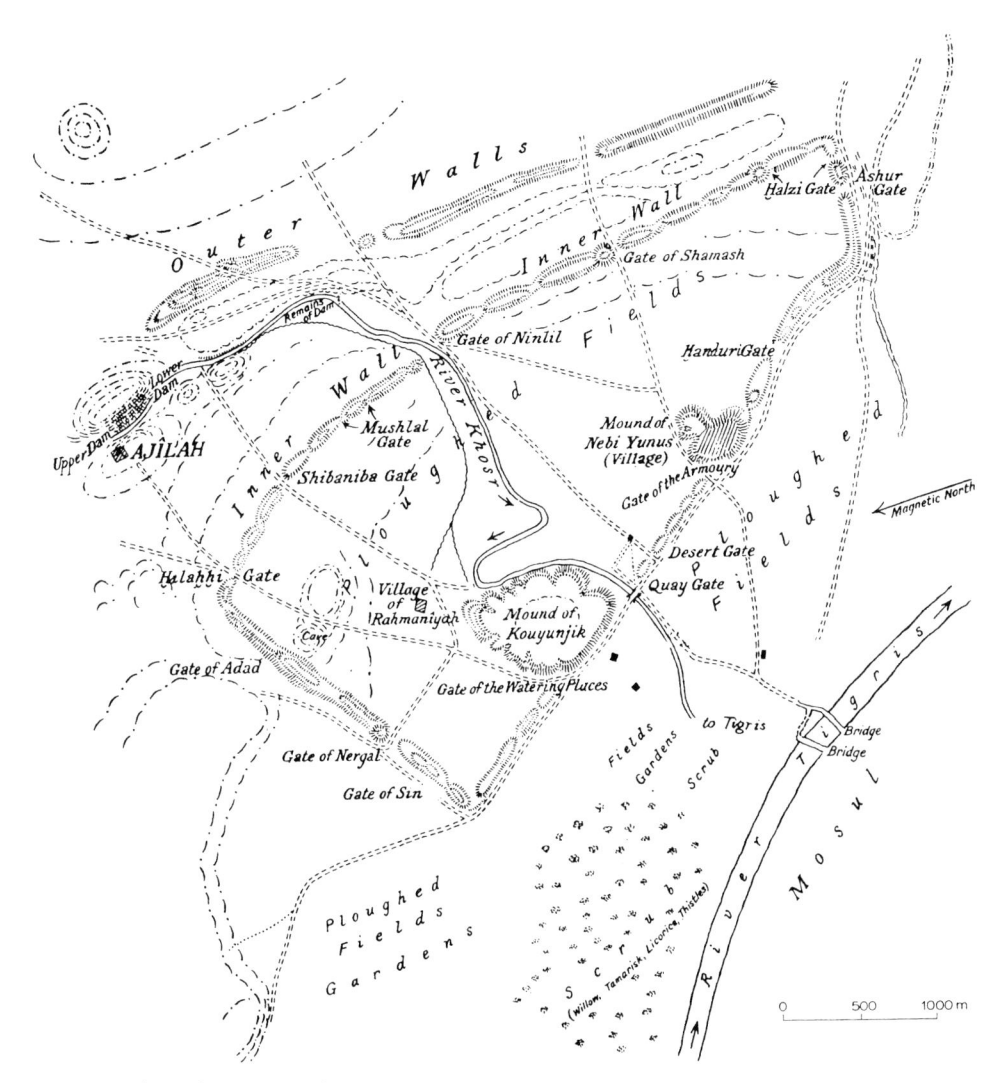

Figure 3: Plan of Nineveh (from R.C. THOMPSON, "Excavations on the temple of Nabu at Nineveh," *Archaeologia*, 79 [1929], pl. 61).

was Kuyunjik.[7] Both mounds stood on the edge of the settlement, against the enclosing wall towards the Tigris valley.

The three capital cities of the Neo-Assyrian empire thus shared common features: they were protected by a line of outer ramparts of a rather regular, squarish shape; they had two separate official quarters built against the enclosing wall; the major official quarter included the royal palace and consisted of several palaces and temples. The site of Dur-Sharrukin, which, as an entirely new city, was not subjected to the same

---

[7] R.C. THOMPSON, "The buildings on Quyunjik, the larger mound of Nineveh", *Iraq*, 1 (1934), pp. 95-104. On Tell Nebi Yunus: G. TURNER, "Tell Nebi Yūnus: The ekal mašarti of Nineveh", *Iraq*, 32 (1970), pp. 68-85.

natural constraints as Kalhu and Nineveh, shows that these features resulted from a deliberate choice and were not accidental.

The originality of this concept, which has already been emphasised by A.L. Oppenheim,[8] will be more apparent if we look at other examples of Mesopotamian urbanism. Assyria itself offers at least one more example of the construction of a new capital city. Tukulti-Ninurta I, in the 13th century B.C., founded a new capital on the left bank of the Tigris and called it Kar-Tukulti-Ninurta.[9] The settlement was roughly square in shape (fig. 4). Two palaces have been identified. One was built in the west corner, on the bank of the river; the other was at some distance to the south, also on the river bank. The temple of Assur was closer to the centre of the site. Such a layout offers some similarities to the later Neo-Assyrian capitals, namely the regular outer shape and the decentralized position of the palaces, but differs notably in the sense that the sacred and administrative buildings do not seem to have been grouped inside one or two fortified areas placed against the fortification wall. Both palaces and temple, as far as we can judge, were part of the urban structure.

The plan of Kar-Tukulti-Ninurta is similar to that of other newly founded Mesopotamian cities. The Old Babylonian city of Shaduppum, for instance, which is the modern Tell Harmal, was also quadrangular with several temples and at least one administrative building integrated into the urban scheme.[10] A similar plan seems to have been adopted for Haradum, in the land of Suhu on the Euphrates, built roughly at the same time.[11] Old cities, which underwent a renovation programme, seem to have adopted a similar plan. The centre of Babylon, for instance, entirely rebuilt in the 6th century B.C., is also contained within a quadrangular enclosure with religious and public buildings erected in various places.[12]

If we now turn to settlements that gradually developed over the centuries, we notice even more dissimilarities between them and the Neo-Assyrian capital cities. Assur itself was significantly different.[13] The old city apparently grew around the temple of Assur, to which temples of other deities, palaces and domestic quarters were added. A new city extended to the south along the Tigris river. The old city, however, cannot be considered as a sort of acropolis, similar to the main administrative complex in the

---

[8] A.L. OPPENHEIM, *op. cit.* (n. 2), pp. 129, 132-135. L. BATTINI, "La città quadrata: un modello urbano nella Mesopotamia del II e I millennio a.C.?", *Orient Express*, 1994/2, pp. 49-50, does not pay enough attention to the differences, outlined below, that existed between Dur-Sharrukin and other Mesopotamian square cities.

[9] See plan in T. EICKHOFF, "Kār-Tukulti-Ninurta", *Reallexikon der Assyriologie*, 5/5-6 (1980), p. 457.

[10] T. BAQIR, *Tell Harmal*, Baghdad 1959, fig. 1.

[11] C. KEPINSKI-LECOMTE, *Haradum, 1, Une ville nouvelle sur le Moyen-Euphrate (XVIIIe-XVIIe siècles av. J.-C.)*, Paris 1992.

[12] R. KOLDEWEY, *Das wieder erstehende Babylon*, new ed. by B. HROUDA, Munich 1990. A.L. OPPENHEIM, *op. cit.* (n. 2), p. 133, notes that the royal palace built by Nebuchadnezzar was part of the fortification system and explains it as an Assyrian influence.

[13] W. ANDRAE, *Das wiedererstandene Assur*, rev. ed. by B. HROUDA, Munich 1977.

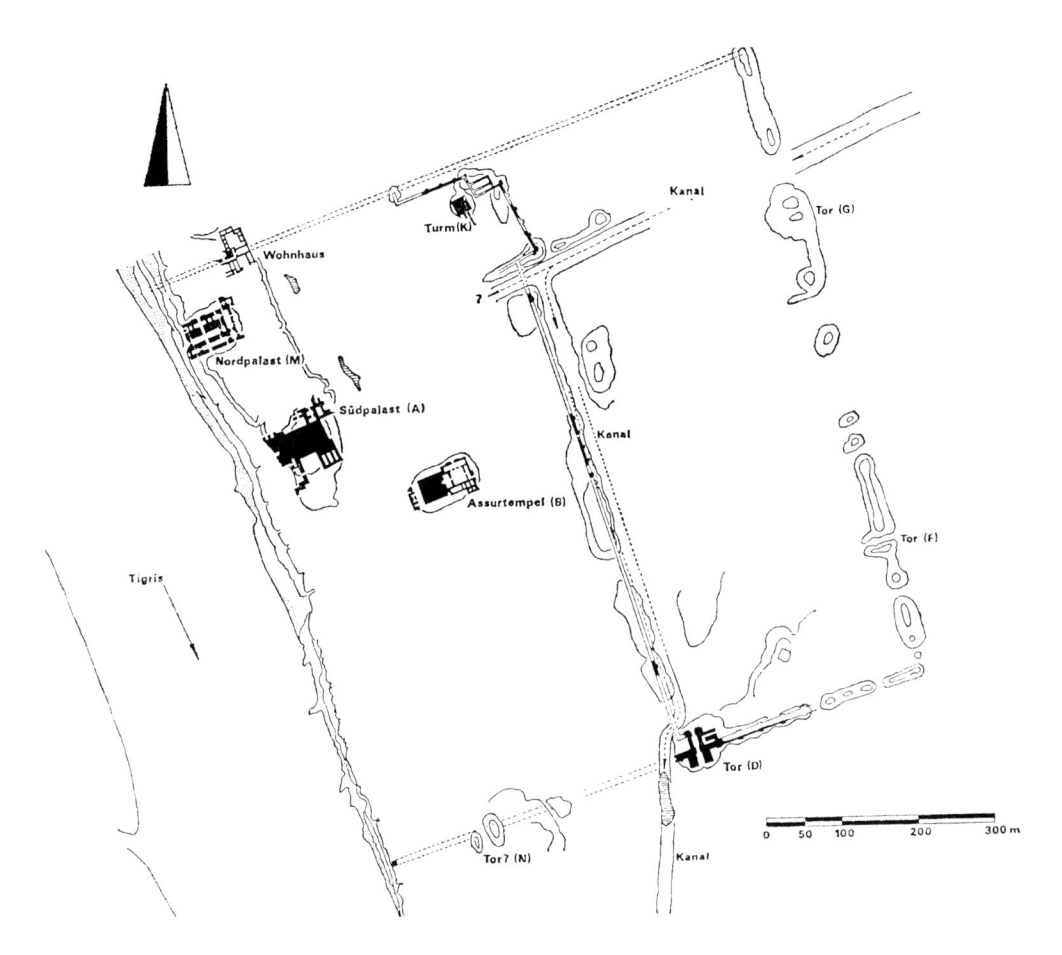

Figure 4: Plan of Kar-Tukulti-Ninurta (from T. EICKHOFF, "Kār-Tukulti-Ninurta", *Reallexikon der Assyriologie*, 5/5-6 [1980], p. 457).

Neo-Assyrian capitals, because it was the city itself. The new city was only an extension of the old one.

The Babylonian centres (e.g. Nippur, Ur, Uruk, Kish, Eshnunna, Isin, Larsa)[14] do not offer a significantly different picture. The overall shape of the settlement was usually irregular and resulted from alterations during the course of history. Temples and official buildings, essentially palaces, could be erected towards the centre of the settlement, or in a more marginal position, but they did not form a distinct and well defined sector placed on the edge of the site. In fact, the opposite situation seems to have been the rule. A.L. Oppenheim noted that the main sanctuary was separated from both the palace and the main wall,[15] and E.C. Stone went as far as to say that

[14] See the discussion and bibliography in E.C. STONE, *loc. cit.* (n. 2).
[15] A.L. OPPENHEIM, *op. cit.* (n. 2), p. 130.

"the locations of temples and administrative centers in Mesopotamian sites suggest a pattern of opposition".[16] The grouping of temples and palaces into one well defined sector seems to be alien to the Mesopotamian tradition.

The Neo-Assyrian capital cities, even though they might have presented some similarities to the Mesopotamian urban tradition (for instance the square plan), were thus remarkably original in their conception.

A.L. Oppenheim explained this originality by the desire of the Assyrian kings to adopt the plan of a military camp.[17] According to him, "representations of Assyrian military camps, rectangular or round, show the royal tent, together with the sacred standards, consistently placed off center, in fact quite near to the stockade which surrounds the rows of tents."[18] It is difficult, however, to see why the Assyrians would have adopted the square plan in preference to the round if both were indifferently used for setting up their camps. It is also difficult to see why the camp must have given its shape to the ideal city and not the reverse. One would rather expect that the camp was reproducing the plan of the ideal city. Indeed, the literary tradition, recently studied by Sylvie Lackenbacher,[19] makes it quite clear that the Assyrians, when they were building new capitals, intended them to be their permanent residence as well as that of the gods. It seems, therefore, that they adopted the quadrangular plan because it was the traditional plan of Mesopotamian new cities, but that they decided to group together temples and palaces and to include them in the fortification system for reasons that still need to be determined.

To find parallels and suggest an explanation for this new practice we must look further west. The site of Tell Halaf, for instance, is strangely reminiscent of Dur-Sharrukin.[20] In the early first millennium B.C. Tell Halaf, called Guzana, had a quadrangular plan with an acropolis built on its northern side on the bank of the Habur river (fig. 5). The acropolis itself included various official buildings. As it cannot be entirely excluded that such a layout resulted from Assyrian interference in the local affairs, we must now consider the Syrian tradition of urbanism, of which Tell Halaf was also part. The use of the architectural form of the porticoed building with a central broad room, usually referred to as *bit hilani*, for the so-called temple-palace on the acropolis, is a clear indication of this western affiliation.

There was a tendency in second millennium Syria[21] to adopt a type of urban settlement plan in which a palace and a temple were located near one of the city

---

[16] E.C. STONE, *loc. cit.* (n. 2), p. 238.
[17] A.L. OPPENHEIM, *op. cit.* (n. 2), pp. 134-135.
[18] *Ibid.*, p. 134.
[19] S. LACKENBACHER, *Le roi bâtisseur: Les récits de construction assyriens des origines à Téglathphalasar III*, Paris 1982, and *Le palais sans rival: Le récit de construction en Assyrie*, Paris 1990.
[20] F. LANGENEGGER, K. MÜLLER & R. NAUMANN, *Tell Halaf*, vol. II, *Die Bauwerke*, Berlin 1950, plan 1.
[21] On urbanism in Bronze Age Syria and Palestine, cf. J.-P. THALMANN, "Les villes de l'âge du Bronze levantin", in J.-L. HUOT et al., *Naissance des cités*, Paris 1990, pp. 75-178.

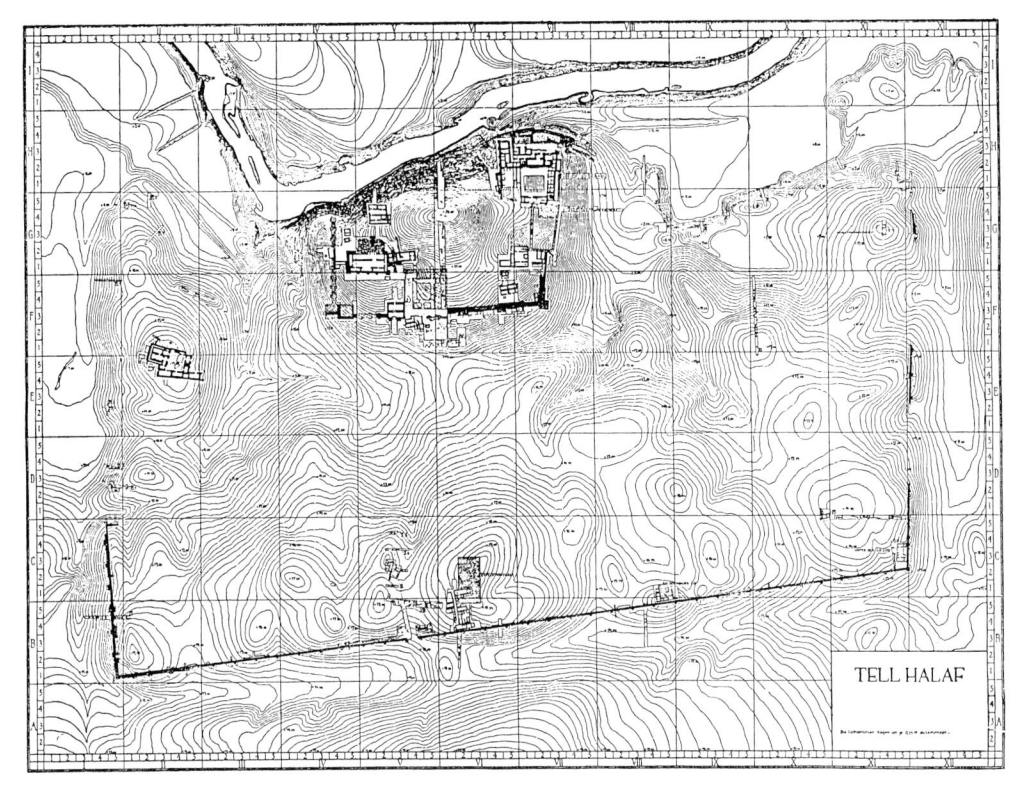

Figure 5: Plan of Tell Halaf, ancient Guzana (from F. LANGENEGGER, K. MÜLLER & R. NAUMANN, *Tell Halaf*, vol. II, *Die Bauwerke*, Berlin 1950, plan 1).

gates.[22] This is first evidenced at Alalakh in the Middle Bronze Age. The palace of level VII, probably dating from the 18th century B.C., was clearly associated with a temple and both were located in the north-western part of the site near a gate (fig. 6).[23] In the Late Bronze Age, still at Alalakh, in level IV dating to the 15th century, the same organization was reproduced but in a more integrated form.[24] The palace was rebuilt closer to the gate and now formed part of a fortified complex that included, besides the palace, a large structure called the "castle" by the excavator, the city gate, an open space between the "castle" and the palace, and an inner gate leading from this complex into the city to the south (fig. 7). The temple was still in the close

---

[22] Cf. A.L. OPPENHEIM, *op. cit.* (n. 2), p. 130, who calls it the "citadel city"; G.R.H. WRIGHT, *Ancient Building in South Syria and Palestine*, vol. 1, Leiden & Cologne 1985, p. 273; J.-P. THALMANN, *loc. cit.* (n. 21), p. 135. For a different interpretation of the gate-palace-temple complex see A. HARIF, "Common architectural features at Alalakh, Megiddo and Shechem", *Levant*, 11 (1979), pp. 162-167. A similar grouping of a palace and a temple near a fortification wall is found at Eshnunna in the early second millennium B.C. (P. DELOUGAZ *et al.*, *Private Houses and Graves in the Diyala Region*, Chicago 1967, pl. 23). Such a grouping seems to be isolated in the Mesopotamian tradition.

[23] C.L. WOOLLEY, *Alalakh: An Account of the Excavations at Tell Atchana in the Hatay, 1937-1949*, Oxford 1955, The buildings of level VII general plan and fig. 35.

[24] *Ibid.*, Level IV general plan, fig. 44 and 57.

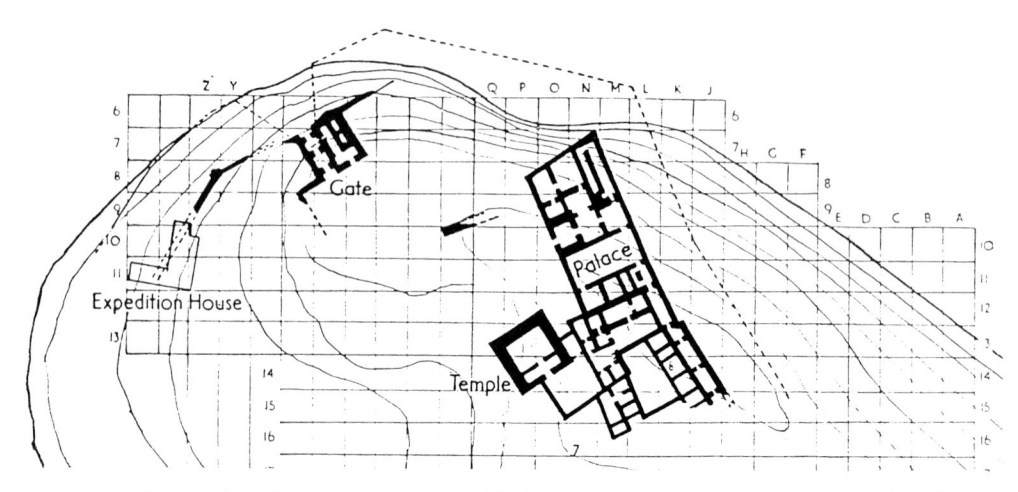

Figure 6: Plan of the official sector of Alalakh, level VII (from C.L. WOOLLEY, *Alalakh: An Account of the Excavations at Tell Atchana in the Hatay, 1937-1949*, Oxford 1955).

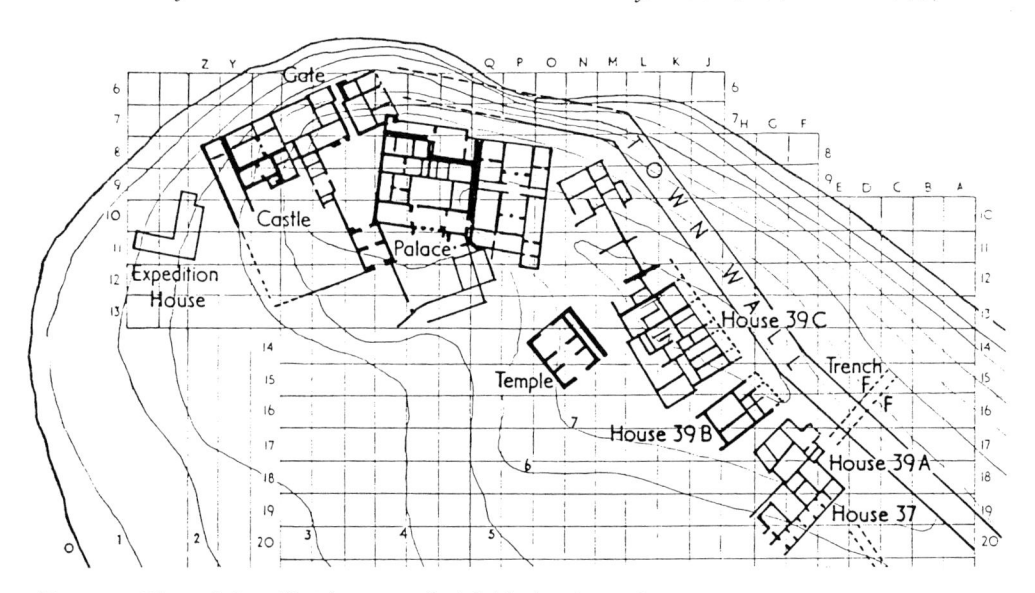

Figure 7: Plan of the official sector of Alalakh, level IV (from C.L. WOOLLEY, *Alalakh: An Account of the Excavations at Tell Atchana in the Hatay, 1937-1949*, Oxford 1955).

vicinity of the palace, although we do not know whether it was included in the same enclosed area as the palace. Alalakh thus offers an early example of an official quarter, separated from the rest of the settlement, and placed on the edge of the site.

The same form of organization is also found at Ugarit in the Late Bronze Age.[25] Here the royal palace stood near the north-western corner of the site. It was part of a

---

[25] See O. CALLOT, "La région nord du palais royal d'Ougarit", *Comptes Rendus de l'Académie des Inscriptions et Belles Lettres*, 1986, pp. 735-755, cf. M. YON, "Ugarit: The urban habitat — The present state of the archaeological picture", *Bulletin of the American Schools of Oriental Research*, 286 (May 1992), pp. 25-26.

larger complex which included a city gate to the west, an open space between the gate and the palace, a temple (the so-called "sanctuaire hourrite") to the north-east and a group of buildings, which probably had a ceremonial function, to the north (fig. 8). This entire complex was isolated from the city by gates that closed the streets running to the north and south-west of the royal palace. The structure was more elaborate than that of Alalakh in level IV and it also included a temple whilst, at Alalakh, the temple might have remained outside the fortified complex. The conception, however, was the same.

More evidence can be found in Palestine. At Megiddo, in area AA in the Late Bronze Age, a palace stood near a gate in the north-western part of the settlement.[26] The excavation reports do not make it possible to say whether there was also a temple in the close vicinity or whether there was an enclosure to isolate the administrative complex. At Shechem, in the Middle Bronze Age, a temple and associated buildings were excavated near a gate, again in the north-western part of the settlement.[27] At Hazor, in the Middle and Late Bronze Ages, the acropolis stood at the south-eastern end of the site. It was fortified and included a temple as well as, possibly, a palace.[28]

This form of urban organization survived in the Iron Age. At Tell Tayinat, which was probably the ancient Kunaluwa in the Amuq plain, two *bit hilani*s and a temple were built on the western part of the tell.[29] A gate gave access to the complex. It should also be remembered that Solomonic Jerusalem seems to have been inspired by a similar model. Solomon built his palace, the palace of the daughter of Pharaoh and the temple of Yahweh in the eastern part of the city, on a terrace overlooking the Kidron valley.[30]

Another, concurrent but similar, model may have affected Syrian urbanism in the Iron Age. Its origin lies in Hittite Anatolia.[31] The site of Hattusha, capital of the Hittite empire in the Late Bronze Age, developed features which are not too dissimilar to those of the Syrian sites just described.[32] Hattusha, in the Middle Bronze Age, grew from an early settlement on the hill called Büyükkale to include a lower city which extended to the north-west of the hill. In the Late Bronze Age, the site extended

---

[26] Cf. A. KEMPINSKI, *Megiddo: A City-State and Royal Centre in North Israel*, Munich 1989, plans 5 to 10.

[27] Cf. E.F. CAMPBELL, "Shechem", *The New Encyclopedia of Archaeological Excavations in the Holy Land*, vol. 4, Jerusalem 1993, pp. 1349-1351 (map of the site p. 1346).

[28] Y. YADIN, "Hazor", *The New Encyclopedia of Archaeological Excavations in the Holy Land*, vol. 2, Jerusalem 1993, pp. 599-600.

[29] R.C. HAINES, *Excavations in the Plain of Antioch*, vol. II, *The Structural Remains of the Later Phases*, Chicago 1971.

[30] 1 *Kings* 3:1, 7:1-12, 9:24. Cf. G.R.H. WRIGHT, *op. cit.* (n. 22), pp. 61-62.

[31] On Hittite urbanism see R. NAUMANN, *Architektur Kleinasiens von ihren Anfängen bis zum Ende der hethitischen Zeit*, 2nd ed., Tübingen 1971, pp. 212-235; J.-P. THALMANN, *loc. cit.* (n. 21), pp. 153-166.

[32] K. BITTEL, *Hattuscha, Hauptstadt der Hethiter*, 2nd ed., Cologne 1983; P. NEVE, *Ḫattuša, Stadt der Götter und Tempel: Neue Ausgrabungen in der Hauptstadt der Hethiter*, Mainz 1993.

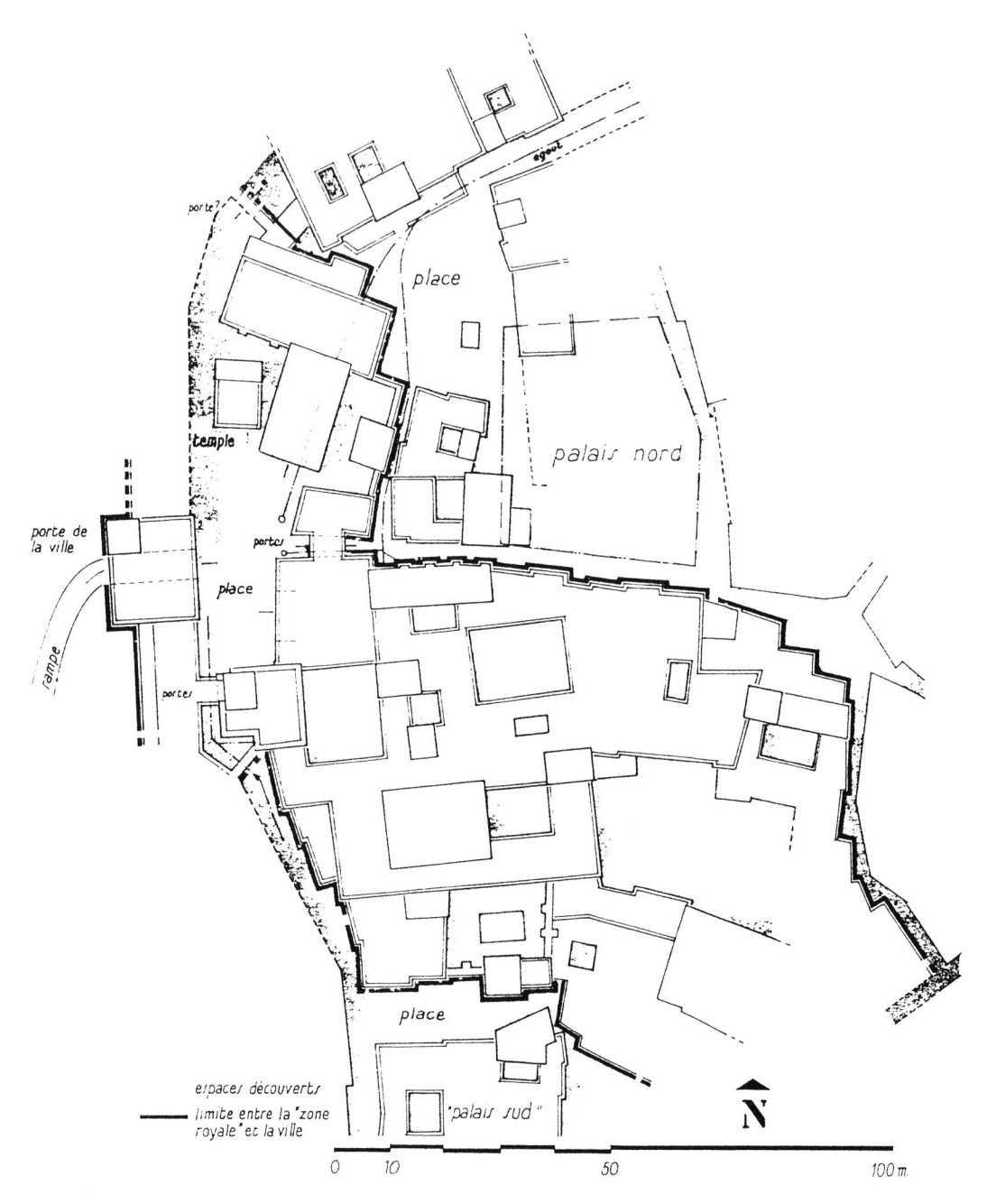

Figure 8: Plan of the official sector of Ugarit (from O. CALLOT, "La région nord du palais royal d'Ougarit", *Comptes Rendus de l'Académie des Inscriptions et Belles Lettres*, 1986, fig. 2, p. 738).

further southwards into the high land that dominated Büyükkale so that, in the imperial period, it consisted of three parts: an acropolis (Büyükkale) with a palatial complex; a lower city with a large temple complex in the middle of domestic quarters; and an upper city with more temples and domestic buildings (fig. 9). The structure of the acropolis is most remarkable in the sense that it does not consist of one palatial structure, or one palace flanked by a few secondary buildings (as, for instance, at Alalakh and Ugarit), but included various buildings probably fulfilling different functions which normally fell within the responsibilities of the palace institution. Also remarkable is the fact that, throughout the history of the site, the acropolis has been on the eastern side of the settlement and that no attempt seems to have been made to place this symbolic structure in the middle of the settlement. Lastly, and contrary to the Syrian model outlined above, no sacred structure seems to have been associated with the palatial complex.

In the Iron Age Carchemish seems to have combined the Hittite and Syrian traditions. The role of Carchemish was crucial in the transmission of the Bronze Age heritage to the Iron Age. It was the Hittite capital of Syria at the time of the empire in the second millennium. It survived the turmoil of the end of the Bronze Age[33] and remained one of the most powerful states of northern Syria until its conquest by the Assyrians in 743 B.C.[34]

Carchemish, as Hattusha, consisted of three parts (fig. 10).[35] An acropolis stood on its north-eastern side dominating the Euphrates river. To the south-west an oval city was enclosed by a wall and, further west, south-west and south, an outer city, also enclosed by a wall, formed the third part of the settlement. The overall shape of the settlement was that of a rough hexagon or a square with rounded or cut angles.

The acropolis displayed some features akin to those of the Syrian tradition. It seems to have had its own gate, which the excavators called the Water Gate. From the Water Gate a street led to a monumental staircase, that gave access to the acropolis, and to a large gate leading into the lower city.[36] On the acropolis there was at least one temple that can be identified as that of Kubaba, the main deity of Carchemish. However, unlike the Syrian tradition but similar to the Hittite tradition, several secular buildings also stood on the acropolis.[37]

In summary, it seems that two urban traditions combined in northern Syria in the early Iron Age to give a well defined type of settlement. The first tradition was of Hittite origin. It associated various palatial buildings, erected on an acropolis which stood on the

---

[33] J.D. HAWKINS, "The Neo-Hittite states in Syria and Anatolia", *The Cambridge Ancient History*, 2nd ed., vol. III/1, Cambridge 1982, pp. 380-381; ID., "Karkamiš", *Reallexikon der Assyriologie*, 5/5-6 (1980), pp. 434-446.

[34] Cf. I.J. WINTER, "Carchemish ša Kišad Puratti", *Anatolian Studies*, 33 (1983), pp. 177-197.

[35] See plan in C.L. WOOLLEY, *Carchemish: Report on the Excavations at Jerablus on Behalf of the British Museum*, Part II, London 1921, plate 3.

[36] See plan in C.L. WOOLLEY, *Carchemish: Report on the Excavations at Jerablus on Behalf of the British Museum*, Part III, London 1952, plate 41a. This plan has been combined with the map of the site by J.D. HAWKINS, "Karkamiš", *Reallexikon der Assyriologie*, 5/5-6 (1980), p. 427.

[37] C.L. WOOLLEY, *op. cit.* (n. 36), pp. 205-214.

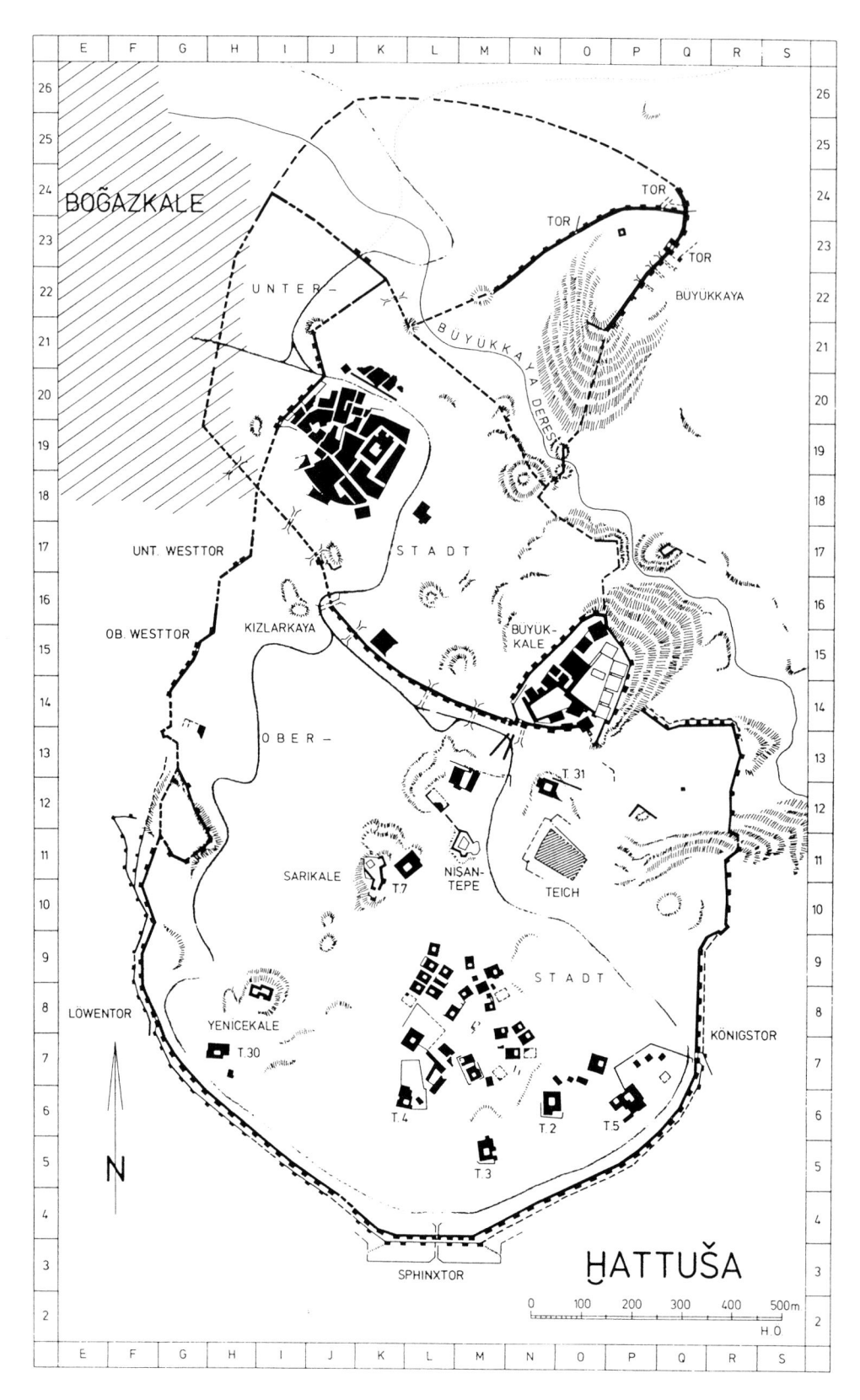

Figure 9: Plan of Boğazköy, ancient Hattusha (from P. NEVE, "Die Ausgrabungen in Boğazköy-Hattuša 1993", *Archäologischer Anzeiger*, 1994, Abb. 1, p. 290).

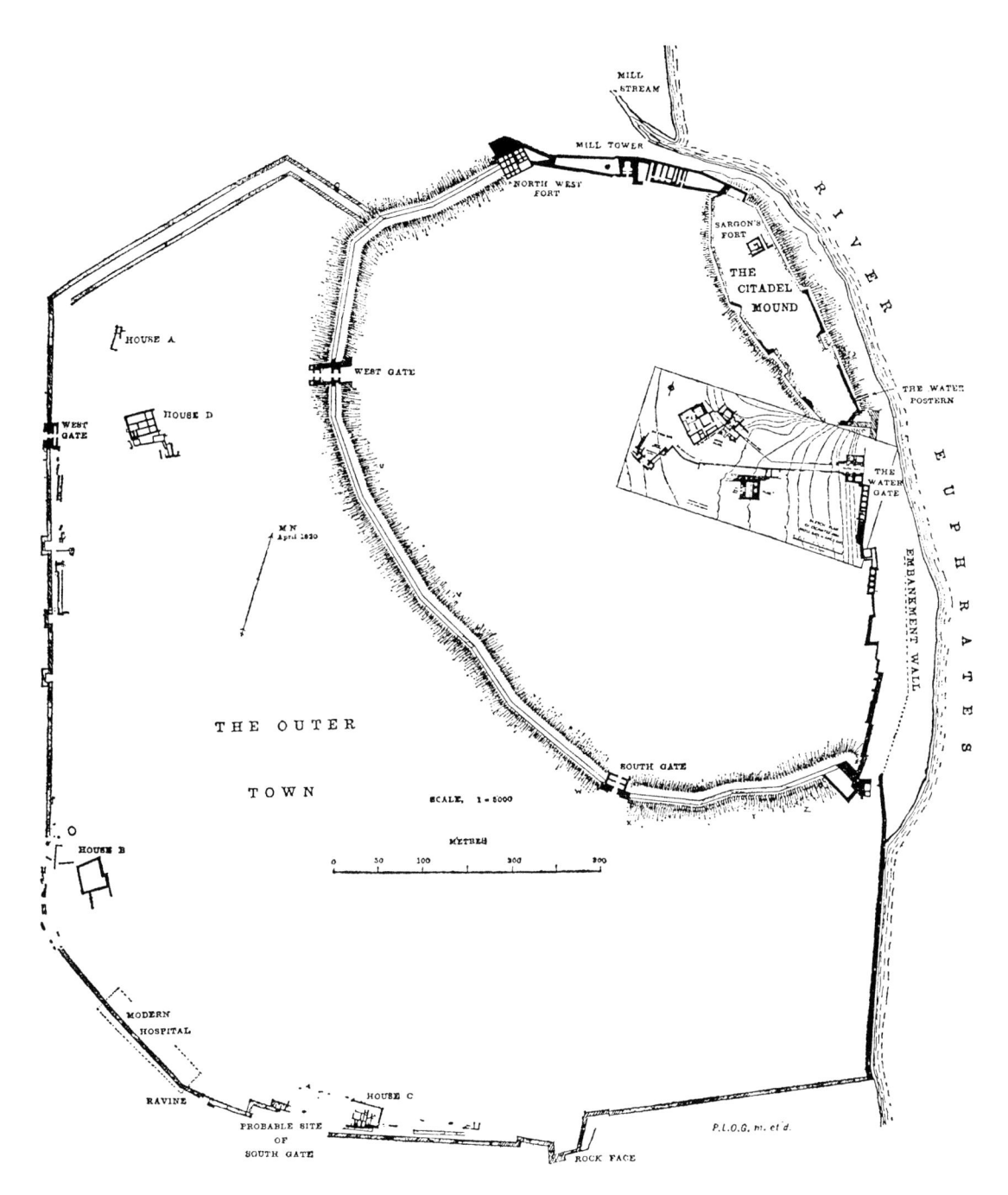

Figure 10: Plan of Carchemish (from J.D. Hawkins, "Karkamiš", *Reallexikon der Assyriologie*, 5/5-6 [1980], p. 427).

side of the settlement, with an inner and an outer (at Hattusha upper) city. The second tradition was of Syrian origin and was best represented at Alalakh and Ugarit. It placed a palace, a temple and a few secondary buildings in a precinct erected near a city gate. The combination of these traditions resulted in settlements with an acropolis, on which several religious and palatial buildings were grouped on the edge of the site, and a simple or double lower city surrounded by a wall of regular, usually quadrangular, shape.

This tradition was not the only one. Sites such as Early and Middle Bronze Age Ebla and Mari in Syria,[38] Middle Bronze Age Alishar and Kültepe in Anatolia and Iron Age Zincirli in the bordering zone between Anatolia and Syria,[39] to mention just a few, show that there were other conceptions of town planning.

Tell Halaf belonged to the combined, Syro-Anatolian, type described above and, given the similarities we observed between Tell Halaf and Dur-Sharrukin, it shows the tradition in the light of which Dur-Sharrukin and the other Neo-Assyrian capital cities should be evaluated. It is remarkable that some Neo-Assyrian provincial centres were probably derived from the same model. Dur-Katlimmu, on the lower Habur river, for instance, was built on a plan that resembled very closely that of Carchemish.[40]

This type of urban layout may have been borrowed by the Assyrians when they came into contact with North Syria in the early first millennium B.C.[41] In doing so, however, the Assyrians were not slavish. As A.L. Oppenheim noted, the entrance to the acropolis complex was through the lower city in Neo-Assyrian capitals.[42] The concept of an association of the palace and temple complex with a city-gate was therefore absent in these cities. On the other hand, the second walled quarter (represented by Fort Shalmaneser at Kalhu, the fortified complex in the south-west wall at Dur-Sharrukin and Tell Nebi Yunus at Nineveh) finds no parallel in Syria nor Anatolia. It must be considered as specifically Assyrian.

P.S. The following book was not avalaible to me at the time of writing: S. MAZZONI (ed.), *Nuove fondazioni nel Vicino antico: Realtà e ideologia*, Seminari di orientalistica, 4, Pisa, 1994.

---

[38] Ebla: P. MATTHIAE, "Architettura e urbanistica di Ebla paleosiriana", *La Parola del Passato*, 46 (1991), pp. 304-371; R. DOLCE, "Tell Mardikh-Ebla da Ur III a Mursili I: una città da riscoprire", *Orient Express*, 1995/1, pp. 10-12. Mari: see the plans in A. PARROT, *Mari capitale fabuleuse*, Paris 1974, pp. 27 and 96, and J.-C. MARGUERON, *Les Mésopotamiens*, vol. 2, Paris 1991, p. 24.

[39] R. NAUMANN, *op. cit.* (n. 31), fig. 293, p. 229 (Alishar); fig. 294, p. 230 (Kültepe); fig.298, p. 232 (Zincirli).

[40] On the urban layout of Dur-Katlimmu see H. KÜHNE, "Gedanken zur historischen und städtebaulichen Entwicklung der assyrischen Stadt Dūr-Katlimmu", *Resurrecting the Past: A Joint Tribute to Adnan Bounni*, ed. P. MATTHIAE et al., Leiden 1990, pp. 153-169; ID., "Vier spätbabylonischen Tontafeln aus Tall Šēḫ-Ḥamad, Ost-Syrien", *State Archives of Assyria Bulletin*, 7 (1993), p. 76 and fig. 4, p. 90.

[41] I.J. WINTER, *loc. cit.* (n. 1), p. 357, was already of the opinion that "it was the initial contact of Tukulti-Ninurta II (890-884 B.C.) and his son, Assurnasirpal II (883-859 B.C.), with the states of North Syria in the first millennium that provided the immediate stimulus for the latter's major building program at Nimrud."

[42] A.L. OPPENHEIM, *op. cit.* (n. 2), p. 133.

CULTURAL INTERACTION IN NORTH SYRIA IN THE ROMAN AND BYZANTINE PERIODS THE EVIDENCE OF PERSONAL NAMES

BY

Graeme W. CLARKE

One possible entry into the question of cultural interaction in an area (e.g. North Syria) is to examine the onomastics to be found within a circumscribed district.[1] This will not necessarily reveal the precise ethnic origins of the individuals named but it will at least reveal some of the ethnic history of the region which gave currency to the names so chosen. Likewise, theophoric names may not in themselves provide evidence for the religious adherence of individuals but they will, again, at least reveal something of the background religious history of the area which allowed currency to the names so bestowed. The choice of language of the recordings (e.g. Greek, Latin, Syriac) will again have a bearing on ethnic and cultural influences. But it has to be borne in mind as a major *caveat* to the whole enterprise that changing fashions in epigraphic habit, not to mention the chance nature of much survival as well as of discovery, do ensure that such sampling will be far from ideal: it may well indeed be misleadingly unrepresentative.

The eleven items listed below pp. 142-143 record individual publications of inscribed surfaces discovered in the course of surveying the environs of Jebel Khalid in North Syria and of excavating the site of Jebel Khalid itself, a Hellenistic site on the West bank of the Euphrates in the middle of the Big Bend, approximately half-way between Jerablus and Meskene. I shall refer to the texts by item number, leaving detailed references to be found in the relevant items of bibliography. What is here attempted is a survey and analysis of all the evidence for personal names thus accumulated within a three to four kilometre radius of Jebel Khalid. None of the texts can be firmly dated: the earliest may be items 9 and 10 (? third/fourth centuries A.D.), the latest (in item 2) even datable to the twelfth century A.D. but the bulk fall within the (vague) range of the late Roman/early Byzantine period — say, fourth to sixth centuries A.D. They do not all therefore form a chronologically homogeneous set neither are they homogeneous in type (though sepulchral inscriptions predominate) — but they can

---

[1] I wish to record my gratitude to the authorities of the Syrian Department of Antiquities and Museums, in particular to Dr Adnan Bounni and Dr Sultan Muhesen, over the last decade during which this research in the region of el-Qitar and Jebel Khalid has been carried out. For further studies on the onomastics of the region see the survey of J.-P. REY-COQUAIS, "Onomastique et histoire de la Syrie gréco-romaine", *Actes du IIe Congrès International d'Épigraphie grecque et latine, Costanza, 9-15 septembre 1977*, ed. D.M. PIPPIDI, Bucharest 1979, pp. 171 ff. and the literature there cited.

still be exploited to disclose something of the changing ethnic, cultural and religious history of life in this rural region of the Middle Euphrates.

I take the funerary monuments first.

Item 4 (fig. 1), a reused *stele* in the graveyard of the present village of Joussef Pasha, records the honorand as Semon (Semitic) and the dedicator as one Abola (? his daughter) — the nearest parallel for the name being Abolus, from Phrygia. The inscription is in large Greek lettering but the control over the language is somewhat shaky (false tense to the verb, mistaken case-ending to the noun). There are what appear to be touches of Christianity (e.g. cross within a phi). This looks to be a monument of a local Syrian family, aspiring to display (not very ably) late Roman levels of culture and Greek literacy (Greek being still regarded as the language for public display), as well as their adherence to Christianity.

Item 5 (fig. 2, 3, 4), a trefoil *hypogeum* near Joussef Pasha, records in Greek outside each of the three *arcisolia* what appear to be the names of their respective owners. One is Hermes (a pagan Greek theophoric), the second is Barachathas (a pagan Semitic theophoric = Blessed of Athē, but assimilated to a standard Greek ending), the third is Marcos Thymos Akebas (that is to say, one Latin praenomen [Marcus] plus two Semitic theophorics, Thymus = TYM [Servant], but assimilated to a Greek-sounding word, and Akebas = 'QB [Whom God Guards], a common Aramaean name, again graced with a Greek termination). If these three names belong to one person, is it a rather bizarre attempt to imitate the Roman *tria nomina*? The MA (? = makarios, blessed) which precedes this third inscription may indicate Christian adherence. All told, a mixture of three Semitic names (all theophoric), one Greek and one Latin personal name, found together in a contemporary setting, written in Greek with Greek terminal forms and despite the theophorics with a strong indicator of Christianity in at least one case.

Item 6 (fig. 5, 6, 7), a similar trefoil *hypogeum* in the same locality, manifests sixteen naming elements (six being repeated), recording presumably the names of inhabitants of the various *loculi*. They range from being Latin in origin, Flavius, Longinus (both twice), through Greek, Gleki(o)s (twice), Stephana, to four Semitic, Vaklios (twice), Vabaios, Baroiaros, Kousatos, plus two that appear to be Iranian in origin, Kareigar, Kamiste(s) (both twice), perhaps a legacy traceable to the Persian period (pockets of Iranizing populations surviving until late Antiquity in Eastern Anatolia, being called Magusaioi by Basil of Cappadocia). Given the intermingling and repetition of the various naming elements this *hypogeum* would appear to have functioned as a family vault — and, as such, reveals some of the ethnic amalgam and political history of the region. The script is in Greek but with a number of orthographical slips (the various hands are not very practised) and with some shaky Greek grammar. There is, in this case, no sign of Christianity.

CULTURAL INTERACTION IN NORTH SYRIA

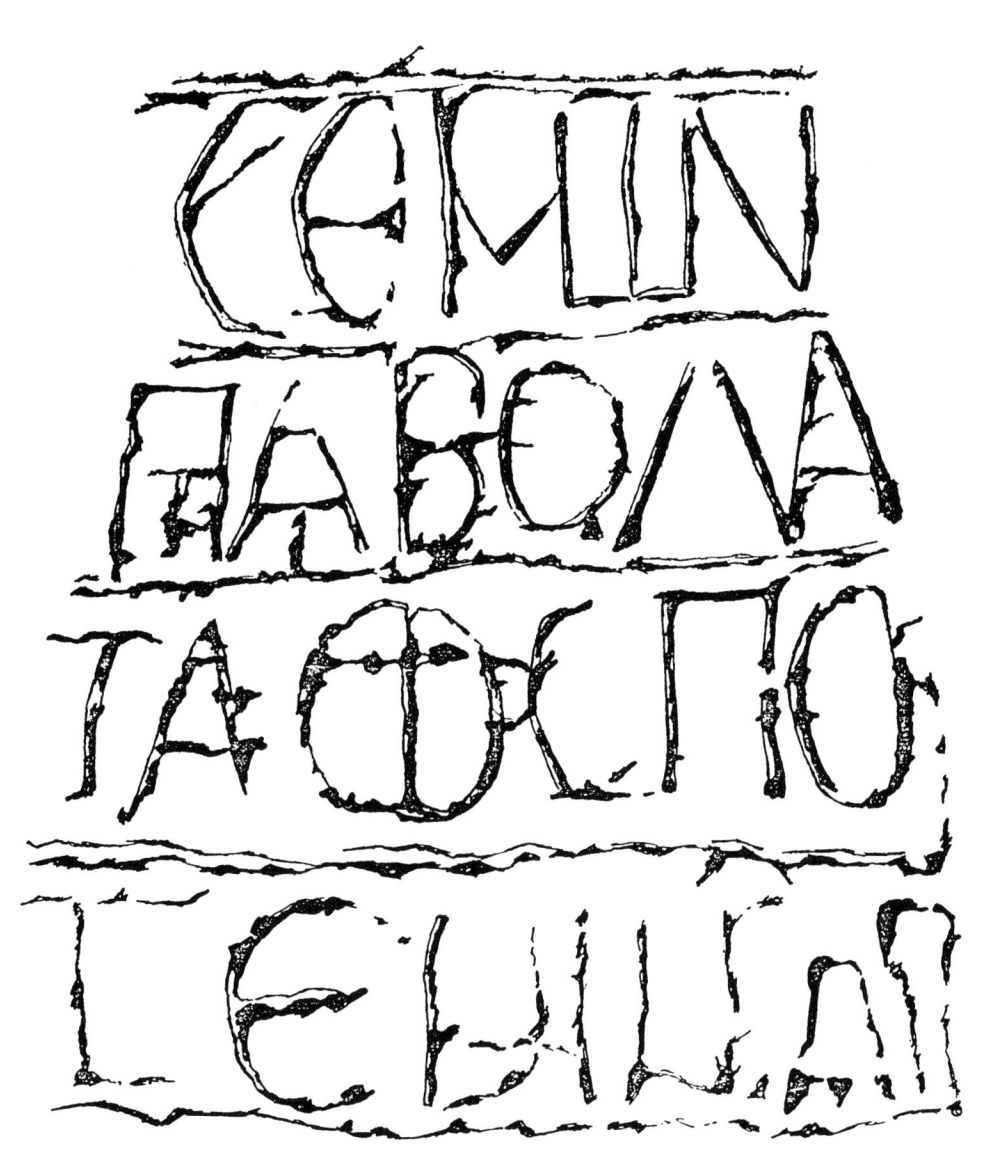

Transcription

1. Ϲ Ε Μ Ω Ν
2. Π Α Β Ο Λ Α
3. Τ Α Φ ο Ϲ Π Ο
4. ι Ε ι [- - - -]

Σεμων/ π(α)τ(ρι) Ἀβολα/ ταφος πο/ιει - - - -

Translation (tentative only):

+Abola makes this tomb + for her father Semon ....

Figure 1

Figure 2

CULTURAL INTERACTION IN NORTH SYRIA 133

Figure 3

Figure 4

Figure 5

Figure 6

Figure 7

Figure 8

Item 9 (fig. 8, 9) reports Greek graffiti found on plaster fragments in the course of excavating the Acropolis Palace on Jebel Khalid. Given the heavy pillaging of this building after it was left derelict and the location of the graffiti themselves (they come from wall blocks originally high up near the ceiling and are most likely to have been inscribed after the blocks had already fallen), they are more likely to be datable to the looting period rather than to that of the Hellenistic inhabitants of the Acropolis. (Some looting can be dated by coin finds in robbed areas to the fourth century A.D.). Only one name, Latin in origin, can possibly be reconstructed, ko[i]ntos, Quintus.

Item 10 (fig. 10, 11) is a fragmentary limestone altar block found at the base of the North face of Jebel Khalid, dating to the middle to late Roman Empire. Its dedicatory inscription, in Latin, may record one Roman name 1UST? (?-us, -ius, -inus, -inius etc.). More likely than not this may be the name of a Roman official, Latin texts being relatively rare in this region. The dedication is pagan (to I[uppiter] O[ptimus] M[aximus]).

Christian presence in the region is well attested, both in the reused Classical building material in the cemetry of the village of Joussef Pasha (see item 4) and in the funerary decoration of tombs in its environs (see item 3: no names are discernible in the fragmentary and largely illegible Greek inscription). This is also the case with Jebel Khalid itself and the village to its immediate North, Kirbet Khalid. Both on the Jebel and in the village Christian graffiti have been found (items 1, 5, 7, 8), largely consisting of a variety of crosses but there are other Christian symbols (e.g. alpha and omega, N : *nikē* = Greek 'victory', IXC = Jesus Christus, all suggesting ultimate Greek origins for Christianity in the region) (fig. 12). But more significantly three Christian Syriac inscriptions have been found, two inside a (?reused) tomb on Jebel Khalid (items 2, 7) and one on a reliquary in Kirbet Khalid (items 8, 11).

The tomb inscriptions are by different hands, one being in mixed Serta-Estrangela style (fig. 13), the other can be accommodated within the Serta tradition. The first may yield the incomplete personal name '.ṢYP', possibly a corrupt spelling of YWSYP', Josephus, whilst the second appears to be written by one ŠYR', Shira (the word is also attested as the title of a convent, which according to Bar Hebraeus, was situated on the banks of the Euphrates). That is to say, two names in the Semitic tradition. The reliquary, in clear Estrangela script (fig. 14), records, unusually, not the names of the saint(s) whose relics lie within nor that of the cleric or patron who sponsored its making but rather of the local craftsmen who fashioned the receptacle. They are KRSṬPRWS, that is Christophorus, a Christian-Greek theophoric, displaying a Semitic adaptation with an internal reduction of vowels, and SKLWN', a Semitic name, variations such as Saikul being recorded by Littman and Wuthnow and the Hellenic — *ona* ending being often attested in North Syria (cf. Sacona, Dadona at

Figure 9a

Figure 9b

Figure 10

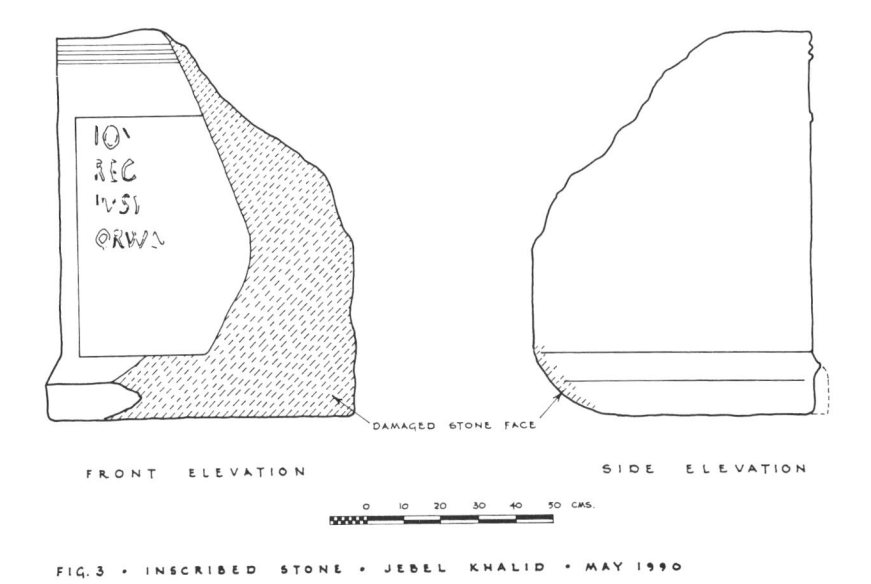

Figure 11

Figure 12

Figure 13

Figure 14

Dura Europos). That is to say this Christian liturgical vessel was made by two local villagers bearing names one Greek, one Semitic but each modified by the other language and they recorded their labour in their local tongue, Syriac.

To summarize, this (very small) sample has produced 30 naming elements, 4 being in origin Iranian, 6 Greek, 7 Roman and 13 Semitic. Or to put this in rough percentage terms 13% are Iranian, 20% Greek, 23% Roman whilst over 43% are Semitic. It needs also to be borne in mind that there is but one inscription in Latin: there are three in Syriac whereas all the rest, the vast majority, are written, with varied degrees of competency, in Greek. Taken together, this may help to give some impression of the racial admixture, political forces, religious traditions and cultural dominances that became fused together to create Syrian culture in this region in late Antiquity.

BIBLIOGRAPHY ON INSCRIBED SURFACES, ENVIRONS OF JEBEL KHALID

Item 1: G.W. Clarke, "Syriac inscriptions from the Middle Euphrates", *Abr-Nahrain*, 23 (1984-1985), pp. 73-82.

Item 2: T. Muraoka, "Two Syriac inscriptions from the Middle Euphrates", *Abr-Nahrain*, 23 (1984-1985), pp. 83-89.

Item 3: G.W. Clarke, "A decorated Christian tomb-chamber near Joussef Pasha", *Abr-Nahrain*, 23 (1984-1985), pp. 90-95.

Item 4: G.W. Clarke, "A funeral stele in the district of Membij: a preliminary report", *Abr-Nahrain*, 23 (1984-1985), pp. 96-101.

Item 5: G.W. Clarke and P.J. Connor, "Inscriptions, symbols and graffiti near Joussef Pasha", *Abr-Nahrain*, 25 (1987), pp. 19-39.

Item 6: G.W. Clarke, "Funerary inscriptions near Joussef Pasha, North Syria", *Abr-Nahrain*, 26 (1988), pp. 19-29.

Item 7: E.C.D. Hunter, "Syriac inscriptions from a Melkite monastery on the Middle Euphrates", *Bulletin of the School of Oriental and African Studies*, 52.1 (1989), pp. 1-17.

Item 8: E.C.D. Hunter, "An inscribed reliquary from the Middle Euphrates", *Oriens Christianus*, 75 (1991), pp. 147-165.

Item 9: G.W. Clarke, "Greek graffiti from North Syria", *Mediterranean Archaeology*, 5/6 (1992/3), pp. 117-120.

Item 10: G.W. Clarke and T. Hillard, "A limestone altar from North Syria", *Mediterranean Archaeology*, 5/6 (1992/3), pp. 111-115.

Item 11: E.C.D. Hunter, "The cult of Saints in Syria during the fifth century A.D.", *Studia Patristica*, 25 (1993), pp. 308-312.

RED TO BLUE: COLOUR SYMBOLISM AND HUMAN SOCIETIES

BY

Claudia SAGONA

A decade ago we began to read into the human use of the colour red, while preparing the publication of archaeological investigations carried out at a Tasmanian Aboriginal ochre mine.[1] By drawing on the scant written accounts and pictorial records of the early nineteenth century for Tasmania, world wide ethnographic parallels and archaeological excavations in which ochre was found, we were able to make inroads into the thought patterns of this intriguing society. There can be little doubt that the Tasmanian use of colour was symbolic, furthermore that their choice of ochre sources, the mining expeditions and processing of the raw material were steeped in symbolic behaviour, probably once ritualistic.

Although red continued to be the favoured colouring for non-complex societies generally, in the Near East there is every indication that there was a gradual shift away from red, or that it continued to be used concurrently with blue in the second millennium B.C. The change appears hand-in-hand with settled communities and the growth and development of infrastructures of centralized governments. This paper presents some of the evidence for blue having a 'value' in symbolic terms, and examines whether it is possible to interpret that value through ancient texts and art, and through the material remains recovered from archaeological excavations.

RED: THE TASMANIAN EXPERIENCE

"The [Aborigines] were extremely anxious to reach the place where the favourite [red ochre] colouring was to be obtained, as proof of which when they arrived at the spot ... they patted [the ochre] with their hands and kissed it."[2]

---

[1] This paper is the result of lengthy discussions between the author and Antonio Sagona; it draws on aspects of our research concerning colour in human society especially surrounding the Toolumbunner mine in Tasmania and our observations in the Near Eastern region.

[2] G.A.R. journals. Field journals of George Augustus Robinson held in the Mitchell Library, State Library of New South Wales, A 7030, vol. 9, pt. 5, 27 April 1832. The reference is to a visit to a Mount Housetop mine. A sound edition of these diaries can be found in N.J.B. PLOMLEY (ed.), *Friendly Mission: the Tasmanian journals papers of George Augustus Robinson 1829-1834*, Hobart 1966; ID., *Friendly Mission ... a supplement*, Tasmanian Historical Research Association Hobart 1971; ID. *Weep in Silence: a History of the Flinders Island Aboriginal Settlement*, Hobart 1987.

"The chief Mannalargenna is overjoyed at the prospect of seeing this celebrated spot. He is in raptures. "By and by me see it — plenty — plenty" [he said]. He is passionately fond of colouring his body with a mixture of ochre and grease."[3]

So wrote George Augustus Robinson in his field diaries during his four year long search for the remnants of the Tasmanian Aboriginal people between 1830 and 1834. It was not until 1982 that the ochre mine now known as Toolumbunner was relocated and a lengthy archaeological investigation of the area was carried out.[4] Behind the exploration of the site were some fundamental questions concerning ochre usage. Was it ochre itself or the colour that was valued? Why this mine above other sources? Why the passionate displays leading up to, during and after the mining the mineral? In what ways was red used in their society and what meaning, if any, did it have?

Robinson was not highly educated and his field notes were written as a daily record — he was, after all, a government man and accountable for his actions and expenses.[5] Hence, comments about Tasmanian culture were incidental. His word lists of their language were kept in order to facilitate their capture,[6] for his task was to locate and remove the Aborigines from their homelands. Yet woven in the journals are the threads we began to follow towards a deeper understanding of their use of red ochre.

As Robinson presented it, the record of usage was extensive. Lumps of ochre were often strewn around abandoned campsites.[7] When the women mined the material, they carted it away in skin sacks so full that Robinson wondered if the average European man could lift the weight.[8] Women generally carried large quantities of red ochre in their baskets as well as the grinding stones used in its preparation.[9]

Ochre was most used in body ornamentation and it took various forms among the Tasmanians, but notably the dressing of hair of the Eastern tribesmen. They plastered their hair and beards and twisted it into clotted ringlets with a paste of ochre and fat. The women often shaved their heads, left a ring of hair, or kept their hair short. Body painting was also practiced not in the elaborate way of mainlanders, but by highlighting specific body parts. There are two portraits of women carrying infants, both depict

---

[3] G.A.R. journals, A7031, vol. 10, pt. 7, 3 July 1834 prior to visiting the Toolumbunner ochre deposit.

[4] The excavation of Toolumbunner was conducted by the University of Melbourne, Victoria, in conjunction with the Queen Victoria Museum and Art Gallery, Launceston, Tasmania. The results are published in A. SAGONA (ed.), *Bruising the Red Earth: Ochre Mining and Ritual in Aboriginal Tasmania,* Carlton 1994; ID., *Bruising the Red Earth: The Catalogue of Finds,* Research monograph of the Department of History, University of Melbourne 1995.

[5] Robinson became Conciliator to the Aborigines, later Commandant of the Flinders Island settlement and Protector of the Aborigines at Port Phillip. N.J.B. PLOMLEY (ed.), *op. cit.* 1966 (n. 2), p. 3; V. RAE-ELLIS, *Black Robinson: Protector of the Aborigines,* Carlton 1988, pp. 18-23.

[6] N.J.B. PLOMLEY, *A Word List of the Tasmanian Aboriginal Languages,* Launceston 1976, p. 23.

[7] N.J.B. PLOMLEY (ed.), *op. cit.* 1966 (n. 2), p. 524, 20 November 1831 or p. 722, 19 May 1833; A. SAGONA (ed.), *op. cit.* 1994 (n. 4), p. 19.

[8] N.J.B. PLOMLEY (ed.), *ibid.*, p. 904, 16 July 1834.

[9] *Ibid.,* p. 531, 26 November 1831.

mother and child with patches of red on the forehead and cheeks.[10] Not all groups in Tasmania expressed body decoration in the same way, suggesting that alone or with combinations of scarification or other colourings, red ochre was used as a tribal marking.[11] Ochre was used at specific times. The underlying reasons may never be known, though an extensive search of the world ethnographic record suggests that the practice carried ceremonial and social meaning as well as being used to enhance one's physical appearance and occasionally it had practical applications.

Conversely, Robinson was told that while in mourning ochre was not used.[12] Unfortunately the edges of clearer understanding are blurred, for on another occasion he writes that it was "evidently a custom and [it] is peculiar to a few tribes".[13] We can not know if those groups he wrote about at this stage (in 1831) were in mourning having been touched by the extensive loss of human life due to European aggression and introduced disease, or whether they rarely if ever used ochre as an expression of their tribal heritage, or more simply, that the right occasion, requiring body adornment, had not presented itself.

When confronted with the prospects of visiting ochre deposits, the Tasmanians began to prepare themselves. Robinson's entries inadvertently record a pattern of song, dance, general lifting of spirits and story telling, and his discussions with them revolve especially around courtship. This was apparent on two occasions — when he visited Toolumbunner and when he went to Swan Island.[14] Robinson took people in his care to the island in November 1830, there, he witnessed nightly scenes of confusion with men carrying knives and pursuing the women. As he does not write of women, wounded or dead, laying about the following day, indicates that their aggressive play formed part of the courtship ritual along with the many hours of mining, preparing and be-daubing the hair and body with ochre. To the extent that he wrote, "this has been their chief employment since they have been on the island."[15]

Charms to cure illness were made from the bones of deceased relatives, smeared in ochre, tied with kangaroo sinews and then applied to the painful area.[16] Ochre had other applications such as rubbing charcoal and the red pomade into freshly cut cicatrices.[17]

---

[10] A. SAGONA (ed.), *op. cit.* 1994 (n. 4), pl. 4-5.

[11] N.J.B. PLOMLEY (ed.), *op. cit.* 1966 (n. 2), p. 501, 4 November 1831. On the 12 December 1831, Robinson indicated that the West Point and West Coast groups did not "use red ochre about their heads", p. 549.

[12] N.J.B. PLOMLEY (ed.), *op. cit.* 1966 (n. 2), p. 892, 29 June 1834. West Coast groups rubbed the pounded cremated remains of their dead kindred over their face as a sign of mourning, p. 625, 1 July 1832.

[13] G.A.R. journals A 7030, vol. 9, pt. 3.

[14] For Toolumbunner G.A.R. journals A 7031, vol. 10, pt. 7, 7 July 1834; Swan Island A 7029, vol. 8, pt. 3, 3 November 1830.

[15] *Ibid.*, A 7029, vol. 8, pt. 3, 19-20 November 1830.

[16] N.J.B. PLOMLEY (ed.), *op. cit.* 1987 (n. 2), p. 229, 12 October 1832. An observation made by James Backhouse.

[17] N.J.B. PLOMLEY (ed.), *op. cit.* 1966 (n. 2), p. 283, 26 November 1830.

Outside Australia, other groups express cosmological belief, or symbolize major physical experiences, and natural occurrences with colour. The colour triad of white, black and red, as well as other ornamentation, take on magical qualities employed to control nature by securing good fortune or effect escape from misfortune. For example, Victor Turner's study of the Ndembu of Zambia indicates that the symbolic values of colour are taught at an early age, while the deeper meanings are conveyed later to the initiate during ceremonies marking the youth's passage into adulthood. In essence, the triad of colours mirror the products of the body: black in the form of mud or charcoal, representing excreta or putrefaction, symbolizes bad things, suffering, disease and death; white, usually white clay, signifies mother's milk and semen, symboling good things, generosity, fertility, reproduction or suckling; red especially red ochre, stood for different kinds of blood, of animals, of mother's (parturition), of women's menstrual and homicidal. According to the Ndembu then, colours are symbolic of the life forces and aggression.[18] Many other examples are documented in the Toolumbunner report as evidence of shared human experience and expression, which suggests that red had far greater meaning than Robinson was aware of.[19]

Tasmanian women may have painted their genitals with ochre as part of the etiquette of courtship, and as indicators of their age and eligibility. But even greater symbolism concerning the fears and hopes of fertility of procreation and acknowledgment of changing states.[20] The reddened hair and body paint for the male was considered alluring to the women, a sign of eligibility, strength and health.[21] With their hair dressed in ochre they likened themselves to the tall trees resplendent with new, bright red growth.[22] Although the ethnographic record for Tasmania is incomplete, we know that their practice of body adornment would have been loaded with meaning to which Robinson was not privy. That he was denied knowledge of Tasmanian ways is apparent from sometimes evasive answers or prohibiting him access to important sites. For example, he was four years in the bush with them before he was allowed to visit Toolumbunner and in so doing considered himself highly favoured.[23] The secrecy surrounding the site is the most salient clue that red substances varied in quality or effectiveness from one source to another as it did within Australian mainland Aboriginal circles. Perhaps the magical qualities of the site had been enriched by successive generations, of tales of battles and bloodshed over the source.[24] Clearly a joyous occasion, the expedition to mine ochre there was enshrined in elaborate song, dance and physical

---

[18] V. TURNER, "Colour classification in Ndembu ritual: a problem in primitive classification", *Anthropological approaches to the study of religion*, ed. M. BANTON, London 1966, pp. 58-61, 81.

[19] A. SAGONA (ed.), *op. cit.* 1994 (n. 4), pp. 10-15.

[20] G.A.R. journals A 7030, vol. 9, pt. 3, 24 October 1831; A. SAGONA (ed.), *ibid.*, p. 21.

[21] A. SAGONA (ed.), *ibid.*, p. 20.

[22] G.A.R. journals A 7029, vol. 8, pt. 3, 19 December 1831 and N.J.B. PLOMLEY (ed.), *op. cit.* 1966 (n. 2), p. 287, 5 December 1830. On this occasion the people adorned their hair with the leaves as they had no red ochre.

[23] G.A.R. journals A 7031, vol. 10, pt. 7, 13 July 1834.

[24] G.A.R. journals A7029, vol. 8, pt. 2, 25 October 1830. Robinson records the story of warfare over the distribution of ochre and breaking of trade agreements between Tasmanian tribes.

preparation before and after Toolumbunner was visited.[25] The twin grinding stones shaped like thick plates and known as *ballywinne* stones[26] were made well in advance on the 8 July 1834, so too were kangaroo skin sacks.

"The skin sacks they prepared for the purpose of packing red ochre in. The natives have been preparing skins for this purpose for some time past and promise themselves a fine harvest".[27]

Language studies further corroborate the commonality of colour usage and symbolism. Recent research into colour terminology parallel the ethnographic evidence that humankind at a similar level of social complexity encode a limited range of colours into their expression of symbolic and social behaviour. That human perception and naming of colour is dependent upon a series of complex biological, social, neurophysiological and psychological factors. Berlin and Kay argue persuasively that basic colour categories are universal to all languages, colour term inventories expanding through time in an ordered, contained manner. People's colour perception results from common neurophysiological processes. Their work rested on a field study of 20 languages and library-based research of 78 other languages. They found between 2 and 11 basic colour categories exist, and from these any given language will use eleven or fewer colour terms even though the human eye can differentiate a multitude of colours.[28]

$$\begin{bmatrix}\text{white}\\\text{black}\end{bmatrix} \to [\text{red}] \begin{matrix}\nearrow [\text{green}] \to [\text{yellow}]\searrow \\ \searrow [\text{yellow}] \to [\text{green}]\nearrow\end{matrix} [\text{blue}] \to [\text{brown}] \to \begin{bmatrix}\text{purple}\\\text{pink}\\\text{orange}\\\text{grey}\end{bmatrix}$$

Figure 1: After P. KAY and C.K. McDANIEL, "The linguistic significance of the meaning of basic colour terms", *Language*, 54 (1978), p. 615

The seven-stage evolutionary sequence can accommodate every colour vocabulary from the simplest at Stage I to the most complex stage VII. All languages have terms for white and black. At the first stage white and black can be expressed in terms of light and brightness, or moist and dry. Other colours are often expressed in qualifying phrases like "fresh leaf" for green. The next stage incorporates a term for red, the brightest colour the human visual system can perceive since it emits the shortest and most intense wavelength. This attracting quality of red may explain in part the human response to it and its place in the colour linguistic sequence.

[25] A. SAGONA (ed.), *op. cit.* 1994 (n. 4), p. 22; G. A. R. journals A 7030, vol. 9, pt. 5; N.J.B. PLOMLEY (ed.), *op. cit.* 1966 (n. 2), pp. 895-905, 13-16 July 1834.
[26] A. SAGONA (ed.), *op. cit.* 1994 (n. 4), p. 122, fig. 42-43, illustrate the *ballywinne* stone as excavated from Toolumbunner and as sketched by Robinson on 8 July 1834.
[27] N.J.B. PLOMLEY (ed.), *op. cit.* 1966 (n. 2), p. 900, 13 July 1834.
[28] B. BERLIN and P. KAY, *Basic Colour Terms: their Universality and Evolution*, Berkeley 1969, p. 4; a summary of recent works on colour in language can be found in A. SAGONA (ed.), *op. cit.* 1994 (n. 4), pp. 26-32.

Languages fall into the subsequent stages when colour terms are present. A modification of the Berlin and Kay sequence was offered by Turton.[29]

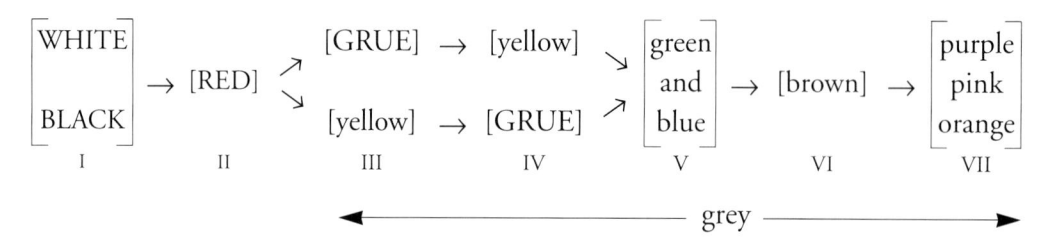

$$\begin{bmatrix} \text{WHITE} \\ \text{BLACK} \end{bmatrix} \to [\text{RED}] \nearrow\searrow \begin{matrix} [\text{GRUE}] \to [\text{yellow}] \\ [\text{yellow}] \to [\text{GRUE}] \end{matrix} \searrow\nearrow \begin{bmatrix} \text{green} \\ \text{and} \\ \text{blue} \end{bmatrix} \to [\text{brown}] \to \begin{bmatrix} \text{purple} \\ \text{pink} \\ \text{orange} \end{bmatrix}$$

I   II   III   IV   V   VI   VII

←——————— grey ———————→

Figure 2: After D. TURTON, *loc. cit.* (n. 29), p. 331.

'Grue' being a term in languages of Stage III which have a term for green/blue. The evidence though quite limited indicates that the Tasmanians were at Stage III in their linguistic development though no term for yellow survives in the record suggest that the focus was on grue and that yellow was considered equivalent to red. Or more simply that the ethnographic record is deficient in that area.[30]

Archaeology has revealed the extreme antiquity of red ochre mortuary and domestic contexts from about 70,000 years ago with Neanderthal burials from Le Moustier, Combe Grenal, La Chapelle-aux-Saints, Le Regourdou and La Ferrassie.[31] Here the deceased were laid to rest with ochre crayons around them and their bodies sprinkled with powdered ochre. The practice persisted into the Upper Palaeolithic at the Balzi Rossi caves east of Monaco, for example, and in Pleistocene Australia at Lake Mungo dated to around 30,000 years B.P.[32]

In Palestine, Natufian cranial burials contained ochre pieces, at other times skulls would be painted red.[33] Ochre burials occur sporadically thereafter into Neolithic times such as those at Çatal Höyük, in Anatolia, and at Jericho, in the Jordan Valley.[34]

---

[29] D. TURTON, "There is no such beast: cattle and colour naming among the Mursi", *Man*, 15 (1980), pp. 320-338.

[30] A. SAGONA (ed.), *op. cit.* 1994 (n. 4), p. 31.

[31] D. PEYRONY, "Le Moustier: ses gisements, ses industries, ses couches géologiques", *Revue Anthropologique*, 40 (1930), pp. 48-76,155-176; F. BORDES, *A Tale of Two Caves*, New York 1972, p. 137; M. BOULE, "L'homme fossile de la Chappelle-aux-Saints", *Annales de Paléontologie*, 6 (1911), pp. 111-172; 7 (1912), pp. 21-56, 85-192; 8 (1913), pp. 1-70; D. PEYRONY, "Le Périgord préhistorique: essai de géographie humaine", *Société historique et archéologique du Périgord*, Périgueux 1949; D. PEYRONY, "La Ferrassie-Moustérien Périgordien, Aurignacien", *Préhistorique*, 3 (1934), pp. 1-92.

[32] L. CARDINI, "Nuovi documenti sull'antichità dell'uomo in Italia. Reperto umano del paleolitico superiore nella Grotta delle Arene Candide", *Razza e Civiltà*, no.1-4 (1942); J.M. BOWLER and A.G. THORNE, "Human remains from Lake Mungo: discovery and excavation of Lake Mungo III", *The origins of the Australians*, ed. R.L. KIRK and A.G. THORNE, Canberra 1976, pp. 127-138.

[33] A. BELFER-COHEN, "The Natufian in the Levant", *Annual Review of Arthropology*, 20 (1991), pp. 167-186.

[34] J. MELLAART, *Çatal Höyük: a Neolithic Town in Anatolia*, London 1967, pp. 205-208. Only eleven of some four hundred burials were sprinkled with ochre as evidence of a moribund practice.

Blue: the Near Eastern sequel

Red colouring and red ochre remained a valued commodity with non-complex societies world wide into the modern era. But there is every indication that red had begun to slip from favour in the Near East, that during the fourth to third millennium B. C. blue appeared frequently on the archaeological scene and took hold, assuming magical properties still unsurpassed in some spheres. It should be noted, however, that in the third millennium, red ochre continued to be traded from deposits in India, through the Persian Gulf merchants to the markets of Sumer. S. Ratnagar indicates that a, "particularly brilliant shade" of ochre is to be found on the Hormuz Island although it is not clear whether the deposit was exploited.[35] Using cuneiform texts, C. Edens has clearly demonstrated that both red and blue, especially red and blue wool, were pivotal in Kassite symbolic practices concerning kingship and the divine in the second and first millennia B.C.[36] As outlined above, the use of red in human symbolic behaviour can be argued to have an antiquity at least as old as 70,000 years B. P., but blue is a relative new comer to the scene.

The first tangible evidence for a shift in symbolic use of colour comes with trade in turquoise and lapis lazuli.[37] Sources of lapis lazuli are rare. Focusing on the Near Eastern sphere, Badakshan in Afghanistan at present remains one of the few sources within reasonable geographic range of Mesopotamia. Even so, the mines there are 3000 kilometres from northern Mesopotamia. Georgina Hermann's study documents the oscillating lapis lazuli trade, indicating that Gawra XIII was central to the early trade. From here, the stone was distributed to northern sites. When the northern monopoly of the stone failed around the late Uruk phase (Gawra IX), the trade in lapis was revitalized from the south during the Jemdat Nasr period.[38]

The earliest turquoise sources to be exploited around the third millennium were located in the Sinai at Wadi Magharah and Serabit el-Khadim, and the Elburz mountains of the inner Kyzyl Kum. Maurizio Tosi drew attention to an interesting phenomenon, namely that turquoise was not popular in Mesopotamia even though long

---

[35] S. RATNAGAR, Encounters. *The Westerly Trade of the Harappa Civilization*, Delhi 1981, p. 106.

[36] C. EDENS, "On the complexity of complex societies; structure, power and legitimacy in Kassite Babylonia", *Chiefdoms and Early States in the Near East*, ed. G. STEIN & M.S. ROTHMAN, Madison Wisconsin 1994, pp. 209-223.

[37] Major contributions in the study of these semi-precious stones can be found in the following landmark essays, G. HERRMANN, "Lapis lazuli: the early phase of its trade", *Iraq*, 30 (1968), pp. 21-55; G. HERRMANN, "Lapislazuli", *Reallexikon der Assyriologie und Vorderasiatischen Archäologie*, Berlin 1980-1983, pp. 489-492; M. TOSI, "The lapis lazuli trade across the Iranian Plateau in the 3rd millennium B.C.", *Gururajamanjarika: miscellanea in onore di Giuseppe Tucci*, ed. A. FORTE, L.P. REMAGGI & M. TOSI, Napoli 1974a, pp. 3-22; M. TOSI, "The problem of turquoise in protohistoric trade on the Iranian Plateau", *Memorie dell'Istituto Italiano di paleontologia umana*, II (1974b), pp. 147-162. See also P.R.S. MOOREY, *Ancient Mesopotamian Materials and Industries: the Archaeological Evidence*, Oxford 1994, pp. 85-92, 101.

[38] G. HERRMANN, *loc. cit.* 1968 (n. 37), pp. 29-36.

distance trade in lapis lazuli was well established after the 4th millennium. For instances it was absent from the Royal Cemetery of Ur. (2500-2000 B.C) even though turquoise was no more difficult to mine, transport or process and was popular on the Iranian market.[39] He wrote "the absence of turquoise in the *decorative products* [my emphasis] of protodynastic Mesopotamia was due to one or more of the following factors:

1. shortage of raw material,
2. absence of specific demand,
3. inefficiency of trade-and-transport systems on the Iranian plateau."[40]

I would argue that seemingly intangible factors which had created an "absence of specific demand" had already elevated lapis lazuli to such an exalted level that it was not merely a *decorative product* — and turquoise was at best a "poor cousin". In his concluding remarks Tosi was faced with the possibility that economic pressures alone could not explain the small demand for turquoise over lapis lazuli and that ideological factors were at play.[41]

The supremacy of Toolumbunner red ochre over other sources in Tasmania springs to mind. It would seem from its appearance in Mesopotamia that lapis lazuli was absorbed into the culture, attaining symbolic values as ochre had done with less complex societies.

There is every indication that lapis was the stone of royal houses, as it had religious value and magical properties. Take "Innana's Descent into the Netherworld" as an example. In this myth, the goddess of light, love and life visits the land of the dead. As preparation she wears a crown, and carries a measuring rod and line of lapis lazuli. She also wears a small lapis lazuli bead necklace, a gold ring, breastplate on her body and garments befitting her status. As she descends she passes through seven gates. At each, an item of apparel is removed, until, naked, she stands in front of Ereshkigal and the seven judges. They fix upon her the look of death.[42]

There is a sense that without the protective apparel she is vulnerable; and the items she wears were no doubt also indicators of her social standing. Her dressing as portrayed in the poem is steeped in ritual. Although Hermmann did not pursue the cultural values placed on lapis lazuli, she remarked that "the vast wealth consecrated to the death of the royal tombs of Ur had a specific purpose and that the materials principally used were lapis, carnelian and gold, that they possessed important ritual values".[43] The array of artefacts from these famous graves and adorning the women of the royal houses reflects the ritual and itemized objects recorded in the poem. In both, the living gird themselves in readiness for voluntary death (in some cases, natural in others) and the ordeals of the after life. In whatever way the apparel aided the divine, so too the magical and symbolic qualities were evoked at the human level. And the objects surviving within the

---

[39] M. Tosi, *loc. cit.* 1974b (n. 37), p. 154.
[40] *Ibid.*, p. 154.
[41] *Ibid.*
[42] S.N. Kramer, "Inanna's descent to the nether world", *Ancient Near Eastern Texts Relating to the Old Testament,* ed. J.B. Pritchard, Princeton 1969, pp. 52-57.
[43] G. Herrmann, *loc. cit.* 1968 (n. 37), p. 54.

archaeological record may not be grave "gifts" or "goods" but the paraphernalia of ritual vital to the successful passage from the realm of the living to that of the dead.

In Egypt, turquoise commodities were found from the late Neolithic, Badarian culture, and precede the lapis lazuli trade with Mesopotamia. The mining of turquoise went hand-in-hand with copper production in the Sinai; so too the copper carbonates, malachite and azurite which were processed for cosmetics. Unlike the settlements of Iran which acted as intermediaries in lapis trade with Badakshan, envoys went directly from Egypt to acquire the commodities of the Sinai.[44]

In a fascinating essay, Professor John Baines illustrates how ancient Egyptian colour terminology fitted into the Berlin and Kay scheme at the third stage having words for black (km), white (hd), red (dsr) and green/blue or grue (söb) and there was also a term for variegated.[45] Interestingly, these colour terms stayed the same from the mid third millennium B.C. to the Middle ages even though Egyptian use of colour increased in complexity through time. Old Kingdom painting was at Stage V, Middle Kingdom at Stage VI and New Kingdom at a partial Stage VII. Language lagged behind colour usage, the increasingly complex range of colours no doubt spoken of in descriptive phrases or terms. Baines documents developments from Old to New Kingdom culture, growing in sophistication and technology with cognitive advances. In the case of Egypt, colour classification expanded independently of language.[46]

We have blue emerging as a favoured colour within two of the major cultural spheres of the ancient Near East. At times it represented rank; at other times it was linked to religion, woven into myth and vital to the establishment of temples. A king of Sumer gained and maintained power through the wealth of his religious centres. Enmerkar's war of words with the ruler of Aratta documents the importance of lapis trade, the stone is spoken of in ecstatic terms,

> "Let the people of Aratta....bring down pure Lapis lazuli
> from the slab, let them bring down precious stones and
> pure lapis lazuli."[47]

The rarity, desirability and social values placed on lapis lazuli are clearly stated in the story; sentiments and mechanics of the trade that are still impressive. In support of the highly desirable nature of lapis lazuli and indicative of the rare quality of blue sought is a lapis lazuli and gold bead necklace held in the Egyptian Museum, Cairo. One flawless bead stands out for the pureness of its colour, so much so, that it carries a dedicatory cuneiform inscription of the eleventh century B.C.[48]

[44] M. TOSI, *loc. cit.* 1974b (n. 37), pp. 148-149.
[45] J. BAINES, "Colour terminology and colour classification", *American Anthropology*, 87 (1985), pp. 282-297. Baines notes that like Egyptian, Sumerian and Akkadian possessed four basic colour terms — black, white, red and grue — and also a term for variegated, pp. 283-284.
[46] *Ibid.*, p. 289.
[47] S.N. KRAMER, *Tablets of Sumer*, Indian Hills, Colorado 1956, p. 20.
[48] The necklace catalogue number is JE 85755 and the bead is JE 85756. A colour photograph appears in C. HOPE, *Gold of the Pharaohs*, Sydney 1988, p. 91.

Blue had an increasing role to play in the rites of passage from life to death, though there are examples where burials testify to converging practices — having both red ochre crayons and blue bead necklaces — such as the cemetery of Zaman Baba in the Kyzyl Kum region.[49] Blue items could be simply two turquoise beads placed at the head and knees of the deceased at Shahri-Sokhta in Iran, or the elaborate funerary furniture with the dead of the Royal Graves at Ur.[50]

Two favoured areas in which blue played a part focused on the eyes and hair. Blue eyes and blue hair often figured in descriptive or visual representations. Like the Tasmanians, depth of meaning was woven into the decorative treatment of hair. When Agga and Gilgamesh, the kings of ancient Kish and Erech respectively, enter into a verbal war, attempts are made to pacify Agga. He is described in glowing terms — stout, gracious and having a beard of lapis lazuli.[51] The art of ancient Mesopotamia is rich in associations between lapis and hair. The symbolic treatment of hair is an entire study in itself, but suffice to say that the sense behind blue hair is something far more controlled, commanding awe and respect far greater than the figure of Enkidu. This wild man of the Gilgamesh epic has locks of hair that sprouted from his head and shaggy hair that covered his whole body, and who, being lost to society, was destined to roam the fields with the animals.[52]

In Egypt, the link between hair and blue is repeated. Take, for instance, the famous gold mask of Tutankhamun. It is significant that while a lapis lazuli shade of blue was applied to the bands of the wig with glass paste, the beard, eyebrows and kohl lines are of the stone itself. Why the distinction? Realism was not an issue. Clearly the colour choice had symbolic value, as did the deliberate use of lapis lazuli. As Baines pointed out "Blue is the most prestigious colour; it is also employed in the most obviously non realistic way....blue acquires discrete symbolism as well as pictorial functions".[53]

There is every indication that the *eye*, eye of the god, eye of the ordinary person had already emerged as an important symbolic feature before it merged with blue. The magical protective qualities of blue eye amulets remain unshaken among those who fear the evil eye and seek to repel it. In all likelihood the spread of this belief was facilitated by the creation of glazed material, especially faience.[54] In a sense, lustrous, shiny vivid blue objects were available to the masses. Blue faience and glass beads, amulets and small trinkets traveled the Mediterranean lands, particularly with Phoenician traders.

---

[49] M. TOSI, *loc. cit.* 1974b (n. 37), pp. 160-161.

[50] *Ibid*, p. 156.

[51] S.N. KRAMER, "Gilgamesh and Agga", *Ancient Near Eastern Texts*, ed. J.B. PRITCHARD, Princeton 1969, p. 46.

[52] E.A. SPEISER, "The epic of Gilgamesh", *Ancient Near Eastern Texts*, ed. J.B. PRITCHARD, Princeton 1969, p. 74; on decorative hair styles and its symbolism see E.R. LEACH, "Magical hair", *Journal of the Royal Anthropological Institute*, 88 (1958), pp. 147-164, and C.R. HALLPIKE, "Social hair", *Man*, 4 (1969), pp. 256-264.

[53] J. BAINES, *loc. cit.* (n. 45), pp. 288-289.

[54] P.R.S. MOOREY, *op. cit.* (n. 37), p. 90.

Returning to the fundamental reason for the shift in colour symbolism to incorporate blue, I believe the heart of the change lies in the nature of *settled* communities in the Near East. Economic success created surpluses and those surpluses could stimulate trade in valuable commodities, notably lapis lazuli, which increased in desirability as it became interwoven in the fabric and symbolism of the culture. The more difficult to obtain, the more it became enshrouded in mystic. Blue was valuable as well as loaded with symbolism. Lapis lazuli blue became the hallmark for those who could obtain, use and hoard the material. In time, the qualities of blue were called upon at all levels of society as a common practice.